Naval Warfare – Dreadnoughts to Drones

World War One – America Vs Japan – Vietnam – Falklands – Gulf War – Ukraine

ABOVE: The USS *Wisconsin* launches a Tomahawk missile at Baghdad during the 1991 Gulf War. (US NAVY)

ABOVE: British naval supremacy around the Falklands Islands was secured when the nuclear submarine, HMS *Conqueror*, sank the ARA *General Belgrano* on May 2, 1982. (MARTIN SGUT)

ABOVE: In the opening days of the Battle for Okinawa, the USS *Bunker Hill* was hit and badly damaged by two Japanese Kamikaze planes. (US NAVY/US NATIONAL ARCHIVES)

ABOVE: US Navy A-4 Skyhawks led the first US air strikes of the Vietnam war in 1964. (US NAVY)

ISBN: 978 1 80282 854 2

Editor: Tim Ripley

Data and Photo Research: Fergus Ripley

Senior editor, specials: Roger Mortimer

Email: roger.mortimer@keypublishing.com

Cover Design: Steve Donovan

Design: SJmagic DESIGN SERVICES, India

Advertising Sales Manager: Brodie Baxter

Email: brodie.baxter@keypublishing.com

Tel: 01780 755131

Advertising Production: Becky Antoniades

Email: Rebecca.antoniades@keypublishing.com

SUBSCRIPTION/MAIL ORDER

Key Publishing Ltd, PO Box 300, Stamford, Lincs, PE9 1NA

Tel: 01780 480404

Subscriptions email: subs@keypublishing.com

Mail Order email: orders@keypublishing.com

Website: www.keypublishing.com/shop

PUBLISHING

Group CEO and Publisher: Adrian Cox

Published by

Key Publishing Ltd, PO Box 100, Stamford, Lincs, PE9 1XQ

Tel: 01780 755131

Website: www.keypublishing.com

PRINTING

Precision Colour Printing Ltd, Haldane, Halesfield 1, Telford, Shropshire. TF7 4QQ

DISTRIBUTION

Seymour Distribution Ltd, 2 Poultry Avenue, London, EC1A 9PU

Enquiries Line: 02074 294000.

ABOVE: The guided missile cruiser USS *Jouett* passing through the Strait of Hormuz during Operation Desert Shield in August 1990 as US forces launched their build up to counter the Iraqi invasion of Kuwait. (US NAVY)

WELCOME

Naval warfare in the 20th and 21st centuries

Welcome to *Naval Warfare – Dreadnoughts to Drones*. We aim to tell the story of naval warfare in the 20th and 21st centuries by describing a dozen or so of the most important naval actions of the modern era.

We will look at the naval battles that changed the course of history, as well as engagements that saw the successful use of new naval weapons. In some cases, these trends came together to be truly revolutionary. However, it has not always the case, and in some instances superior technology has been defeated by more determined or innovative opponents.

The past 120 years has been a period of dramatic technological and political change. In the naval arena alone, it has seen the rise of the battleship and then its replacement by the aircraft carrier as the dominant weapon on the sea.

The aircraft carrier won the war in the Pacific for the United States and its allies but within a decade of the end of World War Two, the first nuclear powered submarines

had put to sea. Less than five years later nuclear tipped inter-continental missiles had been installed on nuclear-powered submarines, ending the dominant role of aircraft carriers in naval warfare.

While nuclear weapons kept the peace between the world's nuclear superpowers, the rapid development of guided weapons was transforming naval warfare. The 1982 Falklands conflict showed the power of these new weapons and less than a decade later the United States Navy demonstrated that long range guided missiles could be used by fleets to strike deep into the heart of enemy territory.

The past 120 years has also seen the fate of nations and empires turn on the outcome of naval battles. In 1905 the Battle of Tsushima, in the straits between Korea and Japan saw the Russian Empire stumble

US nuclear-powered aircraft carriers are the biggest warships ever built and remain powerful tools for crisis management, even if their vulnerability in full scale conventional war is questionable. (US NAVY)

tide of history which was witnessing the end of Western empires. The Anglo-French intervention at Suez in 1956 was a masterful demonstration of the power of modern aircraft carriers and the potential of helicopters to project troops ashore. However, it was geo-political disaster for London and Paris and in less than a decade both countries had given up their colonial possessions across Africa and Middle East.

America's intervention in Vietnam between 1960 and 1975 saw the extensive use of naval power but its dominance proved illusionary against a nimble and determined opponent hiding in southeast Asia's jungles. Fittingly, it was the US Navy and US Marine Corps who were called upon to lead the evacuation of Saigon in the hours before the arrival of communist troops into the South Vietnamese capital.

The opening military strikes of what become known as America's 'Global War on Terror', were spearheaded by the US Navy and US Marine Corps. After carrier-borne aircraft opened the bombardment of Afghanistan in October 2001, it fell to the US Marines to capture America's first base in the central Asian country.

All these conflicts feature in *Naval Warfare,* demonstrating the changing face of war on the seas over 120 or so years. We hope you find the publication stimulating and informative.

Tim Ripley
Editor
November 2023

LEFT: Nuclear powered submarines remain the dominant naval weapon, but their future is being questioned by the rise of robot vessels or drones. (RUSSIAN MINISTRY OF DEFENCE)

BELOW: Tim Ripley aboard HMS *Prince of Wales*, Britain's newest aircraft carrier. (TIM RIPLEY)

when its fleet was defeated by the new military power in the Pacific, Imperial Japan.

Less than 40 years later, naval battles decided the direction of World War Two and particularly the actions between Japan and America. The Japanese air attack on the US naval base at Pearl Harbor brought America into the war but within months, US aircraft carriers blunted the Japanese offensive wave at Midway. In the final months of the global conflict, US and British aircraft carriers brought allied naval power to the coasts of the Japanese homeland.

The Battle of the Atlantic was equally decisive. It was the longest continuous military conflict lasting from 1939 right up to the surrender of Germany, seeing the defeat of the U-boat threat and allowing the build up of US combat power in Britain, ahead of the invasion of occupied Europe on D-Day.

Overwhelming British, French and US naval power during the 1950s, 1960s, and 1970s could not stop the

Battleships to Carriers

From Dreadnoughts to Flat Tops

At the beginning of the 20th century, the steel battleship was the dominant weapon of naval warfare. The smooth bore cannon-equipped warships of the age of sail had given way to ones fitted with breech loading rifled guns. Steam power and iron - then steel - transformed warship design. In this era, heavy warships were divided into two main types. The big bruisers were the battleships, which boasted heavy armour and large gun batteries, positioned along the ship's hulls. They were supported by faster – but less heavily armoured and armed – battle cruisers, which were intended to range ahead of the main battle fleet looking for the enemy.

However, it was not long before these early generation battleships were overtaken by new technology. A new age of warship building culminated in the launching of

LEFT: During the 1920s and 1930s the battleship was still the benchmark of global naval power. The great powers – Britain, France, Japan, Italy, and the United States – tried to prevent a new naval arms race by agreeing the Washington Naval Treaty in 1922 to control numbers of battleships. (US NAVY)

HMS *Dreadnought* in 1906. This was a revolutionary battleship, powered by steam turbine to make her faster than any rival and her armament was mounted in large rotating turrets which could dominate opponents from long range. Overnight every other battleship in the world was obsolete, setting off a global arms race in the years leading up to World War One. Immediately, battleships were classified as Dreadnoughts or pre-Dreadnoughts.

For the first two decades of the 20th century, Dreadnought-class battleships dominated naval warfare. Admirals around the world sought to bring the enemy's fleets to battle so they could be destroyed by superior firepower. This culminated during World War One in the Battle of Jutland, which saw the British and German battleship fleets trade fire in the North Sea in the early summer of 1916. The battle ultimately proved inconclusive and represented the last major battle contested primarily by battleships.

In era of sail and broadsides, naval tactics revolved around the idea of 'crossing the T', in which a line of warships would cross in front of a line of enemy ships to allow the crossing line to bring all their guns to bear while it received fire from only the forward guns of the enemy fleet.

In the late 19th and the early 20th centuries, the advent of steam-powered battleships with rotating gun turrets made it possible to bring all of a ship's main guns to bear. They were able to move faster and turn more quickly than sailing ships, which had fixed guns facing sideways.

Although Dreadnought-class battleships had the firepower and speed needed for these more modern tactics, at Jutland it became apparent that other aspects of naval technology had not kept up. World War One-era battleships still largely relied on efficient observers with telescopes, or binoculars, to spot the enemy fleet on the horizon and then coloured signal flags were employed to order fleet manoeuvres. British and German tactics failed at Jutland because of technological problems. Rapid advances in communications and intelligence gathering soon revolutionised naval warfare. Reliable radio communications, or wireless as it was known, allowed fleets and individual warships to be controlled in real-time on a global basis. As soon as naval commanders realised the potential for using wireless to control their fleets, naval intelligence officers began to see the opportunity to gather information of their enemies' communications. Direction finding ❯

BELOW: The US Navy still boasted a significant flotilla of battleships throughout World War Two to provide air defence cover for its carriers and to bombard shore targets ahead of amphibious landings across the Pacific. (US NAVY)

RIGHT: Some of the US Navy's first experiments with naval aviation before World War One were carried out off the USS *Pennsylvania*, a converted armoured cruiser, which had been fitted with a landing platform. (US NATIONAL ARCHIVES)

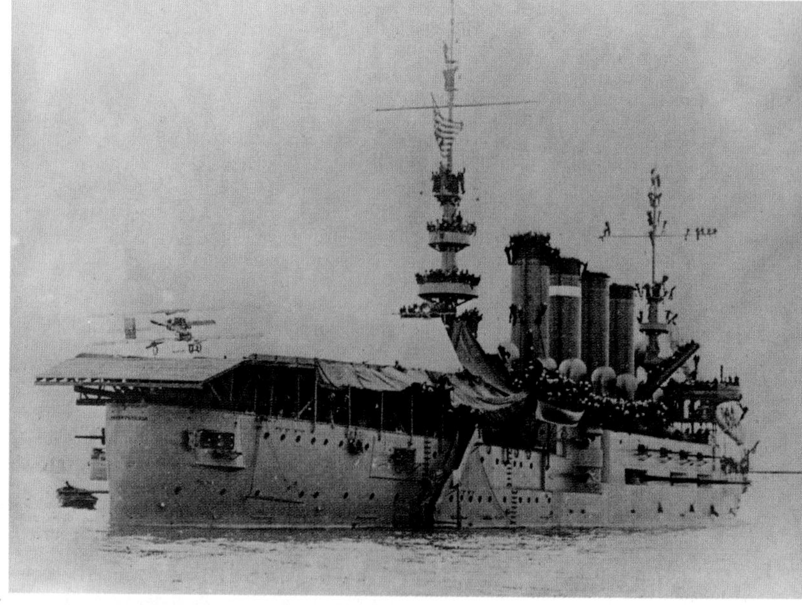

techniques could pinpoint the location of enemy ships transmitting radio messages and eventually code-breakers could read enemy radio traffic. This revolutionised naval intelligence in World War Two and gave fleet commanders – both Axis and Allied - a decisive advantage in many engagements.

After the end of World War One, the battleship continued to be considered the decisive weapon of naval warfare even though technological advances in aircraft, bombs, torpedoes, and submarines would soon make battleships obsolete.

During the 1920s and 1930s, enthusiasts for naval aviation pushed to develop aircraft carriers and strike aircraft that could deliver hammer blows without fleets having to come within sight of the enemy. This had the potential to transform naval warfare but, in the interwar period many senior naval officers were not convinced that the era of the battleship was over.

Flying off the deck of warships has a long history stretching back to World War One when several navies experimented with different methods of launching and recovering aircraft. The first heavier-than-air aircraft was launched off a warship in 1910 when aviation pioneer Eugine Ely flew his Curtiss Pusher off an improvised platform on the forward turret of the USS *Birmingham.* A few months later, he repeated the feat landing on a larger platform on the USS *Pennsylvania* and was then able to turn his aircraft around to take off a few minutes later.

In May 1912, Royal Navy Commander Charles Rumney Samson became the first airman to take off from a moving warship. He lifted off in a Short S.38 from the battleship HMS *Hibernia* while she steamed at 15kts during the Royal Fleet Review at Weymouth, England. Just over two year later, the Royal Navy launched the first ever warship dedicated to operating aircraft. The first HMS *Ark Royal* was originally intended be a merchant ship but midway through her construction, navy chiefs decided to fit her with a flat deck to allow the ship to launch and recover sea planes. Within months, another carrier, HMS *Furious,* was under construction and in 1917, Squadron Commander E.H. Dunning made the first landing on the ship as she was underway in Scapa Flow off Orkney. He was killed five days later, attempting to repeat the feat.

BELOW: The HMS *Ark Royal* of the 1930s was the first aircraft carrier which had hangars and flight deck as an integral part of the hull, instead of an add-on or part of the superstructure. (IMPERIAL WAR MUSEUM)

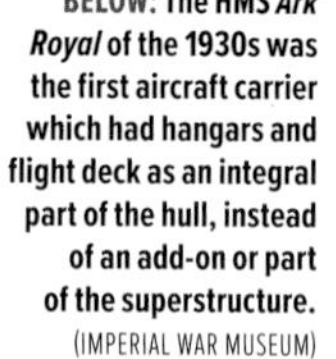

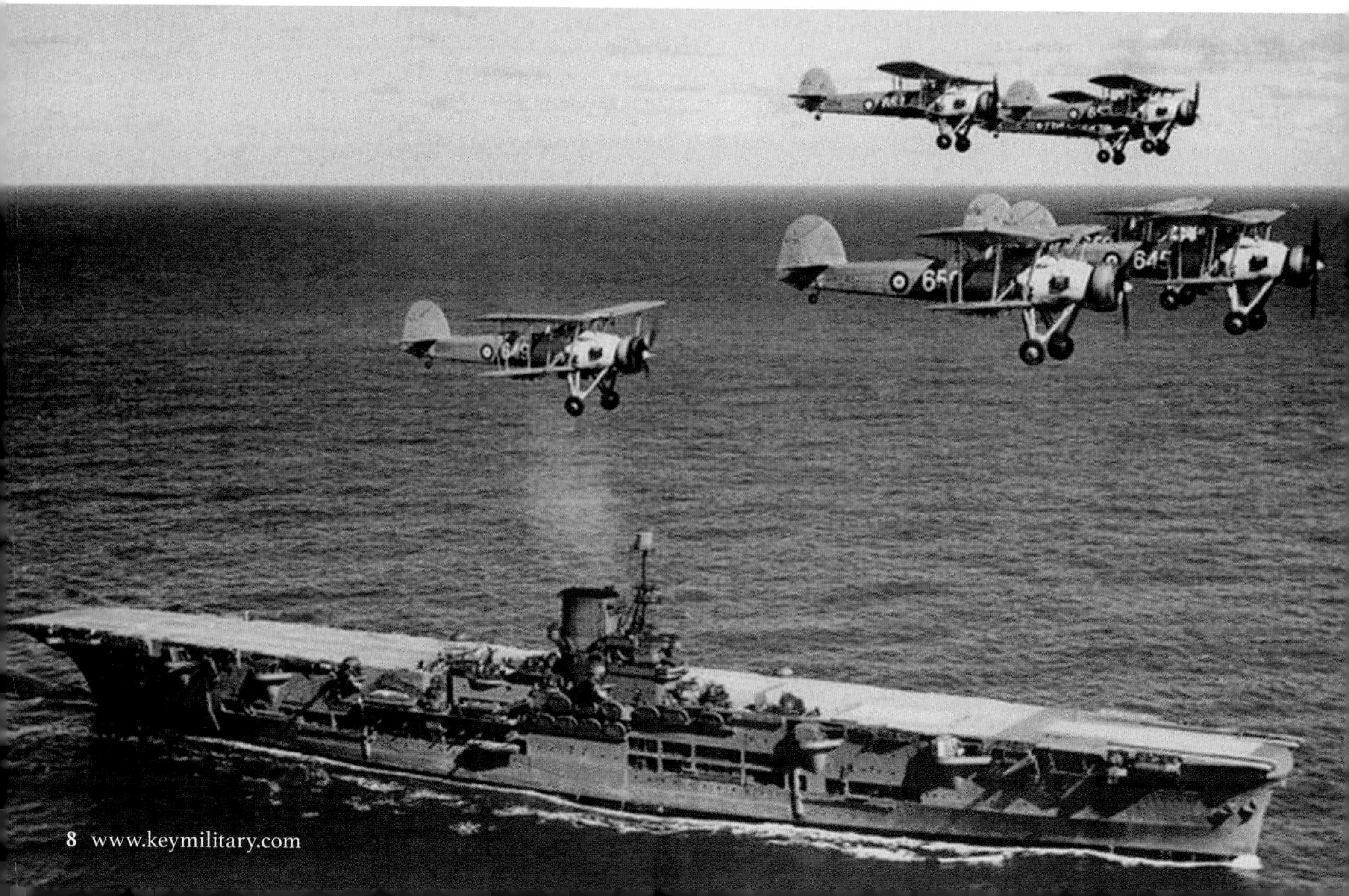

The recovery of aircraft on carriers had yet to be mastered.

HMS *Furious* was used in anger for the first time in July 1918 when she launched seven Sopwith Camel aircraft to drop improvised bombs on the German Zeppelin base at Tondern. Several of the German airships were destroyed or damaged in the raid, but the British naval aviators had no way of landing back on the ship, so either had to ditch in the sea next to HMS *Furious* or land in neutral Denmark.

In the 1920s and 1930s the Royal Navy continued to lead the way, experimenting with bigger and better aircraft carriers, as well as developing the aircraft and weapons to fly off them. The first warship that was able to routinely launch and recover powered aircraft was HMS *Argus,* which for the first time boasted a large flat deck for aircraft to launch and recover on.

This was a period of transition between the dominance of the battleship and the rise of the aircraft carrier, as the main type of capital ship. The British, US, and Japanese navies were the leaders in the drive to build bigger and better aircraft carriers, as well as to field purpose-built aircraft to operate from flat tops. Revolutionary thinkers in navies around the world could see the potential of the carrier and an embarked air group but it had not been proved in battle.

This changed on November 11, 1940, when the carrier HMS *Illustrious* launched a strike force of Fairy Swordfish torpedo bombers to attack the main port of the Italian fleet at Taranto. The Italians were taken by surprise by the daring strike and in a matter of minutes, half the Italian fleet was at the bottom of the harbour. Only two Swordfish were lost in the attack.

The supremacy of British naval airpower was demonstrated again six months later when more Swordfish, launched from the second carrier to bear the name HMS *Ark Royal,* found, and crippled the German battleship *Bismark* in the North Atlantic.

The Japanese attack on the US Navy base at Pearl Harbor on December 7, 1941, put carrier aviation on the map. The crippling of the US Pacific Fleet in a matter of hours showed that the aircraft carrier was now the dominant naval weapon.

ABOVE: The Royal Navy got out of the conventional aircraft carrier business in the 1970s on cost grounds and had to innovate to fill this capability gap by fielding the Invincible-class carriers equipped with the revolutionary Sea Harrier jump jet. (ROYAL NAVY)

The USS *Saratoga* was one of the Forrestal-class aircraft carriers, which was the first class of super carriers, combining high tonnage, deck-edge elevators, and an angled deck. (US NAVY)

Submarines Dominate

From U-Boats to Nukes

The past 120 years have seen submarines transformed from being unreliable craft with short range and limited ability to stay underwater for prolonged periods into the dominant naval weapon.

Although experimental underwater craft had been built through the 19th century, it was not until the 1890s that the Irish inventor John Philip Holland produced the design of what is considered the first modern submarine. His submarine was powered by a petrol engine when on the surface and relied on a battery powered electric motor when submerged. The captain had a periscope to observe the surface, whilst the vessel was underwater, and it had two tubes that could launch torpedoes at ships. He sold his design first to the United States Navy and Imperial Russia.

Famously, when British Admiral Sir Arthur Wilson was offered the design of the submarine for the Royal Navy, he declined, saying submarines were "underhand, unfair and damned un-English." The Admiralty, however, had other ideas and secretly placed an order in 1901 for a version of their own, which was dubbed *Holland 1* by the Royal Navy. The rest as they say is history.

By the start of World War One, all the major European navies had fleets of submarines and they were soon in action. These early submarines now sported conning towers, deck guns, pressure hulls and multiple torpedo tubes. They, however, could only remain submerged for a few hours at a time before they had to surface to recharge their electric batteries and refresh their air. This meant that World War One era submarines only submerged when they were making their final attack and would transit to their operational areas on the surface.

The Imperial German Navy produced the strategy of using its U-boats, or Unterseeboot in German, which literally translated as undersea boat, to strike at British shipping in the North Atlantic. By cutting its sea lanes, the Germans hoped to starve Britain into surrender. At first, individual merchant vessels were picked off easily, but the allies tried to neutralise the U-boat threat by forming convoys of ships that were protected by warships.

In the 1930s, Nazi Germany re-started U-boat production and worked hard to perfect the design of its submarines. Improved battery

technology meant that U-boats could now stay underwater for more than 24 hours at a time. The Type VII – the most common U-boat of the first half of World War Two – could carry 14 Torpedoes and had an 88mm anti-aircraft gun on her deck to take on allied maritime patrol aircraft or fire on unarmed merchant ships. By 1943, the Germans had perfected the design of a snorkel that would allow fresh air to be brought into a submerged U-boat down a pipe. This allowed the U-boat to run its diesel engine while submerged and meant it could spend extended periods underwater.

The Nazi U-boat fleet came close to victory in the Battle of Atlantic but advances in radar, radio direction finding, maritime patrol aircraft and anti-submarine tactics allowed the allies to defeat the submarine menace.

In 1955, the US Navy sailed the world's first nuclear-powered submarine, the USS *Nautilus* and so revolutionised naval warfare. Nuclear-powered submarines did not need to be refuelled during cruises, could

generate their own water, and recycle their air supply so in theory could remain submerged indefinitely. The only limiting factor was the amount of food the vessel could carry to feed her crew. At a stroke, all previous

anti-submarine equipment and tactics were obsolete.

When the United States installed Polaris inter-continental ballistic missiles into the USS *George Washington* it transformed the ❯

ABOVE: Sinking of the SS *Linda Blanche* by *U-21* in January 1915 at the start of the German unrestricted submarine campaign in World War One. (WILLY STOWER)

LEFT: Captured German U-boats outside their pen at Trondheim in Norway, after the Nazi surrender in May 1945. The U-boat campaign brought Britain to the verge of defeat. (IMPERIAL WAR MUSEUM)

RIGHT: The world's first nuclear powered submarine, USS *Nautilus*, has been permanently docked at the US Submarine Force Museum and Library, Groton, Connecticut, since 2008. (US NAVY)

RIGHT: Admiral Hyman Rickover over saw the building of the world's first nuclear powered submarine, the USS *Nautilus*, leading to him being dubbed the 'Father of the Nuclear Navy'. (US NAVY)

BELOW: The USS *Nautilus* got 'underway on nuclear power' on January 17, 1955, to formally to launch the age of nuclear-powered submarines. (US NAVY)

global nuclear stand-off. The US Navy could now strike at the heart of the Soviet Union from a submarine operating in the northern hemisphere. These SSBNs were almost impossible to track and there was little opportunity to build defence systems to intercept their missiles. It meant that there was no chance for the Soviet Union to launch a surprise strike to disarm America's nuclear arsenal by hitting its nuclear armed bombers on their airfields or land-based nuclear missiles in their silos. The Soviet Navy soon fielded its own SSBNs, and this brought stability to the Cold War arms race, epitomised by the concept of Mutually Assured Destruction, or MAD, as it was known. This prompted the first moves towards arms control to limit Soviet and American nuclear arsenals.

While SSBNs ensured peace because of their invulnerability, US, Soviet, British, and French navies started to field new fleets of nuclear-powered attack, or hunter killer, submarines, known as SSNs. They used their unlimited endurance and stealth to dominate the world oceans. Once underway, they would dive deep and detect enemy shipping at long-range using advanced sonar technology. These were the ultimate ship killers, and they had the advantage in almost every sort of scenario, even against

the most modern and best equipped surface warship. The best way to defeat an attack boat was to send another hunter-killer submarine after her.

Unlike in the interwar period, when many navy chiefs had been sceptical about the utility and effectiveness of aircraft carriers, few Cold War naval chiefs had any doubts that nuclear-powered attack submarines would dominate any fleet engagements should the stand-off between East and West ever turn into a real 'hot war'. Both NATO and Soviet fleets quickly became dominated by anti-submarine operations and resulted in most ships, aircraft and helicopters being optimised to hunt and kill submarines. Ships and submarines were fitted with towed sonar arrays to extend detection ranges. Helicopters were fitted with dunking sonar to listen for submarines. Anti-submarine aircraft were equipped to drop and control sonobuoy fields that could triangulate the position of a submarine's sound. New families of torpedoes were fielded that could home in on submarines. The US Navy created arrays of sea-bed based acoustic listening devices, dubbed SOSUS, spread across the North Atlantic and Pacific, to track Soviet submarines.

The power of modern attack submarines was demonstrated dramatically in May 1982 when the British submarine, HMS *Conqueror*, sank the Argentine cruiser, ARA *General Belgrano*. For the rest of the Falklands conflict, the Argentine fleet stayed in port and conceded naval supremacy in the South Atlantic to the Royal Navy.

Land Attack Missiles

The ending of the Cold War in 1989 saw another evolution of submarine operations when the US Navy started firing Tomahawk Land Attack Missiles (TLAM) as part of strategic air campaigns. Hundreds of TLAMs were fired from US submarines during the 1991 Gulf War, 1999 Kosovo War, 2001 Afghan War, 2003 invasion of Iran, and 2011 Libyan intervention. British submarines and ships joined in these operations from 1999 and fired their own TLAMs.

Russian submarines have also fired hundreds of their own Kalibr cruise missiles at targets in Syria between 2015 and 2018, as well as against Ukraine from 2022.

Submarines retain their dominant position in the naval hierarchy but the race for supremacy under the sea remains competitive with global navies searching for technological advantages. A modern SSN costs well over $1bn to design and build, as well as hundreds of millions of dollars a year to operate. So, staying in the nuclear submarine business is very expensive and only a handful of navies can afford the price of entry.

ABOVE: The arrival of submarines capable of firing Polaris intercontinental ballistic nuclear missiles in 1960 transformed the nuclear stand-off between the US and Soviet Union. The USS *George Washington* made her maiden deterrent patrol in 1960 and eight years later the HMS *Resolution* sailed for her first patrol. (ROYAL NAVY)

LEFT: Russian Navy attack submarines, such as this Victor/Project 671 class boat, are now reported to match their western rivals in terms of speed and low acoustic signatures. (RUSSIAN MINISTRY OF DEFENCE)

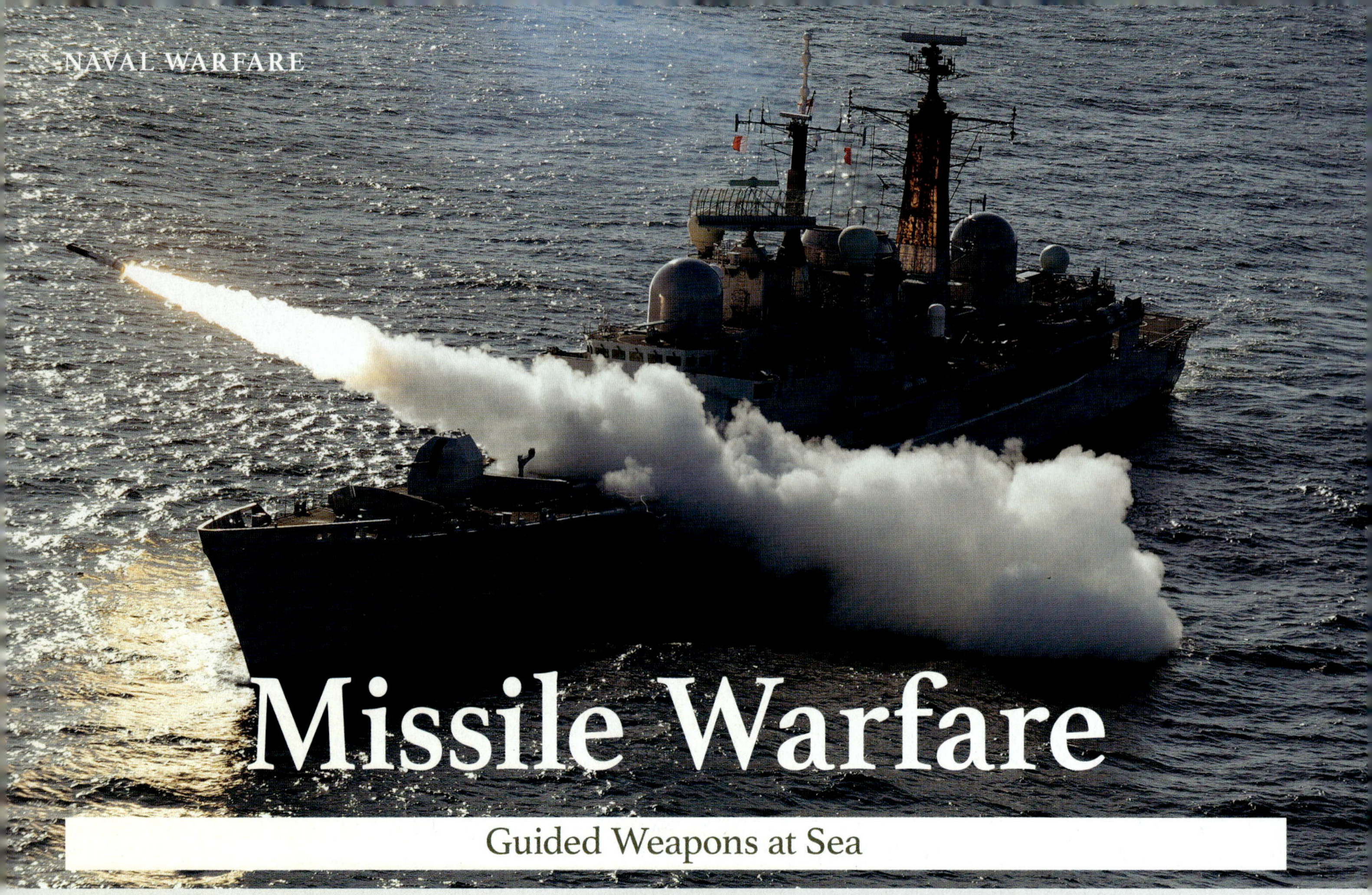

Missile Warfare

Guided Weapons at Sea

ABOVE: Since the 1960s, guided weapons have dominated naval warfare – to strike at enemy ships or targets ashore, as well as to defeat enemy air or missile attacks. Here, HMS *Edinburgh* fires a Sea Dart anti-aircraft missile during a trial. (MOD/CROWN COPYRIGHT)

RIGHT: The Fritz X was the first guided weapon to be successfully used in naval warfare, when in September 1943, a Luftwaffe Dornier Do 217 aircraft used them to sink the Italian battleship *Roma* and damage the battleship *Italia* as they were sailing to surrender to the Allies. (SANJAY ACHARYA)

BELOW: The USS *Savannah* was the first warship to fall victim to a guided weapon when she was hit off Salerno on September 11, 1943, during Allied landings on the Italian coast. (US NAVY)

Warships are notoriously difficult to find, hit and sink. In the first half of the 20th century warships relied on traditional gunnery and torpedoes to engage enemy vessels. Naval aircraft had unguided, or dumb, bombs and torpedoes. All these weapons relied on the attacking ship or aircraft getting as close as possible before releasing their weapons. This invariably brought them within range of the target's own defensive systems.

The answer seemed to be to use radio communications to control and guide weapons to their targets. Radar allowed long range detection of targets and enabled operators to keep their weapons heading in the right direction. Until the 1950s, the electronic industry had yet to develop the necessary components to make guided weapons operate effectively in the maritime environment. However, in the past 70 years the reliability and effectiveness of guided weapons has improved dramatically, and they now allow navies to dominate huge areas of ocean with a few weapons.

The first generation of guided weapons relied on fairly basic radio command systems and a near continuous control link had to be maintained to keep weapons on target. In World War Two, the German *Luftwaffe* carried out the first ever anti-shipping strike using air-launched guided weapons.

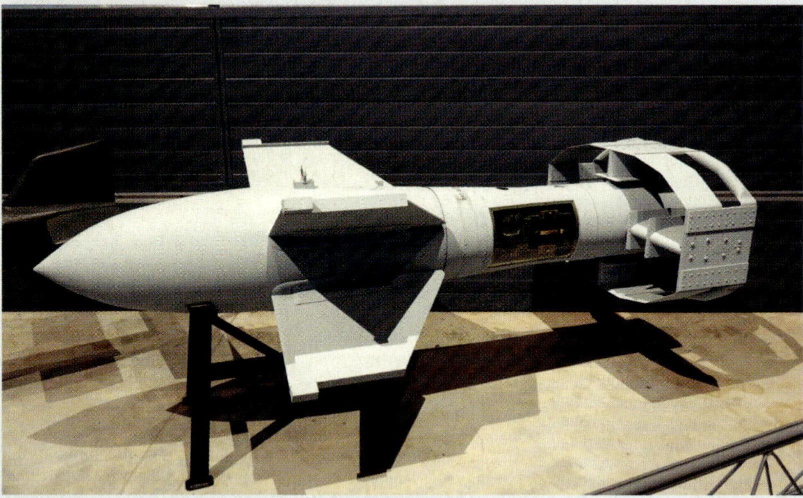

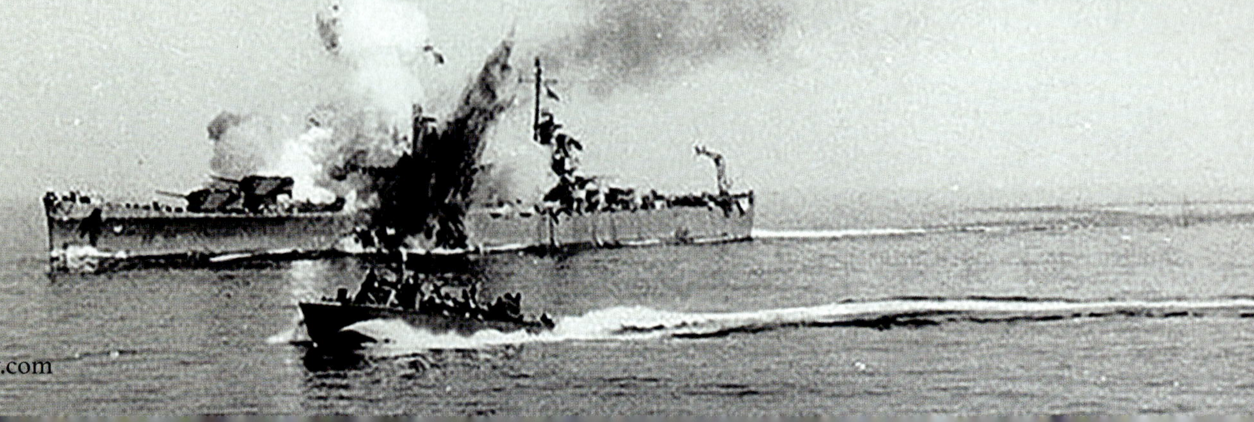

The Fritz X was a guided bomb, which used radio control to direct it towards its target. In September 1943, the weapons scored their first ever hits when six Dornier Do 217K-2s bombers attacked Italian warships, trying to defect to the Allied side. The Italian battleship *Roma* received two hits and one near miss, and sank after her magazines exploded, killing 1,393 men. Her sister ship, *Italia*, was also seriously damaged but reached a safe port.

A few weeks later the Luftwaffe elite unit, Kampfgeschwader 100, was in action against allied ships during the amphibious landing at Salerno in southern Italy. Several ships were hit and badly damaged, including the cruiser USS *Savannah*, the light cruiser HMS *Uganda* and battleship HMS *Warspite.* The allies eventually realised the Achilles heel of the Fritz X and started to jam the radio frequencies used to control the weapons.

The 1950s and 1960s saw a massive interest in developing guided missiles for warships, which went hand in hand with advances in electronics, mini-computers, and radar sensors. The first missiles with their own onboard radars started appearing at this time and they were quickly used in action.

The first ship to be sunk by a modern guided missile, was the Israeli destroyer, the INS *Eilat*, which was hit by three SS-N-2 Styx missiles, fired from Egyptian Komar-class missile boats. The Soviet supplied radar-guided missiles were rudimentary by modern standards, but the Egyptians caught the Israeli warship by surprise by firing their weapons from inside Port Said harbour.

Enter the Exocet

In France, missile makers were working on a more ingenious weapon dubbed the Exocet that was designed to fly at just above wave height to avoid radar surveillance. It had an onboard radar that was used to identify targets and during the weapon's approach to its targets, it was programmed to 'pop-up' briefly to allow the radar to get a good fix on the target and then issue course corrections to its guidance computer.

The Exocet received its combat debut during the 1982 Falklands conflict when two missiles fired from an Argentine Navy Super Etendard jet hit and sank the British destroyer HMS *Sheffield*. Another air-launched missile hit and sank the cargo vessel MV *Atlantic Conveyor* and a land-launched Exocet severely damaged the destroyer HMS *Glamorgan*.

During the 1980s Iran-Iraq tanker war in the Arabian Gulf, Iraqi jets hit several tanks with Exocets and also accidently hit and severely damaged the USS *Stark* in 1987.

The increasing effectiveness of guided weapons prompted navies to look to bolster their air and missile defences. Radar surveillance had proved very effective in World War Two at detecting approaching enemy aircraft and this usually allowed friendly fighters to be launched to intercept the in-bound attackers. Radar coverage around naval task groups always starts to degrade because of the curvature of the earth leading to radar black spots, so in the 1950s the first airborne early warning (AEW) aircraft began to be fielded as part of US and British carrier air groups. This in effect elevated the

ABOVE: France's Exocet sea skimming missile transformed naval warfare in May 1982 when they were used by the Argentine navy to sink the British destroyer, HMS *Sheffield*. (TIM RIPLEY)

BELOW: The USS *Stark* accidently fell victim to an Exocet launched from an Iraqi jet at the heart of the Iran-Iraq war in 1987. (US NAVY)

radar up high and allowed it to 'look down' and negate the curvature of the earth. US Skyraider and British Gannet aircraft were the first examples of carrier-borne AEW aircraft. The Royal Navy, however, stood down its Gannets in the 1970s when its last 'cats and traps' aircraft carrier, HMS *Ark Royal*, was retired on cost grounds. The replacement Invincible-class carriers had no embarked AEW in their first years of service.

RIGHT: The Soviet Styx anti-ship missile was developed in the 1950s. It has since been modified by the Chinese as the Silkworm, which has been used in combat by both Iran and Iraq. (US DOD/JOINT COMBAT CAMERA)

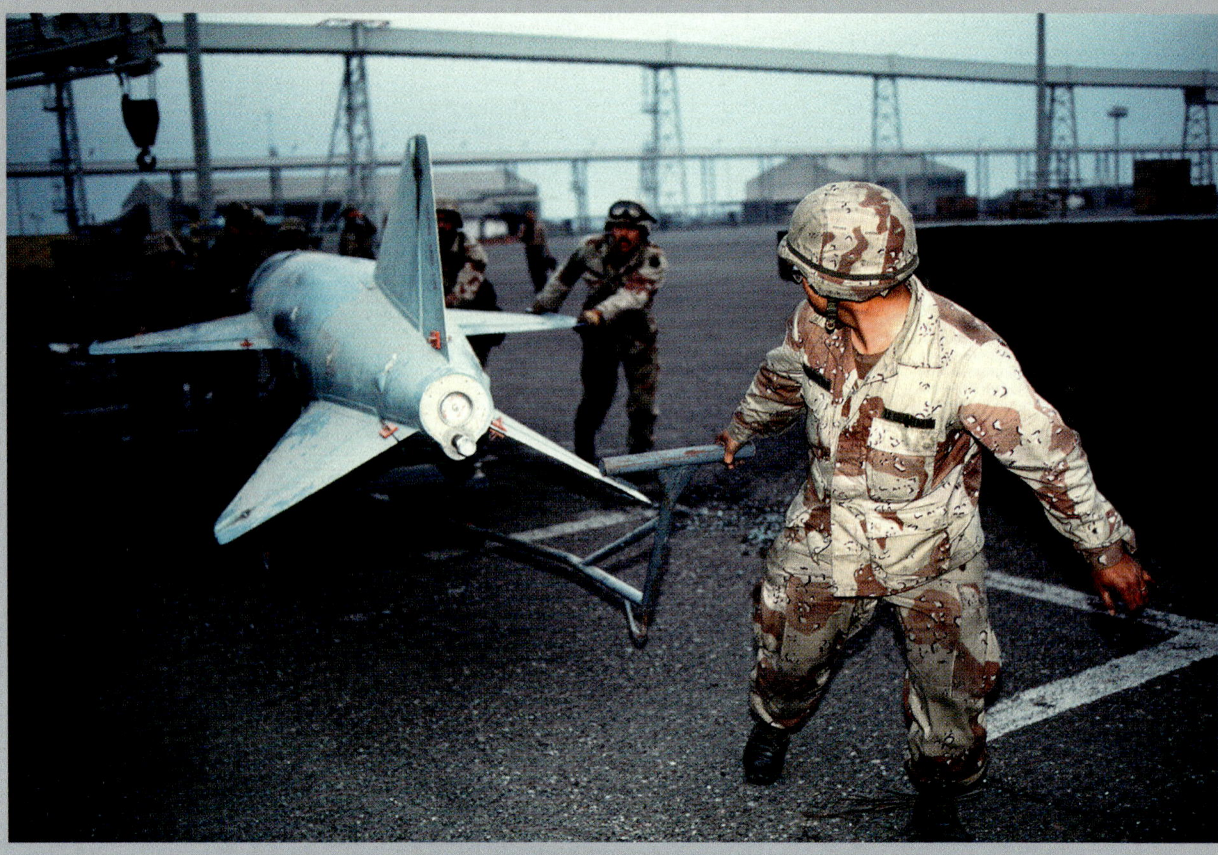

The first effective guided air defence missiles started to be fielded on warships in the 1960s and they generally came in two distinct classes. Long range weapons that relied on radar guidance control from warships were designed to take-out high-flying threats. Simultaneously, aircraft and missiles that got through the outer layer of missiles were to be engaged with shorter range - and more manoeuvrable – missiles. In the 1970s a second generation of weapons that boasted radar homing and lock-on features started to appear on warships.

The Falklands conflict was the first naval theatre of the guided missile age, and the power of these weapons was brutally demonstrated by the aforementioned devastation of HMS *Sheffield* by a French-made Exocet sea skimming missile. While the Argentines achieved an impressive hit rate with their Exocets - five air and one ground launched, hitting three targets – the

BELOW: The US Navy's answer to the Exocet was the Harpoon, which can be launched from warships, submarines, and aircraft. Here one is being launched from the USS *Shiloh* during a training exercise. (US NAVY)

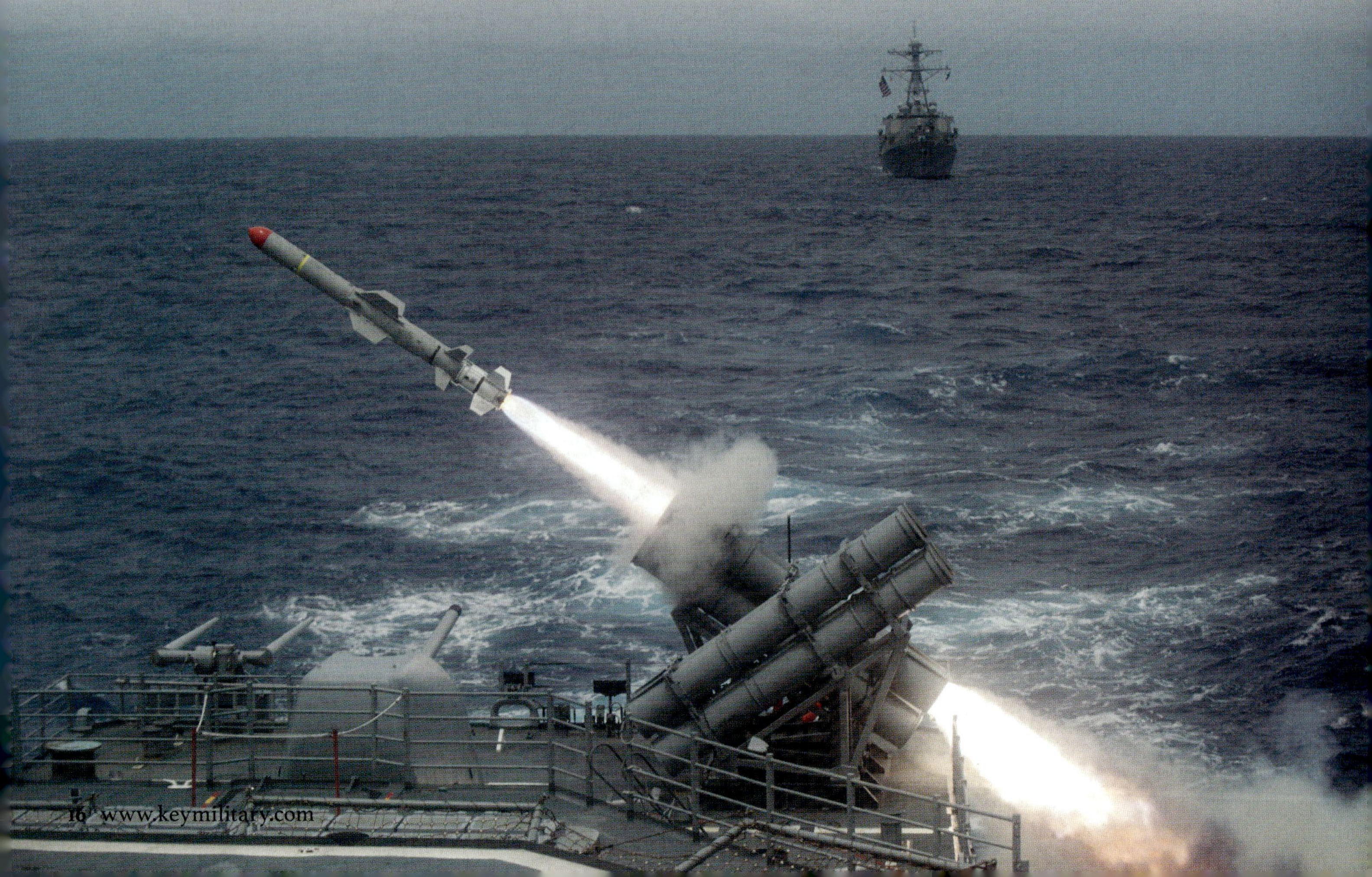

British air defence missiles proved less impressive. Analysis of British missile engagements from ships revealed that the fundamental problem was a lack of reliability of their Sea Wolf and Sea Dart missiles that meant, at critical moments, control switches did not work because of corrosion, software crashing or missiles refusing to fire. During the Battle of San Carlos, the Royal Navy re-learnt the lesson that putting up a wall of machine gun and cannon fire can have a disproportionate impact on incoming strike jet pilots, forcing them to take evasive action and so miss their targets.

In the following decades, the Royal Navy sorted out many of the bugs in their missile systems, warships were fitted with Phalanx gun close-in weapon systems that can shoot down Exocet-type missiles and crucially an airborne early warning helicopter was rapidly brought into service to provide 'over the horizon' radar coverage for naval task groups. In the 1991 Gulf war, the improvements of the Royal Navy air defences were demonstrated when HMS *Gloucester* successfully intercepted Iraqi Silkworm missiles – a derivative of the Styx missiles that had sunk the INS *Eilat* - heading towards the battleship USS *Missouri* as it was bombarding the Kuwaiti coastline. HMS *Gloucester*'s crew detected the Iraqi missile launch and the British ship engaged it with an improved Sea Dart missile.

The dangers to warships from anti-ship missiles have not gone away, as was demonstrated in April 2022 when the Ukrainian navy engaged and sank the flag ship of the Russian Black Sea Fleet, the RFS *Moskva*, with a Neptune missile.

ABOVE: Russia's Kh-47M2 Kinzhal air-launched ballistic missile is the first generation of hypersonic missiles, which have the potential to transform naval war. (RUSSIAN MINISTRY OF DEFENCE)

BELOW: Helicopter-launched anti-ship missiles, such as the Martlet seen here being launched from a Royal Navy Wildcat, are now in widespread use and are very effective weapons to dominate sea zones. (MOD/CROWN COPYRIGHT)

Commanding at Sea

Leading Naval Forces

ABOVE: The 'view from the bridge' of a Royal Navy frigate at the height of World War Two. (IMPERIAL WAR MUSEUM)

When Britain's Grand Fleet and Germany's High Seas Fleet starting trading fire at the Battle of Jutland on the last day of May in 1916, it was the biggest naval action of World War One. More than 150 British warships duelled with just under 100 German vessels. Fourteen British and 11 German warships were sunk, with the loss of more than 8,000 sailors from both navies.

It was the first and last time two fleets of Dreadnought-class battleships clashed in battle. Onboard their respective flag ships, the Royal Navy's Admiral Sir John Jellicoe, and the Imperial German Navy's Vice-Admiral Reinhard Scheer, watched the action unfold. They heard shells flying over their ships and could smell the cordite from the gun turrets. Around them they could see ships exploding.

Jellicoe and Scheer controlled their fleets by radio, or wireless as it was then known, signal lights, and flags. The latter two methods were by far the preferred means of communication for Dreadnought era admirals. They were familiar with them and there was still huge suspicion of the new-fangled wireless. Jellicoe had benefited before the battle with intelligence gained from intercepts of German radio traffic, but he still made most of his decisions during the coming battle on what he could see from the bridge of his flag ship. This would be the last time rival fleet commanders would be able view naval battles for themselves, as they unfolded.

In World War Two, fleet actions involved the launching and recovering of aircraft to strike at the enemy. Battlegroup commanders controlled events from shore headquarters or the map rooms of their flag ships. Signal officers and radio operators worked at a high pace to receive and send messages. Fleet dispositions were laid out on large map tables to allow the commanders and their staff to consider tactical options. Real time intelligence from direction finding posts, radio intercept stations, picket submarines

RIGHT: Admiral Chester Nimitz (left) was the mastermind of America's Pacific naval campaign, which drove the Japanese back to their home islands in World War Two. (US NAVY)

ABOVE: The Japanese naval battle groups at Pearl Harbor and Midway were led by Chūichi Nagumo, who was notoriously indecisive and left his aircraft carriers open to attack. (IMPERIAL JAPANESE NAVY)

sound of the enemy. Victory or defeat depended on the slick passage of information up to battle staff.

In the years following World War Two, command at sea changed very little. When Britain's Admiral Sandy Woodward led the Royal Navy task force to the South Atlantic to liberate the Falklands, he found the experience similar to that of his predecessors, 40 years before.

Information Delays

In some cases, it took days or weeks for crucial messages to be passed and received by senior commanders on ships spread out across the South Atlantic. Only a handful of rudimentary satellite radios were available to the British and the Argentines had none at all. There were no video conferencing links, streaming video, or email to send high resolution satellite reconnaissance photographs of enemy positions. Some warships were equipped with the then-new data links to share radar and submarine ❯

and scout aircraft provided crucial tips at decisive moments in battles. It was now routine for senior fleet commanders never to see sight nor

ABOVE: The Royal Navy's great innovator in World War Two was Admiral Andrew Cunningham, who used carrier-borne airpower to strike at the Italian fleet at Taranto. (IMPERIAL WAR MUSEUM)

LEFT: By the 1970s, warships were commanded from computerised command information centres, where radar returns, and other intelligence was displayed on screens. (US NAVY)

RIGHT: In the 21st century, time critical information is displayed on large screens in warships operations rooms, to give commanders a real-time view of the battlespace. (US NAVY)

BELOW: Rear Admiral Sandy Woodward commanded the British naval task group in the South Atlantic throughout the Falklands campaign, often with little direction or advice from senior commanders in London. (MOD)

tracks, but the technology was in its infancy and often proved unreliable. Long distance communications had to be sent by highly formatted signals that had to be physically typed into message machines.

This communications gap was highlighted by the issue of satellite intelligence. It was widely assumed that the Americans would provide their British allies with huge quantities of images taken by their network of spy satellites. However, it transpired that hardly any of them orbited over South America or the Falklands. The South Atlantic climate meant that for most of the war, key locations such as Port Stanley or Argentine airbases were shrouded in cloud preventing the US spy satellites from taking any useful imagery. Even when the Americans could get decent pictures, the only way they could be delivered to the British task group was for hard copy prints to be flown to the airbase on Ascension Island and then parachuted to Royal Navy warships in the South Atlantic. There was no real-time surveillance of the Falklands. Not surprisingly, Royal Navy officers found the 1981 edition of the famous *Jane's Fighting Ships* naval reference book to be their best source of intelligence on the Argentine navy.

Admiral Woodward made split second decisions based on flimsy information that was often rendered out-of-date when new intelligence arrived days or weeks later. This was the loneliness of command, exercised to the extreme.

The British did have one huge intelligence advantage though. The eavesdropping agency at the Government Communications Headquarters (GCHQ) had cracked both the Argentine diplomatic cables traffic and the radio codes of the Argentine navy. Within hours of key messages being sent by the Junta in Buenos Aires they had been read by the British code breakers in Cheltenham. The Cabinet in London often had advance warning of Argentine moves in the run-up to the war and, once the Task Force approached the Falklands, the Ministry of Defence had early warning of enemy naval moves.

However, the precarious communications with the Task Force in the South Atlantic meant it often took hours or days for this war winning intelligence to reach those who needed it. The events leading up the sinking of the ARA *General Belgrano* epitomised this phenomenon. All the participants were working on out-of-date information, and no one had the full picture.

At crucial moments in the war, the commanders found themselves out of communications and ended up resorting to what is euphemistically dubbed 'best military judgement'. The Falklands war was definitely a conflict fought before the modern information era.

By the 1990s, the modern communications era had finally arrived when satellite television was installed onboard US Navy aircraft carriers, so the crew could watch live television coverage of the wars they were fighting. This was swiftly followed by secure email, broadband-like internet connections, and secure video conferencing. US Navy fleet commanders were now part of a joint force, combining air, land, and sea forces.

LEFT: Despite the proliferation of modern communications and computerised systems, command at sea can never be divorced from the need for good seamanship to ensure warships remain safe and achieve their missions. (MOD/CROWN COPYRIGHT)

BELOW: Captain James 'Sandy' Winnefeld was in command of the USS *Enterprise* on September 11, 2001, when critical decisions were made to position US naval forces to within striking range of Afghanistan. (US NAVY)

Real Time

On the morning of September 11, 2001, Captain James 'Sandy' Winnefeld, the captain of the aircraft carrier, USS *Enterprise* watched the two hijacked airliners crash into the Twin Towers live on television in his cabin. His ship was sailing south through the Indian Ocean towards South Africa. He was immediately able to order his ship to slow down and prepare to change course to move into position to be ready to strike at suspected Al Qaeda bases in Afghanistan. Minutes later he had held a telephone conference with his battlegroup commander and fleet commander, who ordered Winnefeld to bring his carrier about and be off the coast of Pakistan by the following morning.

When the US was ready to strike at Afghanistan a month later, Winnefeld's pilots and aircrew received their orders for the first wave of air attacks in a top-secret email known as an air tasking order. This incorporated all the targets, flight plans, routes, weapons loads, air-to-air refuelling positions and other tactical details for all the aircraft – US Air Force, US Navy, and British Royal Air Force – participating in the first raid, as well as all the targeting data needed by US and British warship and submarine crews to programme the Tomahawk Land Attack Missiles being fired. Once this information was received by USS *Enterprise*'s aircraft squadrons, they set to working getting ready for battle. No longer are naval forces expected to fight on their own.

Tsushima to Jutland

Battleship Action

Battleships were the dominant type of warship in the first decades of the 20th century but surprisingly there were only two major fleet actions, in which rival nations traded fire on the high seas.

The Battle of Tsushima, off the southern coast of Korea in May 1905 can truly be called decisive. It was the first defeat of a European military force by an Asian country and set in train the events that eventually led to the overthrow of the Russian monarchy a decade later.

When Russia and Japan clashed, it was the first war of the industrial era, that pitted rival modern armies and navies against each other. They fielded machine runs, rifled artillery, motor vehicles and iron battleships. The eastward expansion of the Russian empire into Manchuria and Korea prompted the Japanese to strike back. After being opened to western influence by the United States in the 1850s, the Japanese had resolved to build westernised armed forces to prevent the country falling under foreign influence. The Japanese turned to Britain to help build their navy and its first battleships were built in Barrow-in-Furness in Cumbria.

In February 1904, the Japanese launched a surprise attack on the

Russian garrison and naval flotilla at Port Arthur, now Lüshun Port, in northeastern China. This port dominated the western coast of the Korean peninsula, which the Japanese hoped to incorporate into their

growing empire. Japanese torpedo boats attacked and badly damaged two Russian battleships and a cruiser. In April, the two surviving Russian battleships tried to foray out to break the Japanese blockade. Both hit sea

LEFT: Admiral Tōgō Heihachirō on the bridge of his flag ship, *Mikasa*, at the height of the battle of Tsushima. (TŌJŌ SHŌTARŌ)

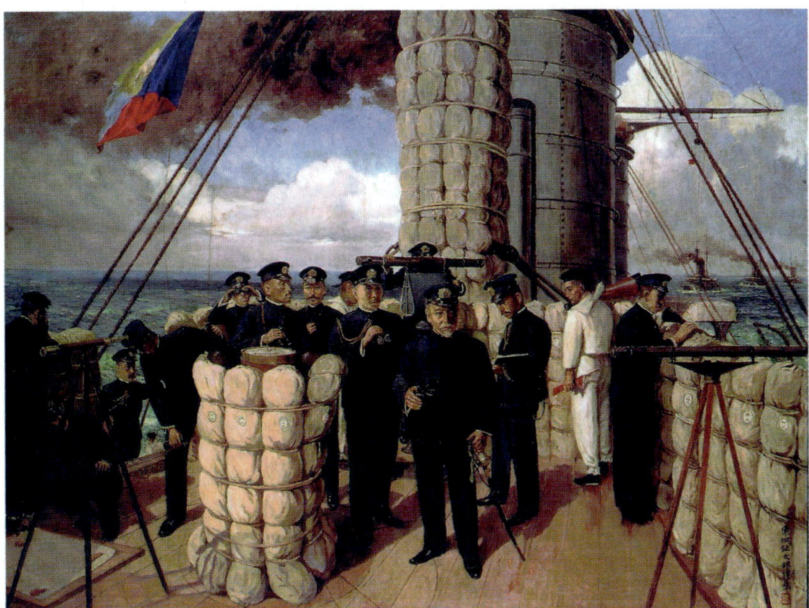

mines and one of the battleships sank immediately, the other limped back into port after being badly damaged. The commander of the Russian navy's Pacific squadron, Admiral Stepan Makarov, died in the incident that effectively bottled-up Russia's remaining fleet inside Port Arthur.

In October 1904, to try to restore the situation and break the Japanese dominance in the Pacific, Tsar Nicholas II ordered the Russian Baltic Fleet to sail to the Far East to engage the Japanese. This was an 18,000nm odyssey around the Cape of Good Hope and through the South China Sea. En route the fleet fired on British fishing boats in the North Sea, almost bringing the British into the war on the side of the Japanese.

By mid May 1905, the Russian fleet was approaching the Tsushima Strait, which separated Japan from the Korean peninsula.

The Japanese Combined Fleet under Admiral Tōgō Heihachirō sailed out to meet Admiral Zinovy Rozhestvensky's Russian squadron of which many vessels were suffering from mechanical problems from their mammoth voyage and could not match the speed of the Japanese warships.

The Russians hoped to reach Vladivostok and establish naval control of the region in order to relieve the Imperial Russian Army in Manchuria. The Russian fleet of 29 battleships and cruisers had a numerical advantage in terms of battleships but was overall older and slower than the Japanese fleet of five battleships and 29 cruisers.

The Russians were sighted in the early morning on May 27, and the battle began in the afternoon when the Japanese effectively 'crossed the T', bringing overwhelming firepower to bear against the columns of Russian warships. The Japanese gunnery devastated the Russian fleet, sinking four of its eight battleships in short order. Just 90 minutes into the encounter the Russian battleship *Oslyabya* become the first ever steel or iron battleship to be sunk solely by naval gunnery.

Rozhestvensky was wounded and knocked unconscious in the initial action and by sunset the Russian fleet was effectively blocked.At night, Japanese destroyers and torpedo boats were unleashed to attack the remaining Russian ships, which

BELOW: Alerted by radio to the presence of Russian warships, the Japanese fleet put to sea in the early hours of May 27, 1905. (SHIGETADA SEKI)

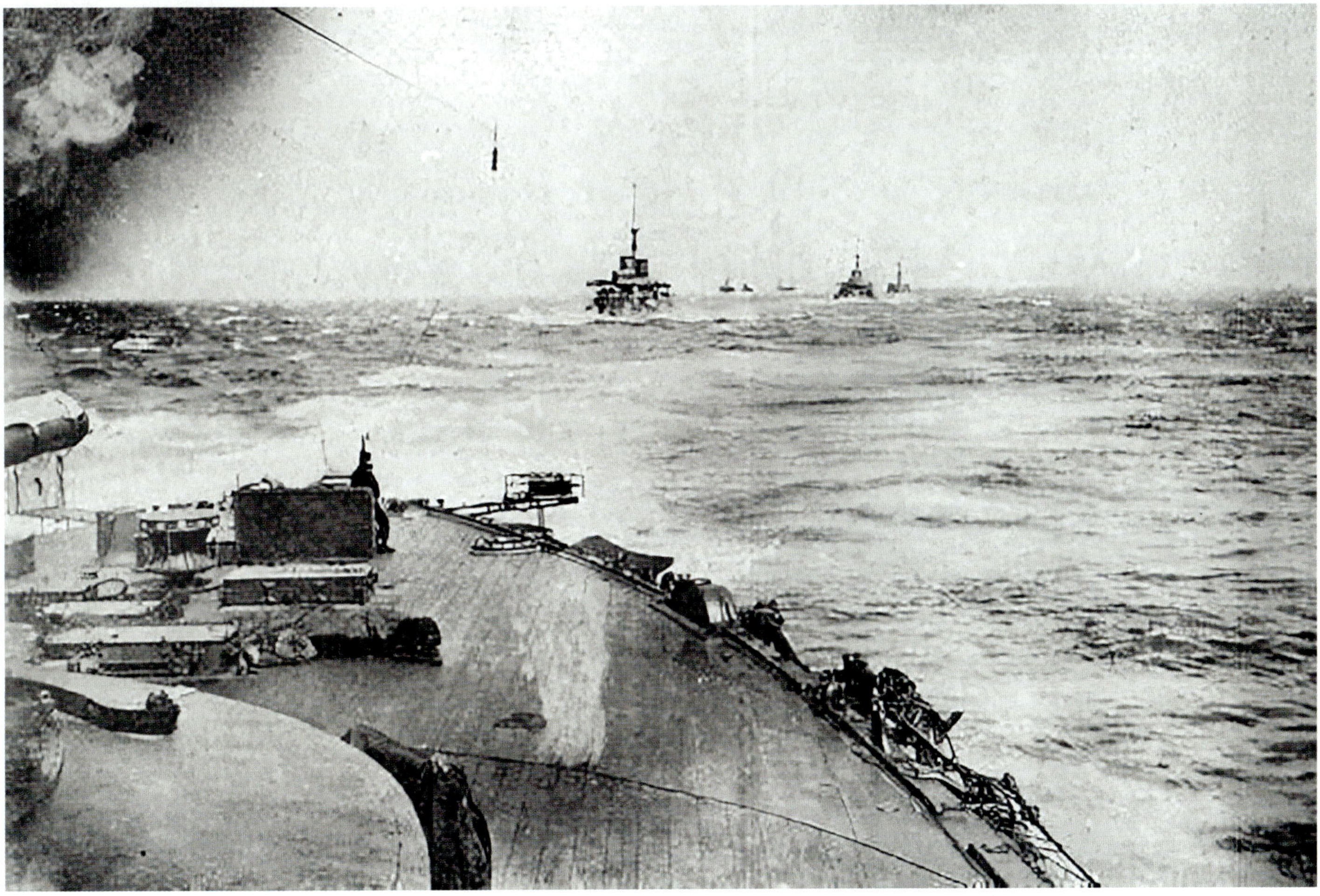

had to scatter to escape. Only three warships managed to break through to reach Vladivostok. The remainder of the Russian fleet, now under the command of Admiral Nikolai Nebogatov, surrendered on the morning of May 28.

All 11 Russian battleships that had taken part in the engagement were lost - seven sunk and four captured. Three cruisers were interned at Manila by the United States until the war was over. Eight auxiliaries and one destroyer were disarmed and remanded at Shanghai by China. Russian casualties were high, with more than 5,000 dead and 6,000 captured. The Japanese, which had lost no heavy ships, had 117 dead.

The loss of almost every heavy warship of the Baltic Fleet forced Russia to sue for peace, and the Treaty of Portsmouth was signed in September 1905. The Battle of Tsushima was described by British colonial administrator Sir George Clarke as "by far the greatest and the most important naval event since Trafalgar."

World War One

When World One broke out there was an expectation that there would soon be a 'Trafalgar for a new century', resulting in a decisive victory for the larger and superior British Grand Fleet over the German High Seas Fleet. Both navies spent nearly two years trying to entice their opponent's main force to come out to fight from their respective anchorages at Scapa Flow in the Orkney Islands and Wilhelmshaven in northwest Germany.

The British Grand Fleet had more than 150 battleships, cruisers, and destroyer, which were considered the most modern and advanced in the world. Small contingents of fast cruisers were based at Rosyth and Invergordon, on the Scottish mainland, to allow them to rapidly respond to German forays to bombard the English west coast. The overall fleet commander, Admiral John Jellicoe, was naturally cautious and he frequently clashed with his cruiser commander, Vice Admiral David Beatty, who wanted to pursue a more aggressive strategy.

The German fleet had considerably fewer battleships and cruisers – 36 – but had twice as many destroyers and large torpedo boats. The German fleet commander, Admiral Reinhard Scheer, objective was to make the British commit their fleet piecemeal so that it could be defeated in digestible chunks. This would eventually allow the German fleet to break out into the Atlantic and cut off Britain from global trade.

On May 30, 1916, the Germans decided to make a foray into the North Sea in the hope of forcing the British to commit at least part of their fleet. Both sides sent squadrons of armoured cruisers ahead of their main force to try to make contact with the enemy, which pitted six Germans warships against five British ones. Jellicoe soon followed with the bulk of the Grand Fleet, with the intention to surprise the Germans and destroy their outnumbered armada.

When the two squadrons clashed on the afternoon of May 31, the Germans came off better thanks to superior gunnery and ship design. After seeing two of his cruisers apparently blown up within minutes, Admiral Beatty famously told a subordinate, "there seems to be something wrong with our bloody ships today." In a further clash, another British cruiser was lost.

The main German and British fleets continued to close on each other, but their commanders had no idea about proximity of their opponent. Early in the evening the two fleets came into view, with the British being able to sail across the German line of advance. However, this successful 'crossing of the T' was only partially effective.

Immediately, Admiral Scheer realised the danger he was in and ordered a 180 degree turn by all his warships. In an impressive show of seamanship, the German

LEFT: In a bid to lure the British fleet out into battle during World War One, the German cruiser squadron launched a raid against the coastal town of Lowestoft in April 2016. (HANS BOHRDT)

LEFT: Admiral John Jellicoe led the British Grand Fleet at Jutland. He was criticised for not being aggressive enough during the battle. (LIBRARY OF CONGRESS BAIN COLLECTION)

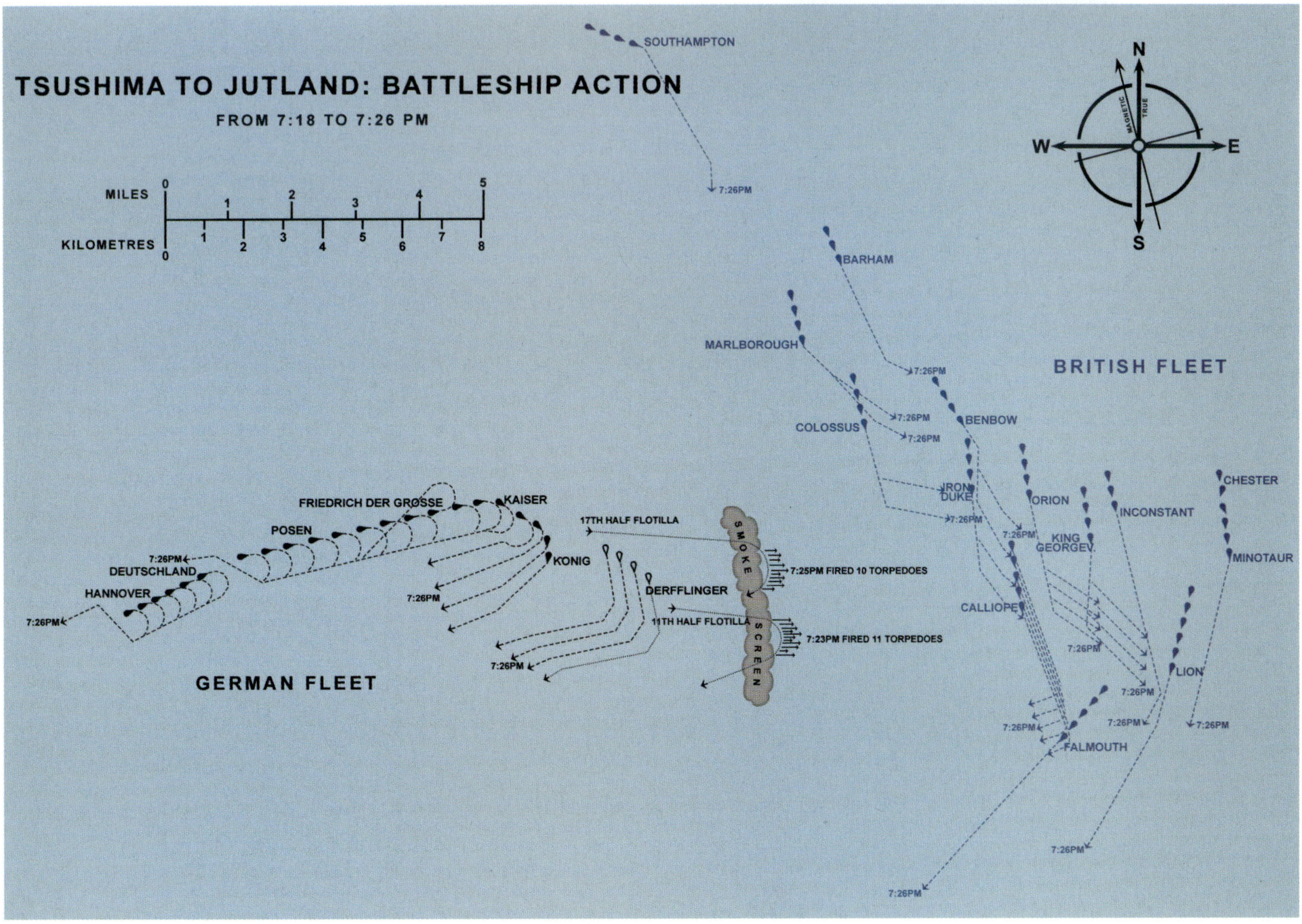

BELOW: The British and German fleets clashed in the North Sea on May 31, 1916, in the biggest fleet action of the battleship era. The Royal Navy managed to 'cross the T', by positioning itself ahead of the German fleet on two occasions, but Admiral Scheer managed to turn his ships around and withdraw in good order. (ANDY HAY FLYING ART)

TSUSHIMA TO JUTLAND: BATTLESHIP ACTION
FROM 7:18 TO 7:26 PM

ABOVE: The battlecruiser HMS *Queen Mary* exploded at the Battle of Jutland, revealing shortcomings in the design of British warships.
(PRIVATE COLLECTION)

RIGHT: Vice Admiral David Beatty led the British Cruiser Force during the Battle of Jutland. He caused controversy after criticising Admiral Jellicoe for being over cautious.
(JOHN BUCHAN)

battleships turned away and escaped the British trap.

Once out of range, Scheer decided to make a dash back to his home port and turned east. Jellicoe had maintained his course, so just under an hour later the German fleet again found itself facing the main line of the British fleet, which for the second time had 'crossed the T'. Scheer again ordered a 180 degree turn but this time the British had already opened fire and the German ships were not all able to see the signal flags in the gloom and smoke. He ordered up his destroyers to launch a mass torpedo attack to give his battleships a chance to break free. The German battle cruiser squadron held off the British, taking 37 hits and suffering heavy damage before being able to break away.

Overnight, the rival fleets manoeuvred to try to gain advantage but there was little significant action, except for when a British cruiser made a navigational error and sailed into the German battle line and was soon sunk. During the early hours of June 1, the German fleet turned for home.

Both sides appeared happy with a bloody but inconclusive draw. The two mightiest fleets of battleships ever to exist had been unable to defeat each other in two days of extended combat. The British lost three cruisers, three armoured

LEFT: The British battlecruiser HMS *Indefatigable* sank after being struck by shells from the German battlecruiser *Von Der Tann*. The first shells exploded in the 'X' magazine and then she was hit by another salvo on the foredeck. The resulting explosion destroyed her. All but two of her crew of 1,119 were killed in the blast. (LT CMDR H T DAY/IWM)

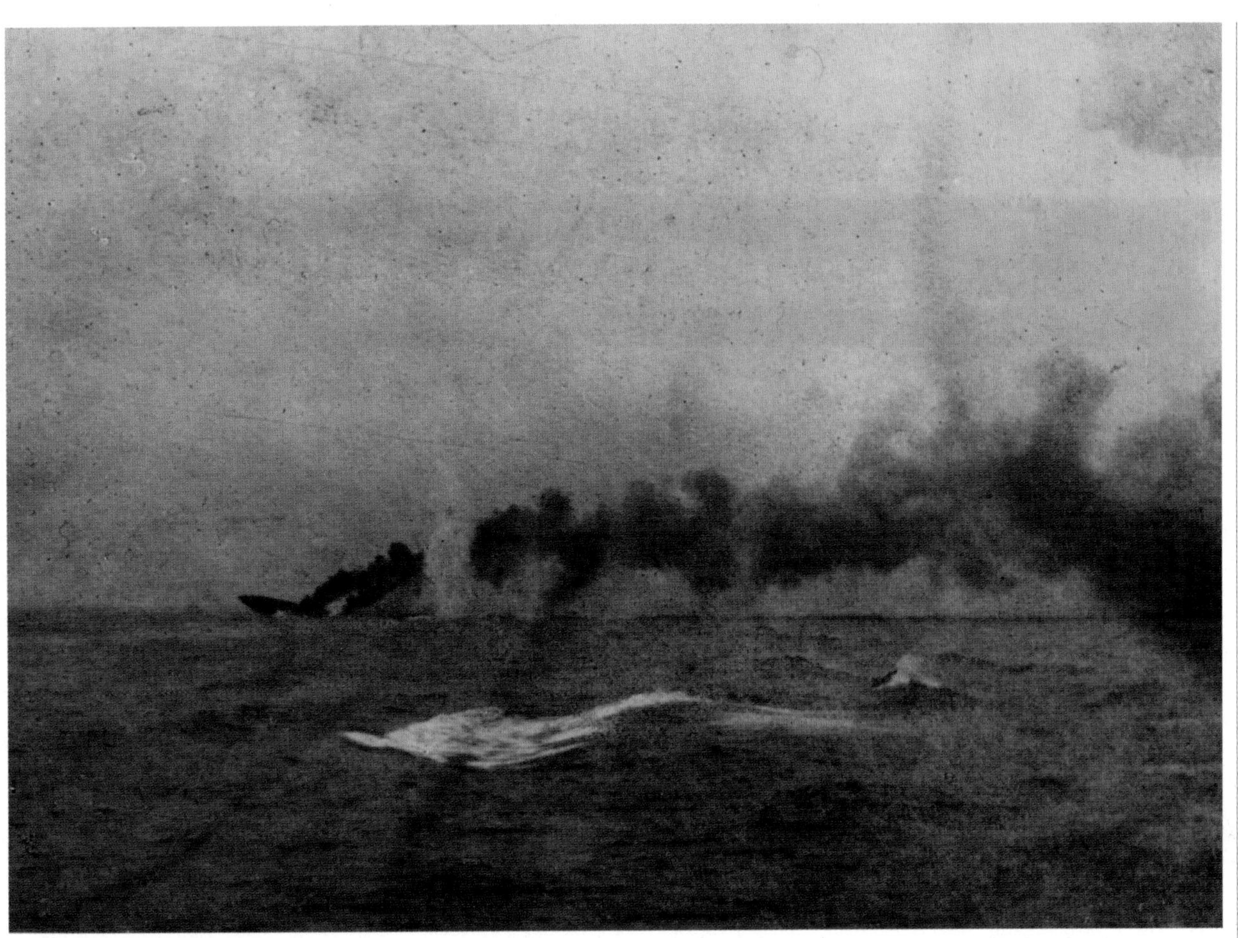

cruisers and eight destroyers out of fleet of 151 warships, with the loss of 6,094 sailors killed. This compared to German loss of one cruiser, one pre-dreadnought battleship, four light cruisers, and five torpedo-boats sunk out of a fleet of 99 warships, with the loss of 2,551 sailors killed.

Although the Germans sank the heavier warships, they were unable to break British control of the exits from the North Sea. The allied naval blockade of Germany remained in place for the rest of the war and contributed the shortages of raw material and food that eventually forced the Kaiser to sue for peace in 1918. Winston Churchill subsequently described the British fleet commander, Admiral John Jellicoeas "the only man on either side who could lose the war in an afternoon." This reinforced the impression that fleets of battleships just cost too much to build to even risk their loss in battle.

BELOW: HMS *Warspite* and HMS *Malaya* seen from HMS *Valiant* at the height of the Battle of Jutland. (PRIVATE COLLECTION)

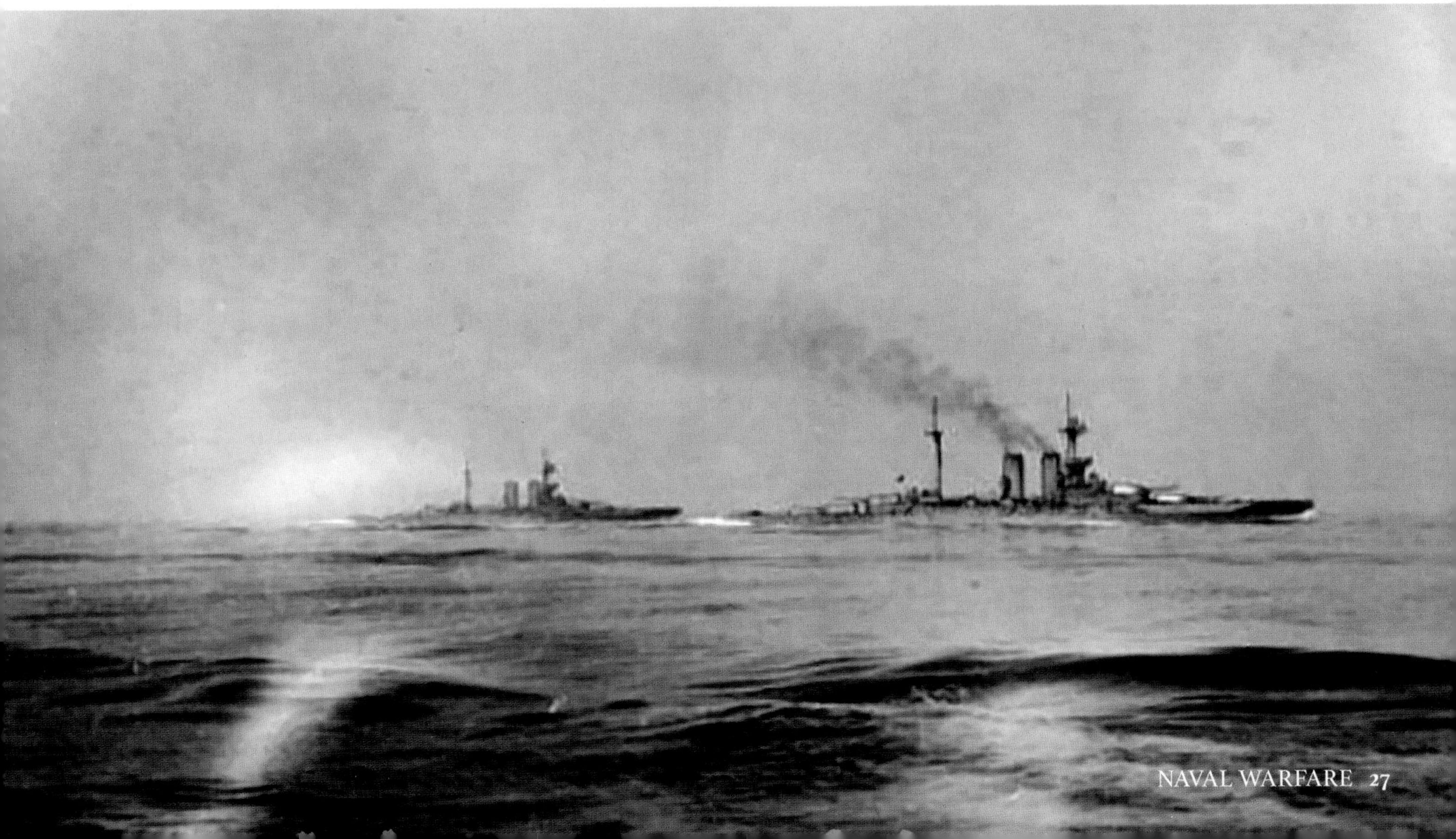

Pearl Harbor

Japan Strikes at the US Pacific Fleet

RIGHT: The USS *Arizona* burns after being hit by multiple Japanese bombs and torpedoes. The pride of the US Pacific fleet was crippled in a morning. (US NATIONAL ARCHIVES)

BELOW: 'Battleship Row' in Pearl Harbor in an aerial photograph from October 1941. The US Navy's biggest base in the Pacific was poorly defended and wide open for a surprise attack from the air. (US NATIONAL ARCHIVES)

December 7, 1941, the day that the Japanese attacked Pearl Harbor, would remain "a date which will live in infamy," declared US President Franklin D Roosevelt.

In the space of a morning, Japanese aircraft, launched from aircraft carriers to the north of the Hawaiian Islands crippled the US Pacific Fleet. The air strikes caught the Americans by surprise and before their defences had to time to react, the anchorage at Pearl Harbor naval base was full of burning warships. Japan's daring attack was only the opening move in a series of offensives across Southeast Asia that in a matter of months would defeat US troops in the Philippines, Dutch forces in their East Indies colonies, and British Empire troops in Hong Kong, Malaya, and Singapore.

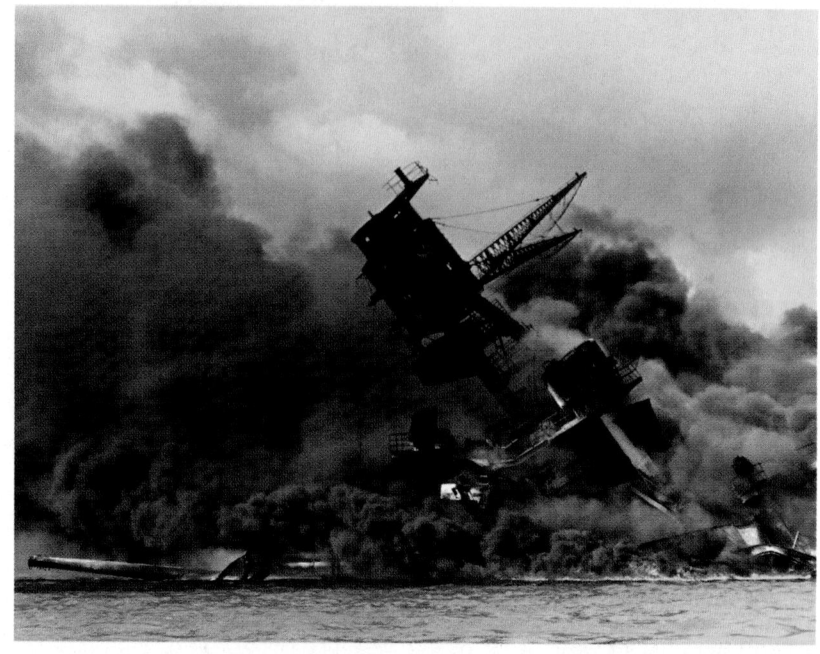

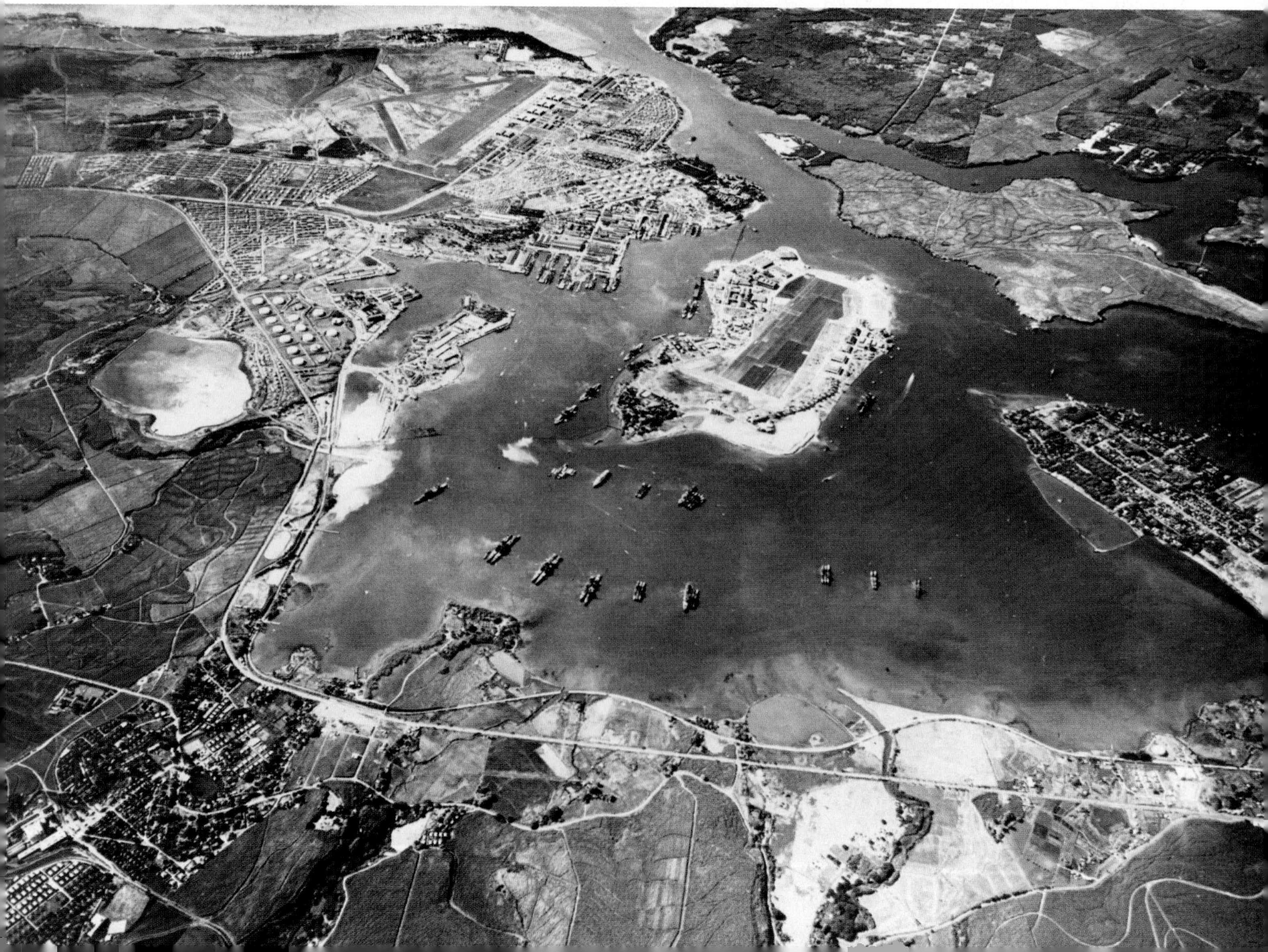

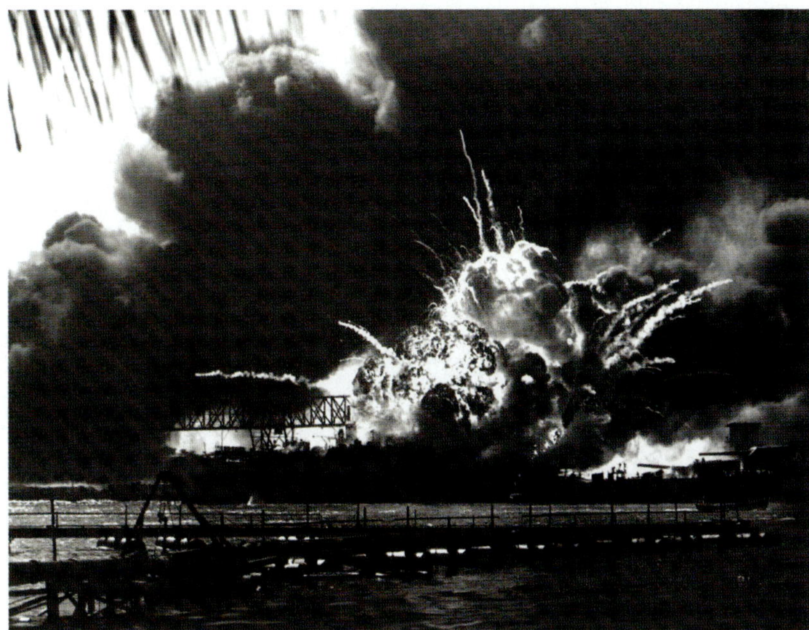

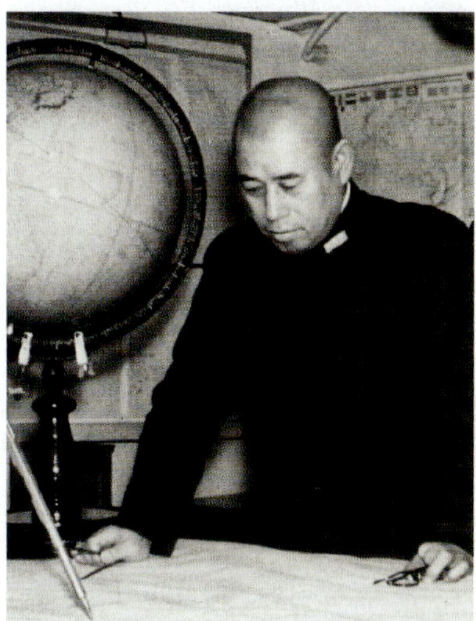

LEFT: The USS *Shaw* explodes after taking several direct hits. (US NATIONAL ARCHIVES)

The seeds of war had been sewn long before as Japan launched an unrelenting war of conquest in China. France's defeat by Germany in 1940 gave the Japanese an opening to move forces into French colonies in Indo-China, now Vietnam. In Washington DC, these moves appeared to confirm Japanese aggressive intentions. During the summer and autumn of 1941, the US government imposed a series of economic and financial sanctions on Tokyo. And alongside an oil embargo announced in November 1941, demanded that the Japanese withdraw their occupation troops from China.

And so began the countdown to war. Japanese military commanders and their political supporters said it would be a national humiliation to give in to American demands. A war council in Tokyo agreed that Japan had to seize the large Dutch oil fields in the East Indies, which are now part of modern Indonesia, to secure its energy independence. Large amphibious task groups were mustered on Formosa, now Taiwan, and in Indo-China, ready to strike south. The oil situation was approaching critical, and the Japanese high command warned that unless the Dutch oil fields were seized by the end of 1941 it would be too late.

Arguments raged about what to do to neutralise the US Pacific Fleet in Hawaii and prevent it interfering with the invasion plans that aimed to

LEFT: Admiral Isoroku Yamamoto was the mastermind of the Japanese surprise attack on Pearl Harbor. (NATIONAL DIET LIBRARY)

BELOW: The Japanese carrier strike group crossed the northern Pacific under a cloak of secrecy and arrived off Hawaii on the evening on December 6, 1941, without being detected. The US Navy's two carriers were also at sea, but they remained undetected by the Japanese. (ANDY HAY FLYING ART)

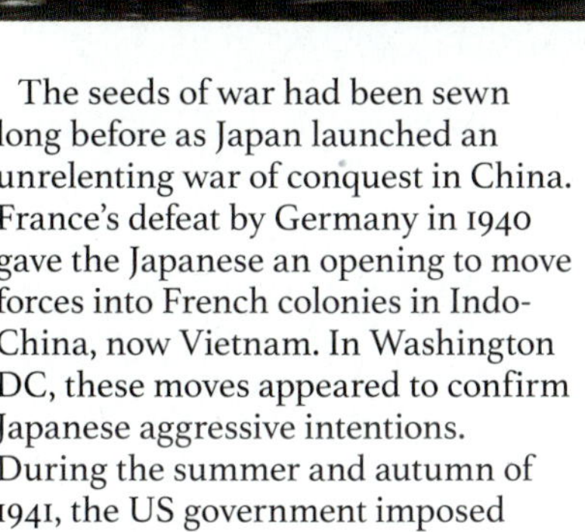

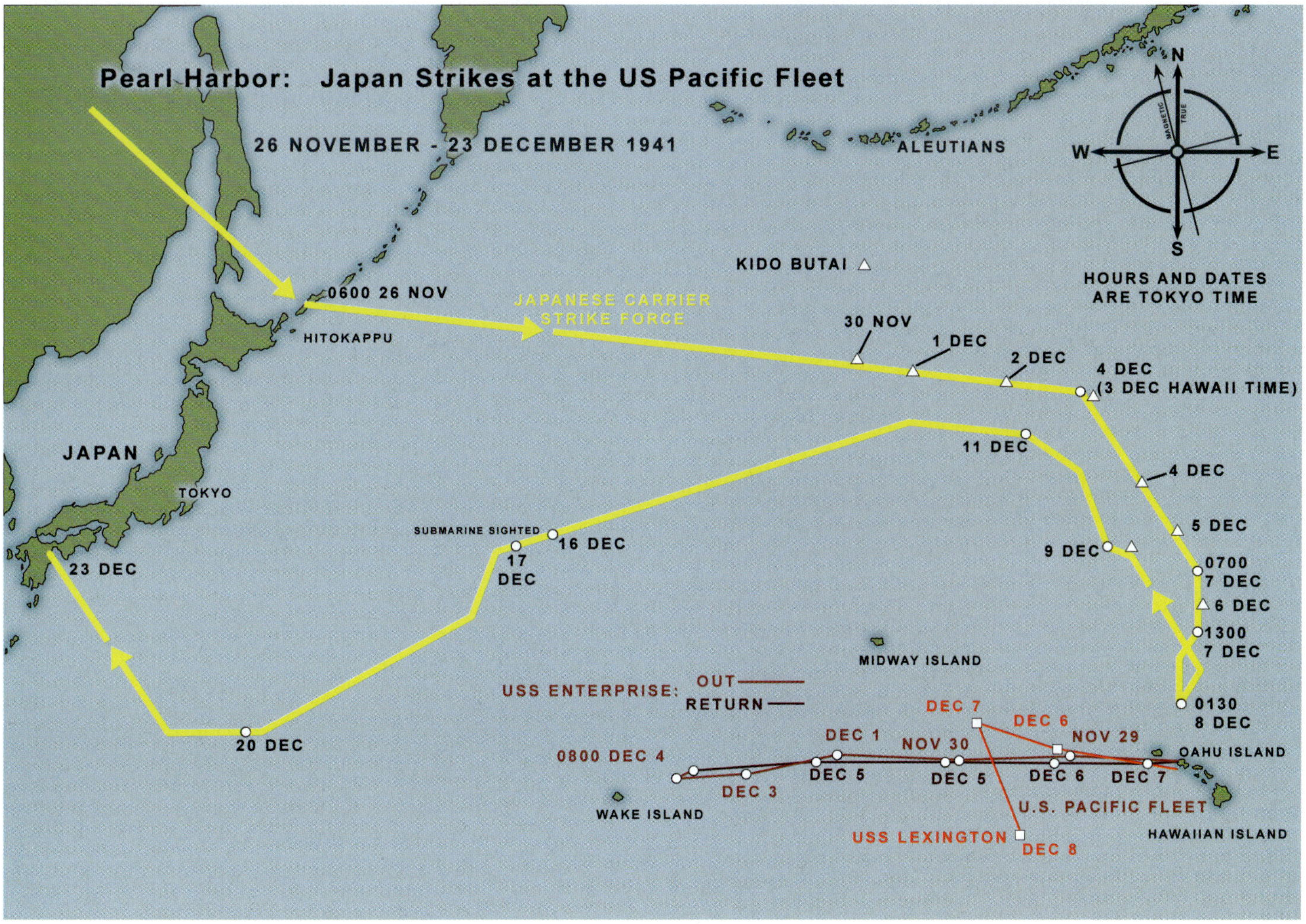

ABOVE: The view of Japanese aircraft as the first wave arrived over Pearl Harbor, with the first explosions visible. (US NATIONAL ARCHIVES)

RIGHT: An Imperial Japanese Navy Mitsubishi A6M2 Zero fighter on the aircraft carrier *Akagi* during the Pearl Harbor attack mission. (US NAVY NATIONAL MUSEUM OF NAVAL AVIATION)

create what was called the Greater East Asia Co-Prosperity Sphere. The commander-in-chief of the Japanese Combined Fleet, Admiral Isoroku Yamamoto, came up with the idea of launching a surprise carrier-borne strike on Pearl Harbor. He had been working on the plans for several months after see the success of the British air attack on the Italian fleet in Taranto harbour in November 1940. Trials of a new air dropped torpedo proved that it would work in the shallow waters of Pearl Harbor. On November 5, the war council agreed to allow Yamamoto to execute his plan as the opening move of the offensive.

To succeed, the attack would have to be undertaken in conditions of great secrecy. The strike group of six aircraft carriers – *Akagi, Kaga, Sōryū, Hiryū, Shōkaku,* and *Zuikaku,* with more than 400 aircraft embarked - was concentrated at Hittokapu Bay on Kasatka Island in the Kuril Islands. All orders were delivered to the carrier group commander, Admiral Chūichi Nagumo, in person and nothing was transmitted by radio for fear it could be compromised to American eavesdropping. For several weeks, the Japanese aircraft carriers had maintained radio silence to ensure that American direction finding monitors lost track of them.

Nagumo received his final orders on November 25, and he set sail the following day. The attack would only go ahead if Japanese intelligence confirmed the presence of the US Pacific Fleet at Pearl Harbor. Agents in the Japanese consulate in Honolulu were tasked every day to drive past the naval base and count the ships tied up alongside. An advanced force of 27 submarines was sent ahead of the fleet to give early warning of any US fleet movements around the islands. Five of these Japanese vessels carried their own mini-submarines that were to attempt to penetrate the harbour defences and attack the US fleet from underwater.

It took over a week for Admiral Nagumo's task group to cross the north Pacific and thanks to bad

weather, it remained undetected. A coded message to the task group on December 1, reading "Climb Mount Niitaka", told the Admiral to proceed as planned and attack on the morning of December 7. The Japanese embassy in Washington DC was sent a coded message to be delivered to the State Department, just as the first wave of aircraft were attacking Pearl Harbor, telling the Americans that Tokyo had rejected their ultimatum and negotiations were over. However, due to a problem decoding the message, the Japanese ambassador was late getting to the secretary of state and the attack was already underway.

Controversy has ranged over why the Americans were caught by surprise on the morning of December 7. US diplomats were bracing themselves to an adverse Japanese reaction to their ultimatum. American code breakers had broken the Japanese diplomatic code, known as Purple, and had been alerted to preparations at Japanese embassies around the world for something to happen. However, the codes used by the Japanese navy high command had not yet been broken so the US code breakers were not getting a complete intelligence picture of Tokyo's intentions.

US naval intelligence did pick up some tell-tale signs of preparation for an attack, such as unusual changing of radio call signs across the Japanese fleet and Yamamoto's carriers observing radio silence for more than a month. However, US intelligence analysts, military commanders, diplomats, and political leaders

did not join the dots. There was no 'smoking gun' in the intelligence that said Pearl Harbor would be attacked on the morning of December 7. This culminated on the fateful morning with American intelligence decoding the infamous 'negotiations are over' message that had been sent to the Japanese embassy before the embassy cipher staff had transcribed it. However, it did not say specifically what would happen once negotiations were over. Japanese security precautions protected Admiral Naguma's fleet from discovery. So beyond vague suggestions to enhanced vigilance, no action was

taken to alert US commanders on Hawaii that war was imminent.

On the evening of December 6, Admiral Naguma summoned the crew of his flagship, the carrier *Akagi*, onto her flight deck to hear the details of their mission. Flying from the ship was the historic signal flag that had flown from Admiral Togo's flagship during the Battle of Tsushima, 36 years before. Japan's navy would soon have another date with destiny. The carrier strike group was then ordered to turn south to bring the Hawaiian islands within range.

Shortly after 6.30am, the first strike wave launched in a mass take-off ➤

ABOVE: The USS *West Virginia* soon settled on the bottom of Pearl Harbor after being hit multiple times and set on fire. (US NATIONAL ARCHIVES)

RIGHT: The USS *Pennsylvania* and two destroyers in dry dock were badly damaged during the second wave of Japanese attacks. (US NATIONAL ARCHIVES)

BELOW: Two waves of Japanese aircraft swept over Hawaii, striking at the US fleet in the Pearl Harbor naval base and American airbases across the island of Oahu. (ANDY HAY FLYING ART)

and formed up to head towards their target, just as the sun was rising. The strike formation was led by 43 Mitsubishi A6M Zero fighters, who were protecting 50 Nakajima B5N Kate high level bombers armed with 1,750lb armour piercing bombs to punch through the decks of warships and 40 Kate torpedo bombers, who had the job of hitting as many US capital ships as possible. A wave of 51 Aichi D3A Val dive-bombers armed with 550lb bombs completed the strike force. The first wave was led by veteran naval aviator, Commander Mitsuo Fuchida, who positioned his bomber at the front of the formation of aircraft.

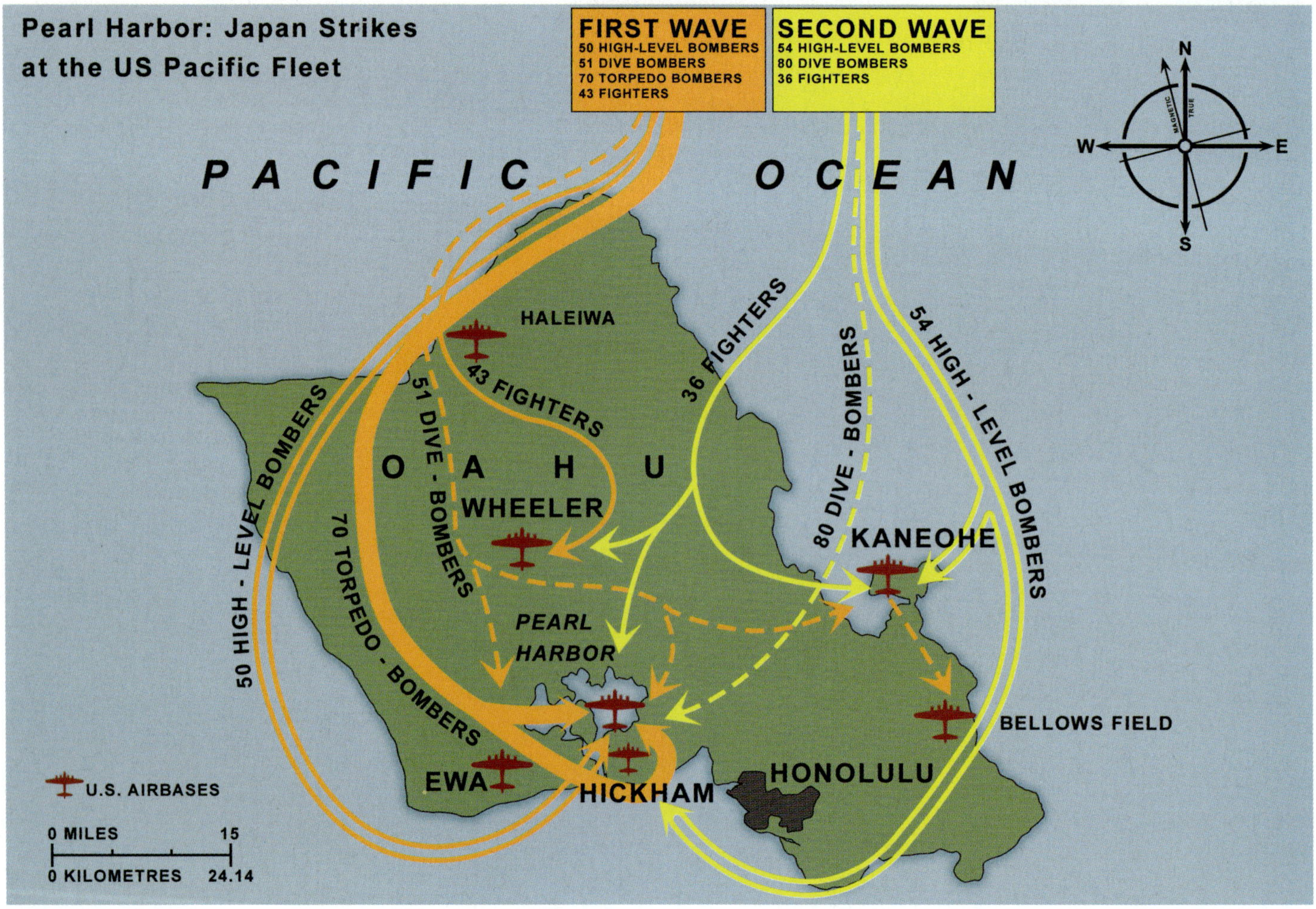

Pearl Harbor: Japan Strikes at the US Pacific Fleet

LEFT: Japanese aircraft prepare to launch from the aircraft carrier *Akagi* for the second wave of attacks on Pearl Harbor. (US NATIONAL ARCHIVES)

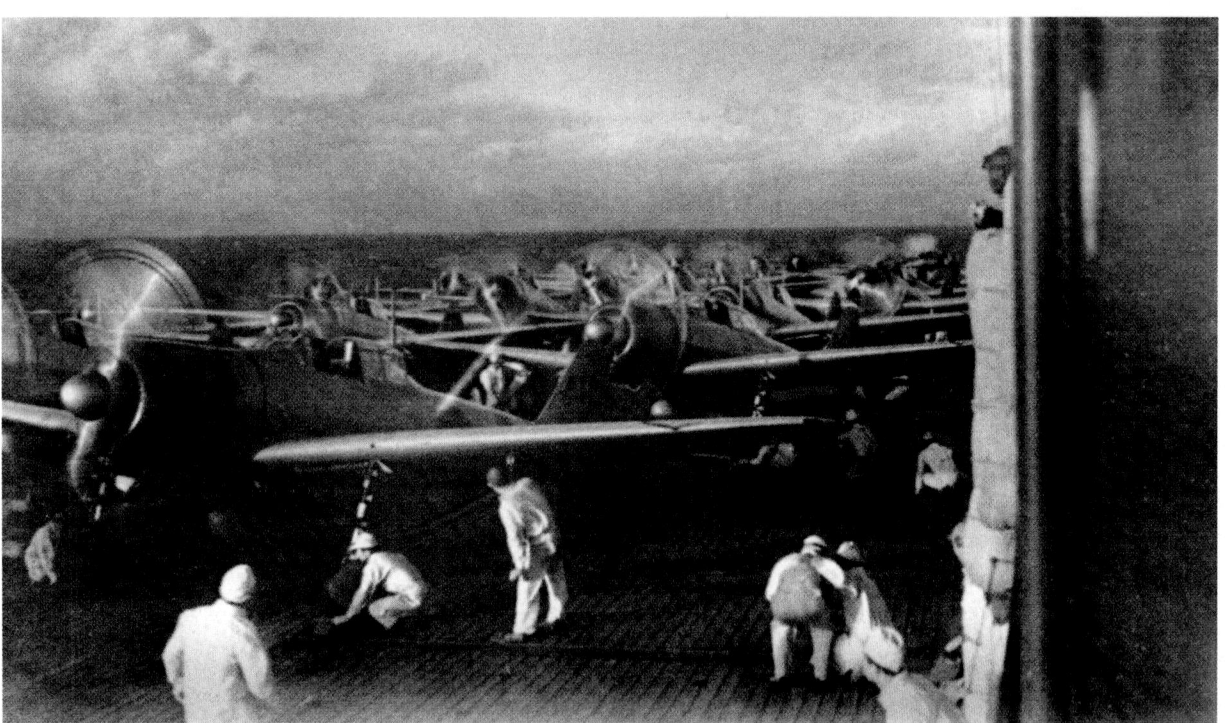

First Engagement

The first shot of the day was not fired by the Japanese, but from the destroyer, USS *Ward*, which spotted the periscope of a submarine in the channel leading into Pearl Harbor. Just before 7am the target was depth charged and it was subsequently found to have sunk the Japanese vessel. A flash message was sent to the fleet headquarters, but it arrived only minutes before the first attacking aircraft were over the islands. Another opportunity to raise the alarm was missed when the US Army radar post on Oahu's highest peak picked up the approaching Japanese aircraft but the operators were told to disregard the track – they were described as US B-17 Flying Fortress bombers en route to Hawaii from California.

At 7.50am, Commander Fuchida got his first sight of 'Battleship Row' in the centre of the Pearl Harbor anchorage. As predicted by Japanese intelligence, there were eight battleships and dozens of other vessels in port that Sunday morning and he ordered his squadrons to attack their designated targets.

Bombs rained down on US aircraft lined up wing-tip to wing-tip on the airfield on Ford Island. Dozens of aircraft were blown up in the initial attack and then the Zeros swooped down to strafe any surviving aircraft that tried to get airborne from Wheeler air base, Hickam Field and Barber's Point airfield at Kaneohe.

There would be no aerial challenge to the Japanese attackers. In the first minutes of the attack only a handful of the anti-aircraft guns on the warships were manned or had ammunition to hand. It was Sunday morning and large numbers of sailors had liberty, or leave, to stay ashore with their families. The Japanese could strike at will.

Next to strike were the torpedo bombers who lined themselves up to deliver their deadly cargo against each battleship and heavy cruiser in the harbour. Seconds later five battleships – the USS *West*

BELOW: The aircraft carrier *Akagi* was one of the oldest Japanese carriers. She was originally laid down as a battle cruiser but finished as a carrier and entered service in 1927. (US NAVY NATIONAL MUSEUM OF NAVAL AVIATION)

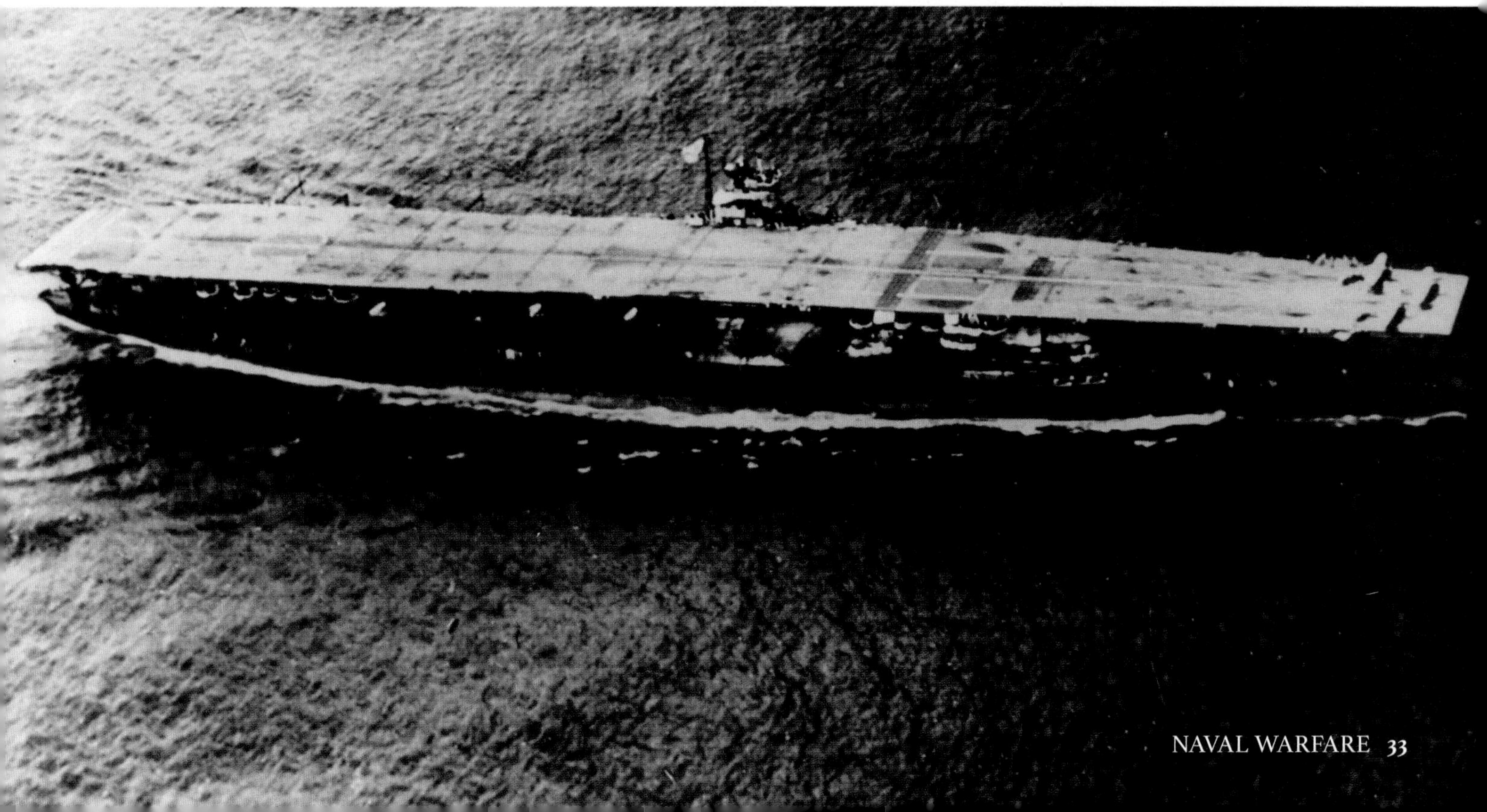

Virginia, *Arizona*, *Nevada*, *Oklahoma*, and *California* – were hit. Two lights cruisers, USS *Raleigh* and USS *Helena*, along with redundant battleship, USS *Utah*, were also hit. Now the dive bombers started to work over the US fleet to inflict more damage and prevent repair teams bringing the fires under control. The coup d'grace was delivered by the high-level bombers, who dropped armoured piercing bombs on the USS *Tennessee*, *Mary*, *Arizona*, and *California*. Huge explosions ripped through the warships as their magazines or gun turrets exploded.

In less than half an hour, Commander Fuchida's squadrons had finished their deadly strike and he ordered them to return to their carriers. The attack had caught the Americans totally by surprise and only nine aircraft had been lost to enemy fire.

Admiral Nagumo was not finished yet. A second wave of aircraft had been launched an hour after the first, led by Lieutenant Commander Shimazaki. It boasted 54 high level bombers, 80 dive bombers and 36 fighters. When they arrived over Pearl Harbor the Americans had managed to get many of their anti-aircraft guns into action. The Japanese aircraft were met by heavy fire but still managed to cause extensive damage. The USS *Pennsylvania* and two other destroyers in dry dock were badly damaged. The USS *Nevada*, which its crew had got underway and were trying to get out to sea was hit and forced to beach to avoid blocking the channel into the harbour. Aircraft and hangars at the Hickam Field, Kaneohe, Ford Island, and Barbers Point airfields were all hit by bombers.

When Shimazaki and his airmen returned to their ships, they reported that the American defences were now fully alerted. They had lost 20 aircraft to the Americans, including six to enemy fighters. Commander Fuchida and other officers pressed Admiral Nagumo to launch a third wave to finish off the American Pacific Fleet by knocking out its dry docks, fuel stores and any remaining undamaged warships. The task group commander decided against it. The heavy losses made him cautious about pushing his luck, particularly as the two American carriers, the USS *Lexington* and USS *Enterprise*, had been at sea on the morning of December 7. Admiral Nagumo wanted to save his pilots and aircraft for the inevitable showdown with the American navy's aircraft carriers.

Just after 10am on December 7, Admiral Nagumo ordered his fleet to turn northwest and head back to Japan. However, his decision to pull back may have lost the Japanese the opportunity to deal a knock-out blow against the Americans. The dockyards and repair facilities which had been left largely undamaged were rapidly put to good use to bring many of the damaged US warships back into service. They would otherwise have had to be towed to naval bases in California to be repaired. More importantly, the Japanese missed the chance to catch and sink the USS *Enterprise*, which was approaching Pearl Harbor from a mission to deliver US Marines fighters to Wake Island in the central Pacific. The carrier's air group was vastly outnumbered by Admiral Nagumo's fleet of more than 350 aircraft, and there is a strong possibility the USS *Enterprise* would have been quickly sunk if it had needed to take on the four Japanese carriers on its own.

Despite these missed opportunities, Admiral Nagumo had inflicted a devastating blow on the US Pacific Fleet and at a stroke put it out of action, just as it was needed to challenge the Japanese drive into southeast Asia. Within three months, the Japanese Greater East Asia Co-Prosperity Sphere was a reality.

In the space of 90 minutes, the Japanese attack was over. It left 2,008 US sailors dead and 710 others wounded. In addition, 218 soldiers were killed and 364 wounded, along with 109 Marines killed and 69 wounded. A further 68 civilians were killed and 35 wounded. In total, 2,403 Americans were killed, and 1,178 were wounded during the attack. Eighteen US Navy ships were sunk or run aground, including five battleships.

Out of 402 American aircraft in Hawaii, 188 were destroyed and 159 damaged, 155 of them on the ground. Only eight US Army Air Force pilots managed to get airborne during the attack and six were credited with downing at least one Japanese aircraft.

Fifty-five Japanese airmen and nine submariners were killed in the raid, and one was captured. Some 350 Japanese aircraft were taking part in the raid and 29 were lost. Nine went down in the first wave - three fighters, one dive-bomber, and five torpedo-bombers - and 20 in the second wave - six fighters and 14 dive-bombers. A further 74 Japanese aircraft were damaged but managed to make it back to their carriers.

By the time the Japanese aircraft had turned for home, the American defenders of Pearl Harbor were emerging from cover and surveying the damage. On the evening of December 8, the USS *Enterprise* entered Pearl Harbor to take on supplies. Such was the fear of a repeat attack that the replenishment, which normally would have taken a day, was completed in only seven hours to allow the carrier to put back to sea.

In Washington DC, President Roosevelt and his military chiefs were in a state of shock. Four days later, the Nazi leader Adolf Hitler declared war on the United States, in solidarity with its Axis partner Japan. America was now well and truly at war and there was no going back. The architect of the attack on Pearl Harbor, Admiral Yamamoto is famously quoted as saying that despite the short-term success, he feared Japan's long-term prospects of victory were low, given America's superior technological and industrial potential. He is portrayed

RIGHT: US President Franklin D. Roosevelt signing the declaration of war against Japan, December 8, 1941. It was a pure formality and set in the train the mass mobilisation of the America's armed forces, industry, and people to fight Germany and Japan
(US NATIONAL PARK SERVICE)

LEFT: The air commander of the Japanese assault, Mitsuo Fuchida send the code words Tora! Tora! Tora! back to the carrier *Akagi*, to say complete surprise had been achieved. The 1970 film about the Pearl Harbor attack adopted the phrase as its title. (20TH CENTURY FOX)

in the 1970 film *Tora! Tora! Tora!* as saying: "I fear that all we have done is to awaken a sleeping giant and fill him with a terrible resolve."

Many historians doubt he actually said those words, but he did send a message to a fellow naval officer in January 1942, saying: "A military man can scarcely pride himself on having 'smitten a sleeping enemy'; it is more a matter of shame, simply, for the one smitten. I would rather you made your appraisal after seeing what the enemy does, since it is certain that, angered and outraged, he will soon launch a determined counterattack."

LEFT: Visitors to Pearl Harbor can pay their respects to the 1,102 sailors and marines who died on the USS *Arizona* during the attack on Pearl Harbor. (VICTOR NY)

BELOW: The Commemorative Air Force Gulf Coast Wing's Tora! Tora! Tora! Gang flying restored Zero, Kate, and Val aircraft during an air display. The legacy of Pearl Harbor is long lasting. (EBDON)

Midway 1942

Carrier vs Carrier Action

RIGHT: SBD-3 Dauntless bombers of VS-8 overfly the burning Japanese cruiser *Mikuma* on June 6, 1942. (US NATIONAL ARCHIVES)

BELOW: Aerial view of Midway Atoll on November 24, 1941, as the US military began to reinforce its defences. (US NATIONAL ARCHIVES)

The Japanese attack on the US naval base at Pearl Harbor on December 7, 1941, was a dramatic demonstration of the power of Tokyo's aircraft carrier fleet and it signalled that naval air power would dominate the struggle in the Pacific.

Although the Japanese air strikes devastated the US Pacific Fleet - sinking four battleships and severely damaging 14 others, as well as destroying 188 aircraft, and damaging a further 159 others – the US Navy aircraft carriers were at sea and escaped without a scratch.

Japan's naval supremo, Admiral Isoroku Yamamoto, wanted to finish off the American carriers. This set the scene for the Battle of Midway in

suffering from what is termed 'victory disease'. They became convinced their run of victories would continue. So, when Admiral Yamamoto produced his plan to strike at Midway there was little dissent. However, he fatally underestimated the resilience of the US Navy to re-build its strength and, more importantly, his plans were compromised by US code breakers.

Yamamoto planned to launch an amphibious attack on the island of Midway, some 2,100km to the west of the Hawaiian Islands to draw out the remaining US carriers in the central Pacific. Once the Americans had taken the bait, Yamamoto would unleash his four carriers, which were to be lurking nearby, to sink the US flat tops. In a bid to weaken the American fleet,

LEFT: Admiral Chester Nimitz was the mastermind of the American victory at Midway and went on to lead America's campaign in the Pacific theatre. (NATIONAL PORTRAIT GALLERY)

June 1942. Although this was not the first engagement that involved rival fleets of aircraft carriers striking at each other, without getting sight of the enemy, Midway would prove to be the turning point in the war in the Pacific. The Battle of Coral Sea in May 1942 has the distinction of being the first carrier vs carrier, but it ended inconclusively. Rather than destroying the American aircraft carriers, at Midway the US Navy turned the table on Yamamoto and sunk the cream of the Japanese aircraft carrier fleet.

Yamamoto's plan to attack Pearl Harbor had dramatically opened the Japanese offensive that rolled up Hong Kong, Malaya, Singapore, the Philippines, and the Dutch East Indies over the next four months. The US, British Empire, and Dutch forces in their way put up pitiful resistance. For the Imperial Japanese Navy, this was an electrifying period. Its aircraft carriers had devastated the US Pacific Fleet, the battleship HMS *Prince of Wales* and the battle-cruiser HMS *Repulse* had been sunk by Japanese land-based aircraft off Malaya, and a British aircraft carrier had been sent to the bottom of the Indian Ocean, off Ceylon, by Japanese carrier-borne strike aircraft. The leadership of the Japanese navy appeared to be

LEFT: At two days notice, Admiral Raymond Spruance took over as commander of the two carriers of Task Group 16 in the central Pacific after Admiral William Halsey was struck down with severe shingles. (US NAVY)

BELOW: In April 1942, the famous Doolittle Raiders launched from the USS *Hornet* to bomb the Japanese mainland. This audacious attack put huge pressure on the Japanese navy to destroy the US carrier fleet as quickly as possible. (NATIONAL MUSEUM OF US AIR FORCE)

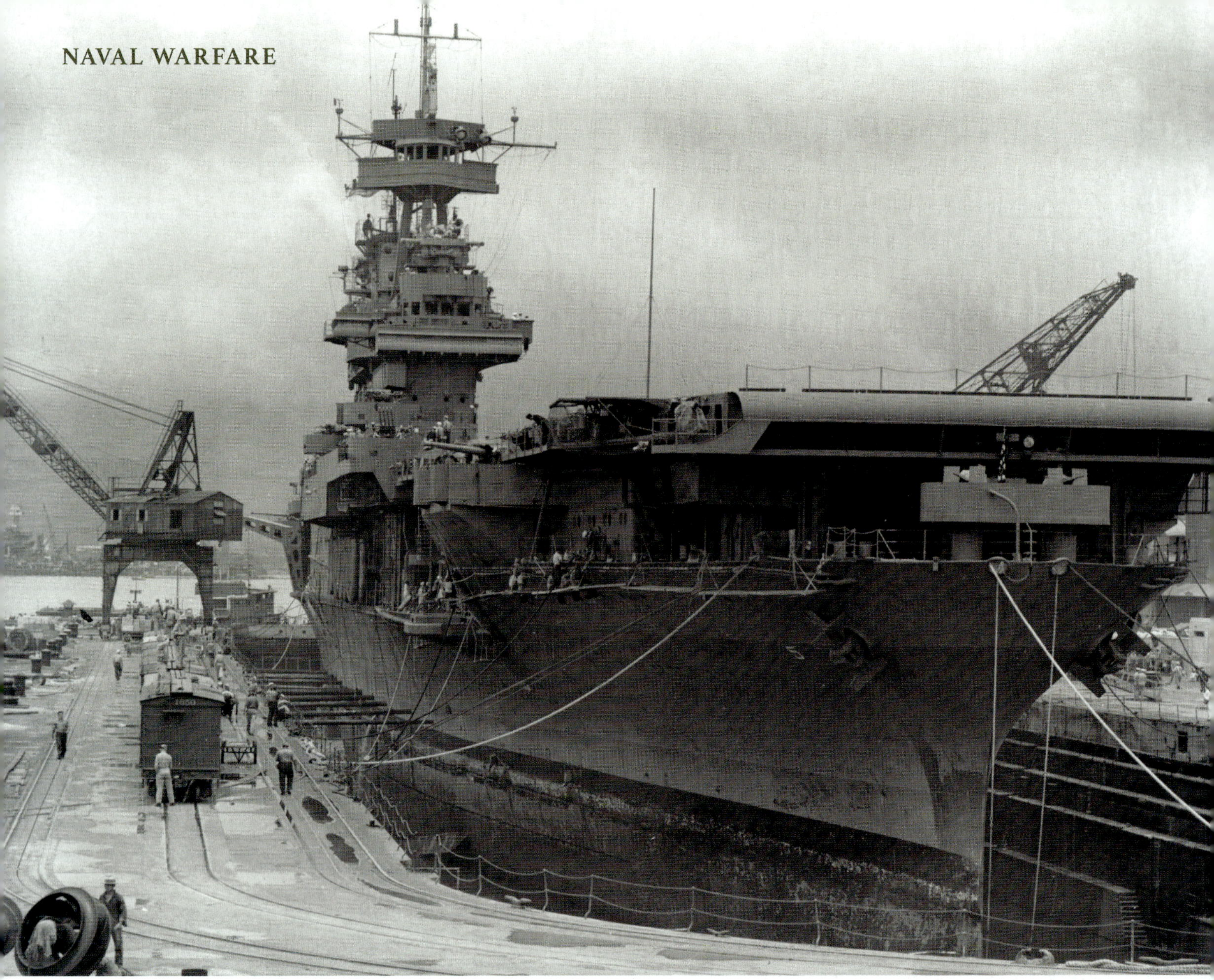

ABOVE: The USS *Yorktown* in dry dock at the Pearl Harbor Naval Shipyard, May 29, 1942, during her rapid repair ahead of the Battle of Midway. (US NATIONAL ARCHIVES)

a feint was ordered against the Aleutian Islands, off Alaska. Two Japanese aircraft carriers supported this manoeuvre, which only served to fatally weaken Yamamoto's main fleet.

Fortunately for the American naval commander, Admiral Chester Nimitz, US intelligence had at last broken the Japanese naval code, JN25, and had worked out Yamamoto's plan. Nimitz did not fall for Yamamoto's Aleutian diversion and the bulk of the US Pacific fleet was massed off Midway.

Nimitz not only beefed-up defences on Midway with US Marines, backed up by Army Air Force fighters and

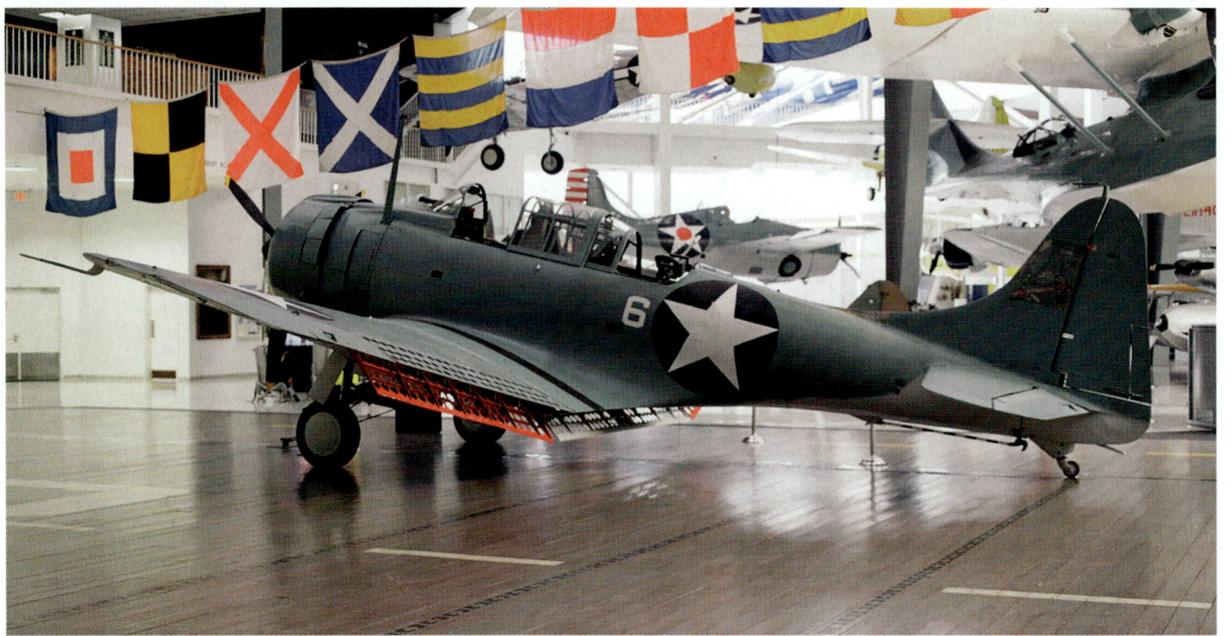

RIGHT: A US Navy Douglas SBD-2 Dauntless on display at the US National Museum of Naval Aviation at Pensacola, Florida. On June 4, 1942, it was one of 16 SBD-2s of VMSB-241 that launched to attack Japanese aircraft carriers to the west of Midway. After unsuccessfully attacking the carrier *Hiryū*, enemy fire holed the plane 219 times. It was one of only eight SBD-2s of VMSB-241 to return from the attack on the Japanese fleet. (US NAVY NATIONAL MUSEUM OF NAVAL AVIATION)

bombers to hold off the Japanese invasion, but he sent his aircraft carriers to intercept the Japanese fleet. Dockyard workers at Pearl Harbor worked around the clock to repair the USS *Yorktown,* which had been badly damaged in the Battle of the Coral Sea. They completed the work in just three days so Nimitz had three carriers to spearhead his counter-move.

The Japanese forces made their move at dawn on June 4 with heavy air attacks on Midway by aircraft launched from the carriers *Akagi, Kaga, Sōryū,* and *Hiryū.* In response, US Marine Corps fighters took off from the island to take on the attackers, but the Japanese Zeros proved more than a match for the obsolete American Buffalos and all but a handful of them were shot down. The American airfield was then hit, with Japanese bombs destroying hangars, oil tanks, and power plants.

Before the bombs fell, the US land-based bombers – Avenger and

Midway 1942: Carrier vs Carrier Action

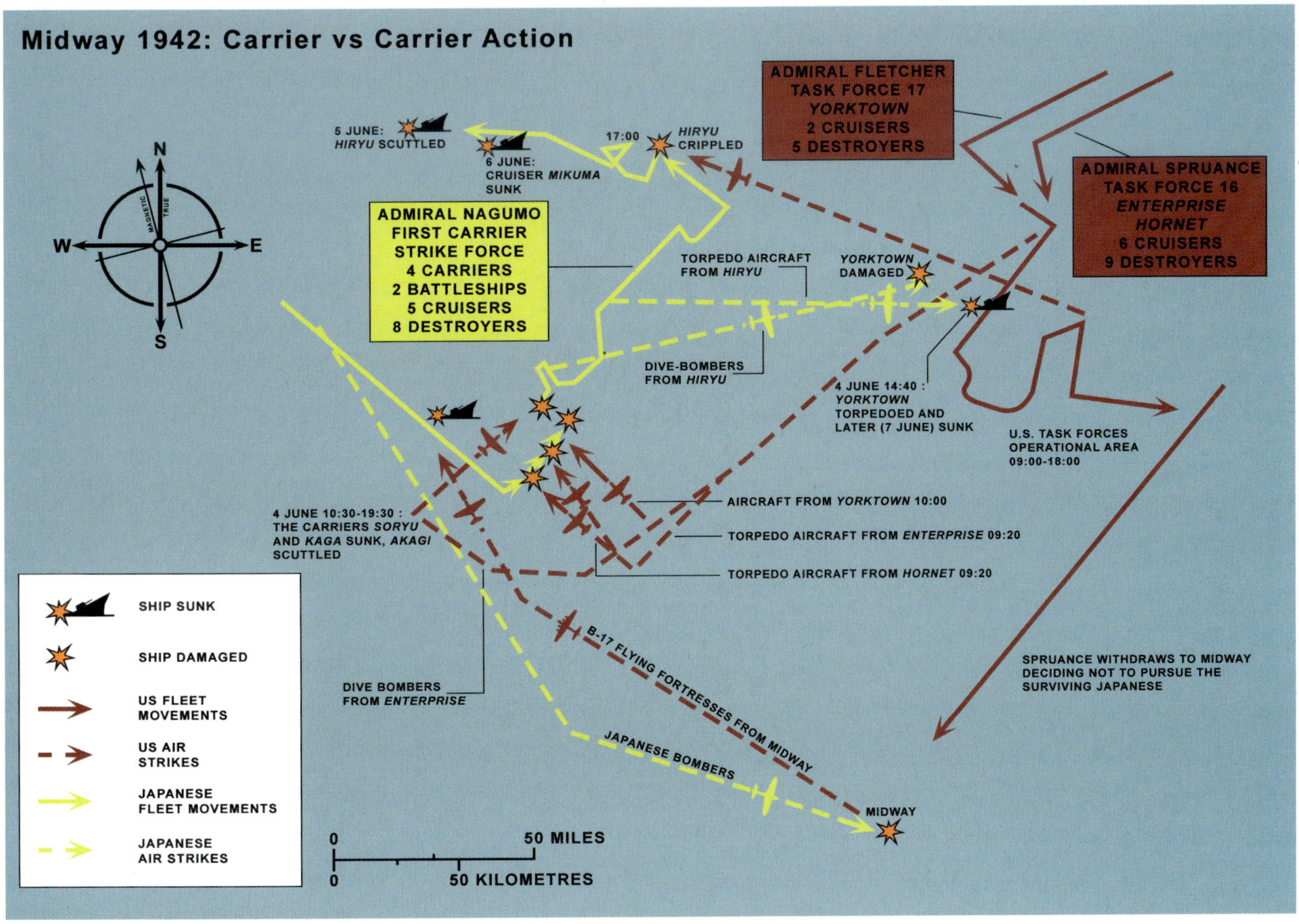

ABOVE: The USS *Yorktown* came under heavy Japanese air attack on June 4, 1942, and was seriously damaged. (US NATIONAL ARCHIVES)

Marauder torpedo-bombers and B-17 Flying Fortress heavy bombers – managed to get airborne and head towards the Japanese carriers. They failed to land any hits on the enemy flat tops and suffered heavy losses to Zeros defending the Japanese fleet. The torpedoes of the land-based American aircraft were later found to be faulty.

So far everything was going to plan for the Japanese. When the planes returned to their carriers, the task group commander, Admiral Chūichi Nagumo, ordered them to be rapidly rearmed with bombs to continue the strikes on Midway. However, just as this was underway, Japanese scout planes spotted the American carriers approaching from the east. Nagumo now ordered his planes be re-armed with torpedoes and armour piercing bombs so they could strike the American ships.

The commander of the US carrier group, Rear Admiral Raymond Spruance had also launched his scout planes from the USS *Hornet* that morning to try to find the Japanese

carriers. He decided to launch a mass strike with every plane that could be mustered from USS *Enterprise* and USS *Hornet*'s air group. Fearing the Japanese carriers would slip away if he delayed, the US Navy squadrons did not wait to form up into a big formation before heading away from the fleet on their attack. As a result, the American attack was split into several waves that arrived above the Japanese fleet over an extended period. The aircraft from the USS *Yorktown* would eventually join the attack when the carrier had recovered and re-armed its scout planes.

The delay in re-arming the Japanese planes meant they were not prepared when the first wave of 116 US aircraft from the USS *Enterprise* and *Hornet* arrived overhead. Dozens of the Japanese planes were still in the hangar decks.

The sky soon became a swirling series of confused and desperate dogfights. As American torpedo bombers lined up to make their low-level runs against the Japanese ships, they were jumped by Zeros. American Wildcat fighters tried their best to

keep the Zeros at bay, but there were just too many of them. The handful of American aircraft that survived the Zeros were soon confronted by walls of flak from exploding shells fired off by anti-aircraft batteries on the Japanese fleet.

This first attack by two squadrons of US torpedo-bombers was thwarted by 50 Zeros, with all the attackers being shot down. Most of the American naval aviators went down with their aircraft but three baled out and were captured by the Japanese. It subsequently emerged that their captors threw them overboard, while bound and loaded down with weights. Only one pilot survived by hiding under wreckage until the Japanese fleet had sailed away, when he inflated his life raft. A US flying boat eventually picked him up.

The next wave of US torpedo-bombers was larger and more co-ordinated. Aircraft from the USS *Enterprise* attacked the *Kaga*, and pilots from the USS *Hornet* took aim at the *Soryu* from the other flank. The multi-prong attack on the Japanese fleet drew its defending fighters in different directions but no hits were recorded by the Americans. Only a handful of US planes managed to escape.

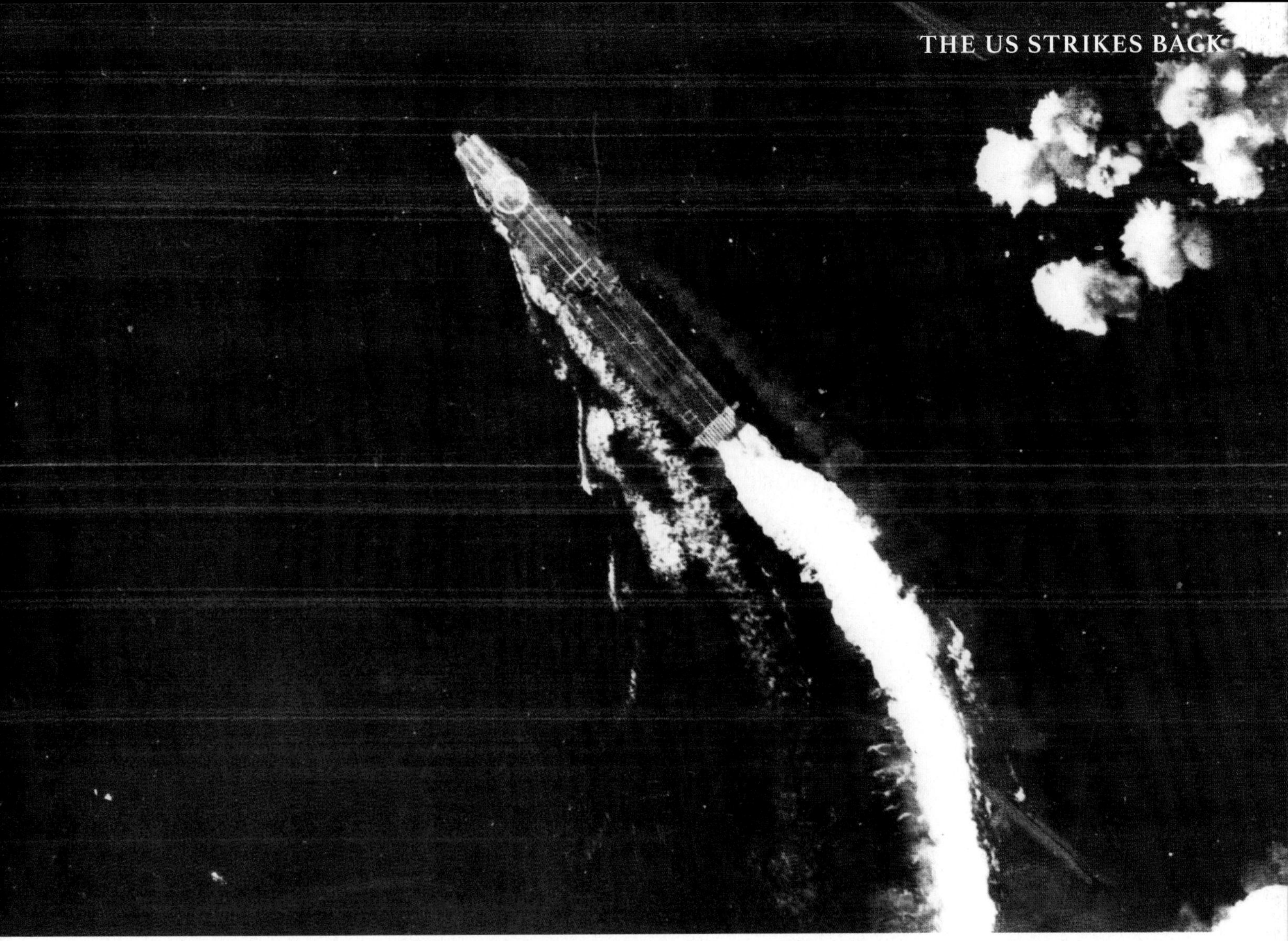

However, the mass low level attack by the American torpedo-bombers focused the attention of the Japanese defenders during a crucial moment of the battle. High above the Japanese fleet, 37 dive-bombers from the USS *Enterprise* had massed ready to attack.

The first wave of three dive-bombers from the *Enterprise* took aim at the *Akagi* and swooped down to put 1,000lb bombs onto the deck of Admiral Nagumo's flag ship. These penetrated through the carrier's flight decks and exploded inside the hangars where the Japanese aircraft were still being re-armed. Bombs and torpedoes were stacked around the aircraft, causing massive explosions. The admiral had to make a swift exit from the carrier, which was now ablaze in multiple places.

The rest of the dive-bombers from the USS *Enterprise* now took aim at the *Kaga*. They only got four bombs on target, but they caused massive devastation. One hit a fuel tanker parked next to the superstructure, setting a fuel tank on fire, which exploded and devastated the bridge.

The carrier's captain and command staff were all killed. The other bombs exploded among the rearmed and fuelled aircraft parked on the flight deck. Soon the carrier was ablaze from stem to stern. The game was up when the crew evacuated the Emperor's portrait, signalling there was no hope of saving the ship.

It was now the turn of the USS *Yorktown*'s air group to enter the fray. They took aim on the *Sōryū,* with a co-ordinated strike from three directions. All the aircraft released their bombs simultaneously and three hit the ship. Just as with the other attacks, Japanese aircraft were parked closely together on the flight deck as they were preparing to launch. The result was the same and within seconds of the bombs hitting the carrier, it was ablaze. After 20 minutes, the captain ordered his crew to abandon ship. No American aircraft were lost in this attack.

In the space of five minutes, three Japanese carriers had been devastated in three attacks. They all stayed afloat for several hours but, for all intents and purposes the pride of Japanese carrier fleet had been put out of action. The *Akagi* was eventually scuttled and torpedoed by

accompanying Japanese destroyers and the *Kaga* was sunk by a US submarine. The *Sōryū* eventually sank of its own accord. Its captain refused to abandon his ship, remaining on his burning bridge, sword in hand, as the ship slipped beneath the waves.

ABOVE: The Japanese aircraft carrier *Hiryū* manoeuvres to avoid US bombs on June 4, 1942.
(USAF)

LEFT: Admiral Frank 'Jack' Fletcher, commander Task Force 17, led by the USS *Yorktown* during the Battle of Midway.
(US NAVAL HISTORICAL CENTRE)

ABOVE: Japanese aircraft carrier *Hiryū* was badly damaged and later sunk, effectively marking the end of the battle and Japan's ambitions to dominate the central region of the Pacific.
(US NATIONAL ARCHIVES)

From his new temporary flag ship, Nagumo ordered aircraft from his surviving carrier, the *Hiryū*, to pursue the retreating US aircraft and strike at the American carriers. A wave of 10 Japanese torpedo-bombers and 18 dive-bombers struck the USS *Yorktown*. American fighters dealt with the first wave of attackers, but three dive-bombers got through. One was hit by the anti-aircraft barrage and crash landed on the flight deck, starting several fires. A second bomb penetrated into the engine room, putting five of *Yorktown*'s six boilers out of action. The final aircraft got a bomb on target that started fires near the carrier's magazine.

Damage control crews appeared to have brought the fires under control and got the USS *Yorktown*'s engines working again when the Japanese torpedo-bombers appeared. Five were shot down but the remainder of the formation got through and dropped their torpedoes only 500 yards from the carrier. She stood no chance. Two hit her port side and soon the carrier was listing badly.

During the afternoon of June 4, a new American attack found the *Hiryū,* and she was badly damaged. Twenty four US Dauntless dive-bombers found the Japanese carrier and despite frantic efforts to evade the attackers it was soon ablaze after four bombs found their mark. One hit the ship aircraft lift, which was blown upwards into its bridge and the remainder penetrated the hanger deck. The Japanese carrier was soon ablaze and although she stayed afloat, was eventually abandoned by most of her crew. She sank a day later, after being torpedoed by a Japanese destroyer.

The American carrier task force commander, Admiral Spruance, realised that he had achieved his objective by sinking the four Japanese carriers and decided to pull his fleet back to the east to protect it for future operations. However, Admiral Yamamoto had not given up on his plans to bring the American fleet to battle. He ordered a cruiser squadron to sweep ahead of his battleship squadron, but disaster struck when two of the cruisers misread signal lights during a night manoeuvre and collided. One cruiser, the *Mikuma*, was badly damaged and fell behind. After dawn, it was found by American aircraft and dive-bombers struck. One bomb penetrated her engine room and exploded. She sank soon afterwards, and Yamamoto ordered a full retreat.

The Americans launched search aircraft to try to find the remaining Japanese surface vessels, but they slipped the net. The Battle of Midway was over, but the human drama was not.

Heroic efforts were underway to try to save the USS *Yorktown* and allow her to be towed back to Pearl

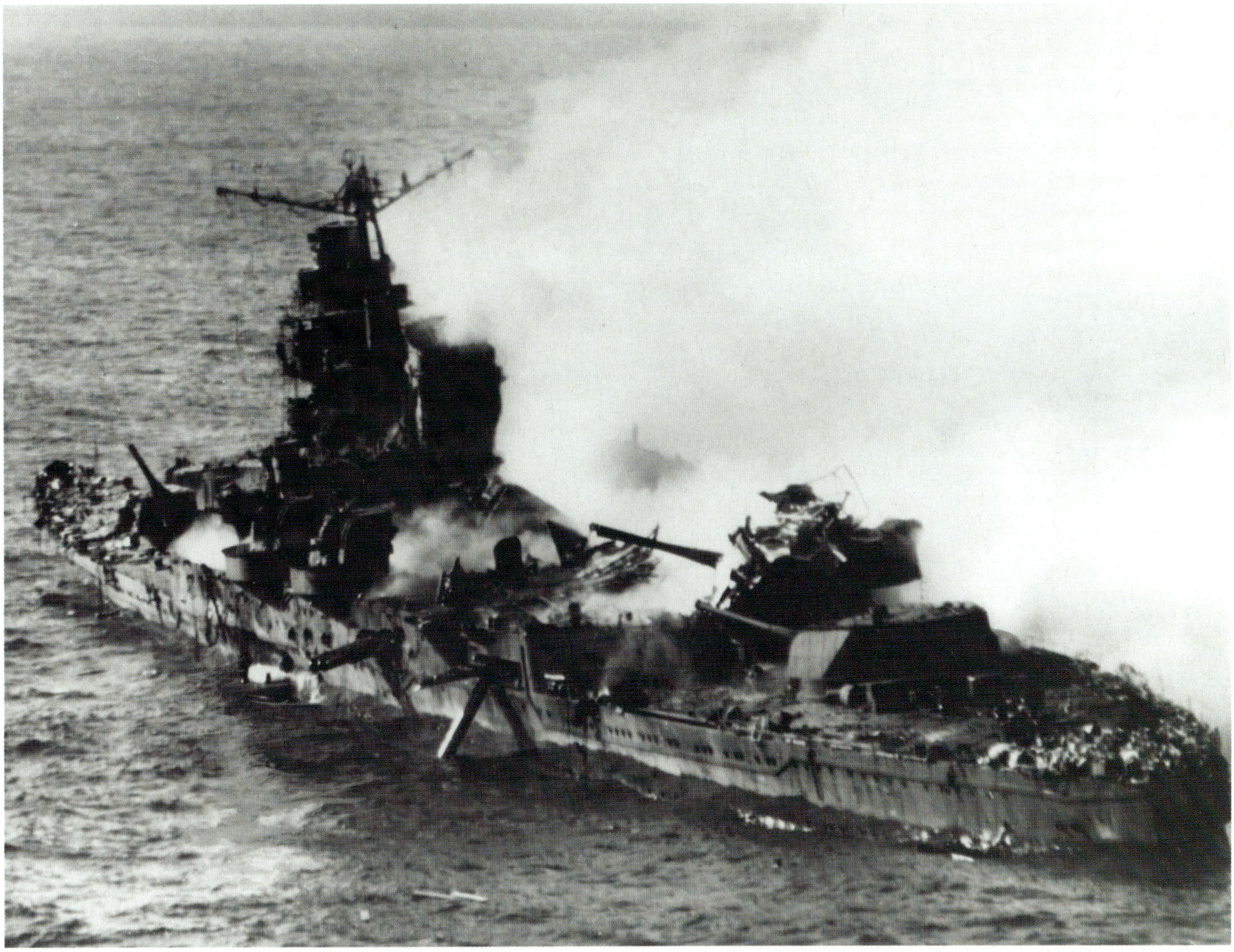

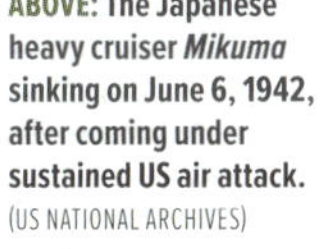

Harbor for repairs, but a Japanese submarine found the stricken carrier, put two torpedoes into her, and sank an escorting destroyer. The carrier started to list heavily, and all the damage control teams were evacuated overnight. On the morning of June 7, she rolled upside down and sank.

The sad end of the *USS Yorktown* notwithstanding, Nimitz and Spruance had won a victory that changed the balance of naval power in the Pacific. They opened the way for the US offensive that eventually brought American forces to the coasts of Japan. This American victory was predominately due to its superior use of carrier airpower - the age of the aircraft carrier as the dominant weapon in naval combat had arrived.

When understanding Midway, the role of US code breakers cannot be underestimated, and US admirals based their plan almost entirely on intercepts of Japanese communications. Meanwhile, Yamamoto had no idea that the US was reading his radio traffic, so rather than setting a trap for the Americans, it was Yamamoto who was surprised and cornered.

The loss of four aircraft carriers at Midway crippled the Japanese navy's strike power. No longer would the Japanese be able to form a mass strike group that even stood a chance of challenging American aircraft carrier dominance. During World War Two the US would eventually build more than 100 aircraft carriers. The Japanese just did not have the industrial capacity to rival this. Admiral Yamamoto's fears about awakening the 'sleeping giant' of America would soon be proved true. The American success at Midway speeded this process, crippling the Japanese carrier strike force and putting them on the defensive.

ABOVE: The Japanese heavy cruiser *Mikuma* sinking on June 6, 1942, after coming under sustained US air attack. (US NATIONAL ARCHIVES)

LEFT: A rescued US Navy flight crewman is carried on a stretcher from a Consolidated PBY-5 Catalina on Midway Islands following the Battle of Midway. (COMMANDER JOHN FORD, USNR)

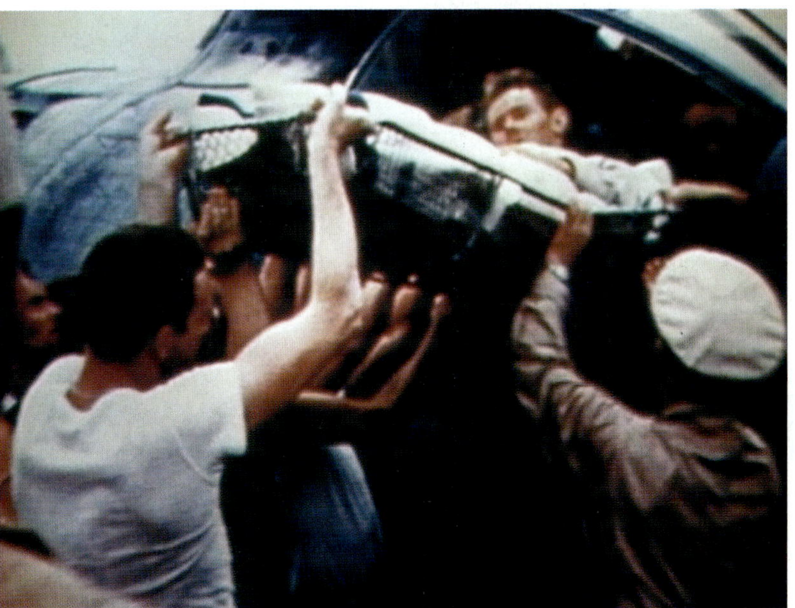

1943 Battle of the Atlantic

Defeating the U-boats

RIGHT: The German U-boats hunted in packs and for the first three years of World War Two threatened to strangle the sea lanes that kept vital supplies of food and raw materials flowing into Britain from the new world. (US NATIONAL ARCHIVES)

The Battle of the Atlantic was the decisive naval engagement of the war against Nazi Germany and unlike many of the battles that feature in this publication, it lasted for years. Allied naval and air forces defeated the attempt by the Nazi submarine force - the infamous U-boats - to cut off Britain's vital maritime supply lines from North America and the wider British Empire. However, this campaign, turned in the first half of 1943 when the allies brought improved tactics and technology to bear to break the back of the U-boat fleet. With the defeat of the U-boats the build-up of US troops in Britain ahead of the D-Day landings in northern France in 1944 was able to accelerate. If the U-boats had not been crushed, then there would have been no D-Day.

BELOW: U-995 has been preserved at the naval museum in Laboe near Kiel in Germany, as part of a memorial, honouring the country's sailors who died in World War One and World War Two. In 1954, the memorial was rededicated to honour sailors of all nationalities who were lost at sea and as a memorial for peaceful sailing in open seas. (DARKONE)

A few simple data points explain how pivotal the first months of 1943 were for the Allies. Up to then they were losing more merchant shipping to the U-boats than could be replaced. At the same time, the Germans were able to replace each of their U-boat losses with two or three newly built submarines. In 1942, the allies lost 1,664 merchant ships but

German only lost 87 U-boats. U-boat production was surging to replace these losses so in the first months of 1943 the German Kriegsmarine boasted 240 U-boats, of which 112 were operational in the North Atlantic. This compared to September 1939 when only 26 U-boats were fit to go to sea out of fleet of 41. The logic of war pointed to Britain being cut off and starved within the year if

U-boats continued to run amok in the North Atlantic.

By 1943, the U-boats were hunting in large groups, known as Wolf Packs, to sink allied merchant ships heading for British ports loaded with food, raw materials, and arms to keep Britain fighting. The Royal Navy – assisted by the Canadian, United States, and other Allied navies – was locked in a deadly

duel against the U-boat force, led by veteran U-boat commander Karl Dönitz.

The institution of convoys in late 1939 that forced merchant ships to travel across the Atlantic under naval escort did much to help stem losses. And a key breakthrough was provided by the Ultra code breaking organisation at Bletchley Park which allowed the Admiralty to track the U-boat's movements in real-time and enabled convoys to be routed away from the wolf packs.

Despite these advantages, merchant shipping losses continued to rise and in 1942 more than 650,000 tons of shipping was sunk by U-boats. The British were critically short of escort vessels because the Royal Navy was thinly spread around the world – fighting the Germans and Italians in the Mediterranean, escorting convoys to Russia and battling the Japanese in the Far East. It crucially lacked escort frigates with the range and endurance to operate effectively in the centre of the North Atlantic. This meant the convoy escorts were so thinly spread that when U-boats attacked, they could not be pursued and sunk. Escorts had to remain with their convoys. So, the Royal Navy was just not able to inflict losses on the U-boats, who could slip away, re-group and attack again with near impunity.

ABOVE: Admiral Erich Raeder, commander-in-chief of the Kriegsmarine, presents medals to the crew of U-99 in 1940, just as the U-boat campaign was gathering momentum. (BUNDESACRIV)

The Gap

An added problem was the shortage of maritime patrol aircraft that had the range to cover an area in the middle of the North Atlantic, known as 'the gap'.

U-boats had to spend a long time on the surface re-charging their batteries and refilling their air banks so they could operate submerged, transmitting/receiving radio messages, or transferring supplies from so-called 'mother' submarines. In 'the gap', U-boats were able to operate on the surface without risk of attack and mass together to plan and launch attacks on convoys. They could save their precious air and battery power for the close quarter attacks and many U-boat captains felt so confident they would even attack convoys on the surface.

The Admiralty had recognised these weaknesses. A crash programme to build long range anti-submarine frigates was launched. These new ships were to operate in so-called support groups so they could be detached from convoys to pursue U-boats to destruction. They were progressively equipped with new acoustic, or sonar, sensors that could detect and identify submerged U-boats. Radio direction finding equipment on escorts gave convoy commanders early warning of imminent U-boat attacks. Forward fire depth charge dispensers were added to increase the firepower of the escorts.

In the spring of 1943, the US Army Air Force (USAAF) and Royal Canadian Air Force (RCAF) deployed long range Consolidated B-24 Liberator maritime patrol aircraft (MPA) in a bid to close the mid-Atlantic gap. At the same

LEFT: When the US entered the war against Germany in December 1941, the country's shipbuilding industry started to ramp up production, but it would take time until production outstripped losses to the U-boats. (US NATIONAL ARCHIVES)

time, Royal Air Force Coastal Command aircraft operating from Scotland, Iceland, Northern Ireland, Cornwall, and the Azores covered the rest of the Atlantic to complete Allied air patrol dominance. Nowhere was to be safe for U-boats to operate undetected from the air.

However, this build up was slow and, in the winter of 1942 and 1943, many of these key assets were diverted to escort troop convoys carrying US and British troops to the Allied invasion of North Africa - Operation Torch. The first months of 1943 would be perilous for Allied convoys cross the North Atlantic. This peril was magnified by the fact that in the first weeks of 1943, German intelligence's B Service broke the British naval codes being used in the North Atlantic and were soon reading all the radio traffic to two large convoys, code named SC-122 and HX-229, which were heading to Britain from Canada and United States.

Dönitz began mobilising his U-boats to intercept the convoys that contained 98 merchant vessels, some of which could not make more than 10kts in the heavy Atlantic storms, and which were protected by a total of 13 escort vessels. The U-boat commanders expected easy pickings.

First Dönitz had to confirm the exact position of the convoys and then mass his U-boats from three wolf packs, each containing more than a dozen submarines, to strike at them as they moved west from March 6. He ordered

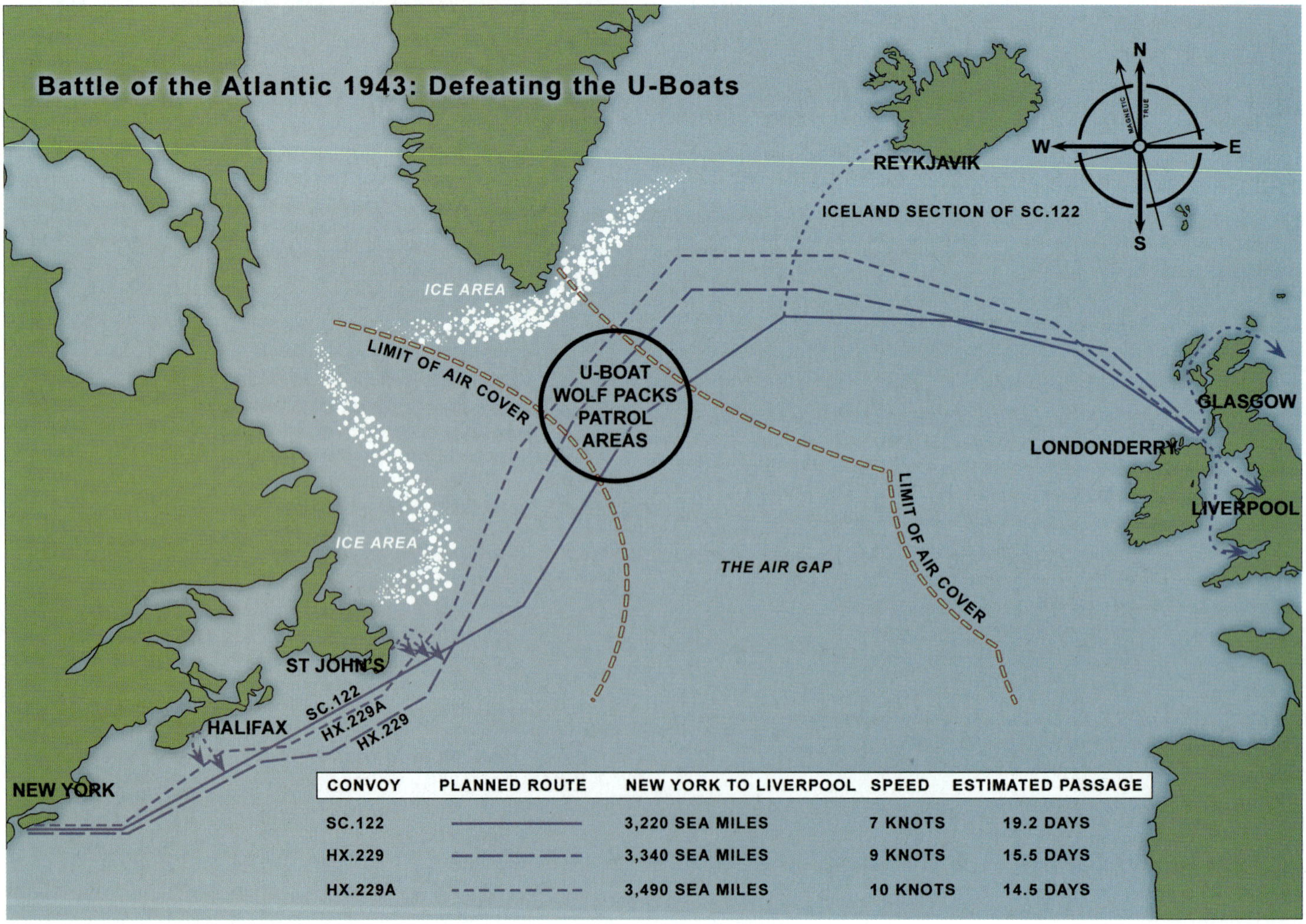

CONVOY	PLANNED ROUTE	NEW YORK TO LIVERPOOL	SPEED	ESTIMATED PASSAGE
SC.122	————	3,220 SEA MILES	7 KNOTS	19.2 DAYS
HX.229	– – – –	3,340 SEA MILES	9 KNOTS	15.5 DAYS
HX.229A	- - - -	3,490 SEA MILES	10 KNOTS	14.5 DAYS

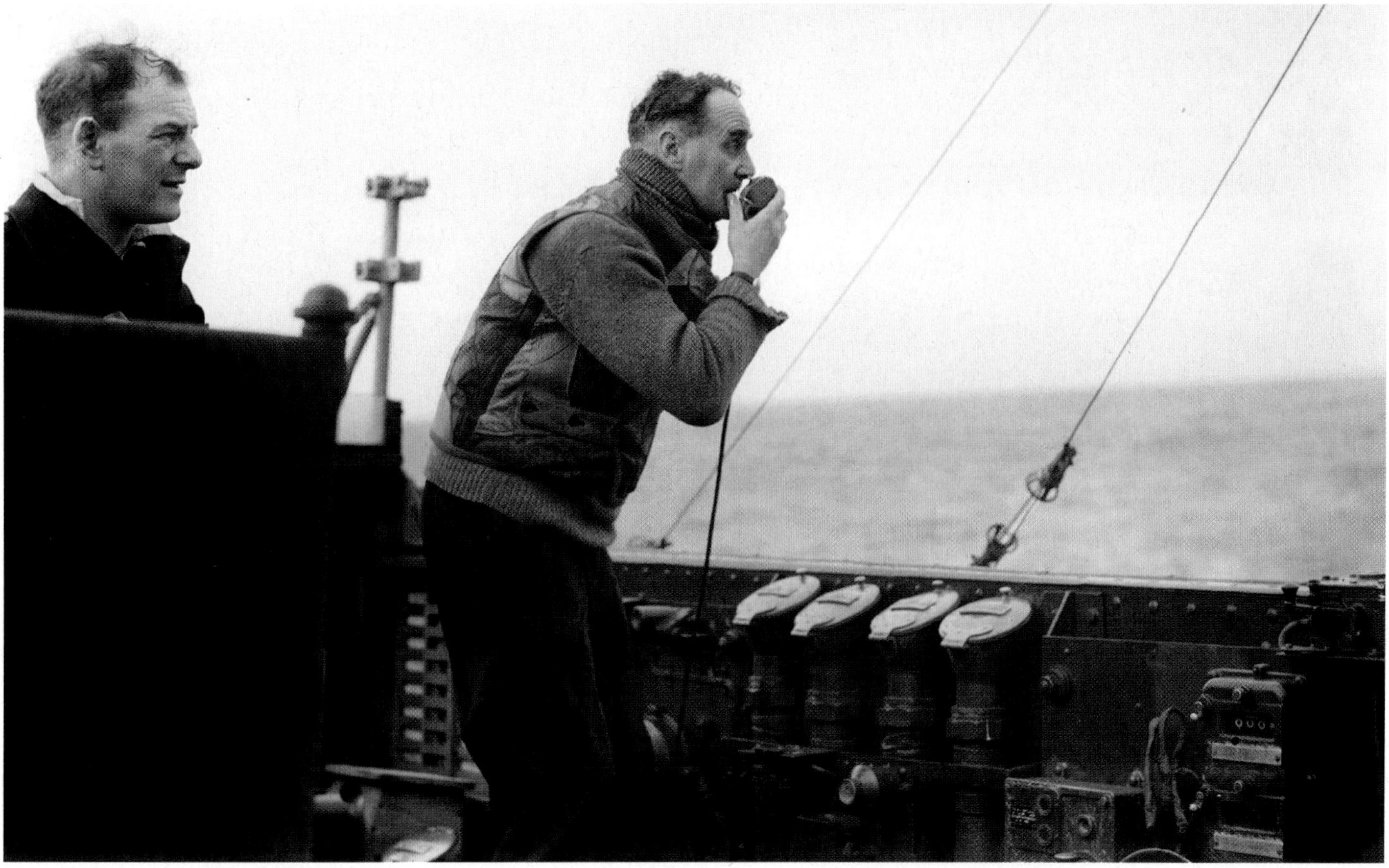

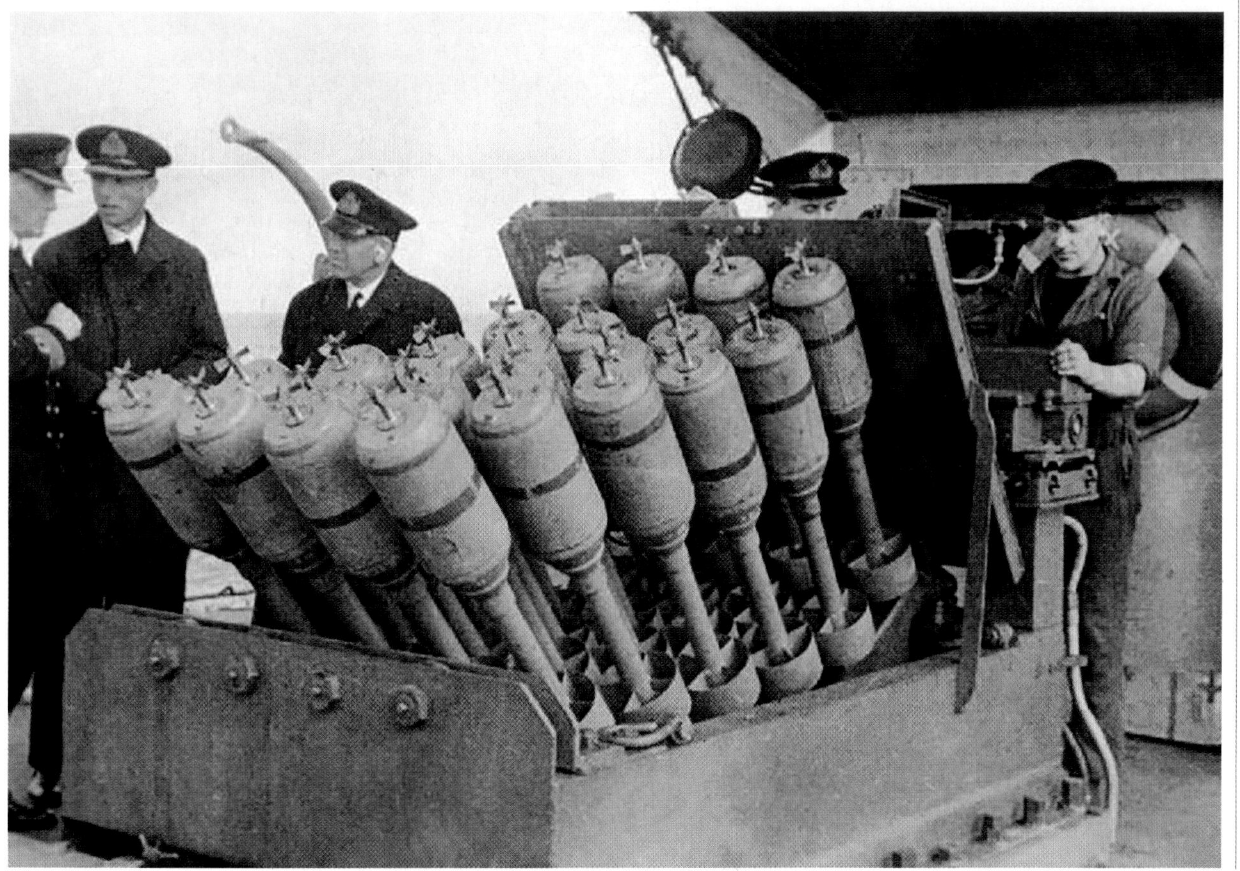

the nearest U-boats to move to intercept and then radio contact information so that the wolf packs could strike. The winter weather initially helped protect the convoys, but the elite U-boat commanders knew their trade and soon had targets in their sight.

One U-boat stumbled on SC-122 by accident in the storms and quickly reported its position. In the gloom of the early hours of March 16, the U-boats struck and by dawn eight ships had been sunk or abandoned by their crews. The following night another wolf pack attacked HX-229 and sunk another four merchant vessels. Another vessel fell prey to a daylight attack during March 17.

Fortunately, SC-122 had now crossed the gap and maritime patrol aircraft from Iceland

ABOVE: Captain FJ Walker, the most successful Royal Navy U-boat hunter of World War Two, directs an attack from the bridge of HMS Starling. (IMPERIAL WAR MUSEUM)

LEFT: Royal Navy frigates were re-equipped with forward firing 'Hedgehogs' to drop patterns of depth charges over submerged U-boats. (IMPERIAL WAR MUSEUM)

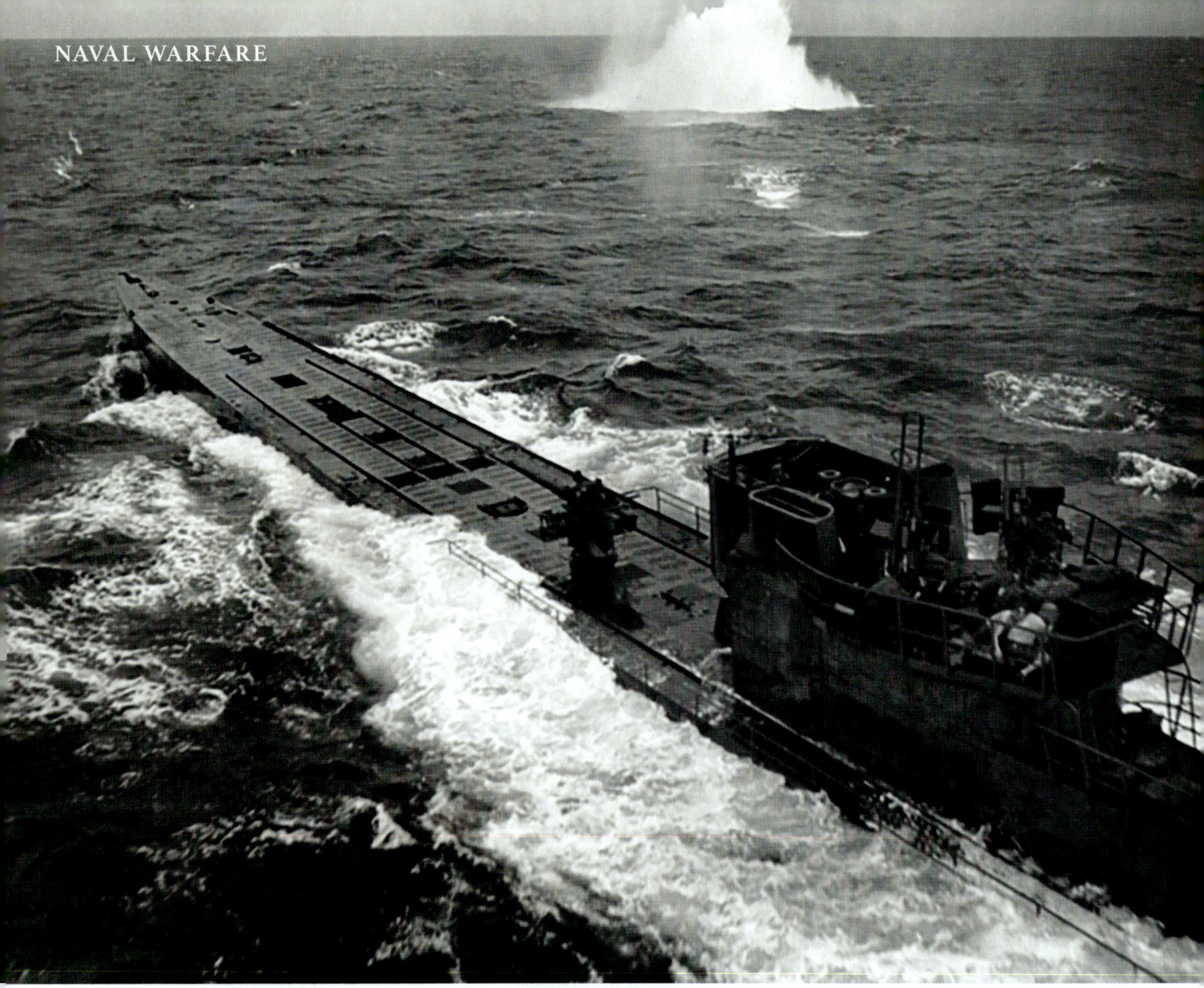

ABOVE: After 1943, the U-boat fleet was put on the defensive and for the remainder of the war became a hunted prey. Here the crew of a U-boat take cover as they come under attack from a US Navy Catalina flying boat. (US NAVY)

arrived overhead to escort it for the remainder of its journey. The pursuing U-boats fell back and concentrated their attention on HX-229. Eleven U-boats had been massed for the attack and struck during daylight on March 17. The bad weather meant the U-boats could attack on the surface, with little chance of being spotted. During the course of eight hours, 10 ships were hit, setting them on fire and forcing their crews to abandon ship. The hard-pressed escort vessels struggled to pick-up the traumatised survivors from the freezing sea. There were no warships available to counterattack against the U-boats. It was only when the first Allied aircraft arrived overhead in the late afternoon that the first U-boat was forced to dive to avoid attack and the wolf pack broke off its attack to regroup, refuel and rearm.

Another wolf pack had caught up with SC-122 and positioned itself to attack at night, when the Allied aircraft could not protect it. And during the night of March 17, the

RIGHT: To close the Mid Atlantic 'gap' in 1943 many different types of aircraft were pressed into service, such as this RAF-crewed Boeing B-17 Fortress IIA bomber, based at Lajes in the Azores. (IMPERIAL WAR MUSEUM)

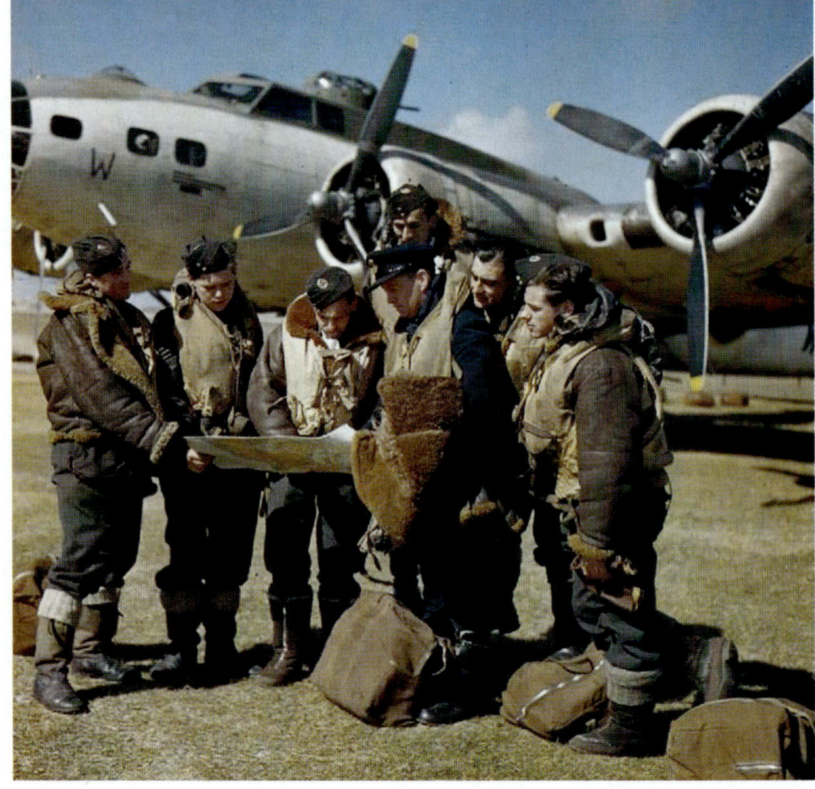

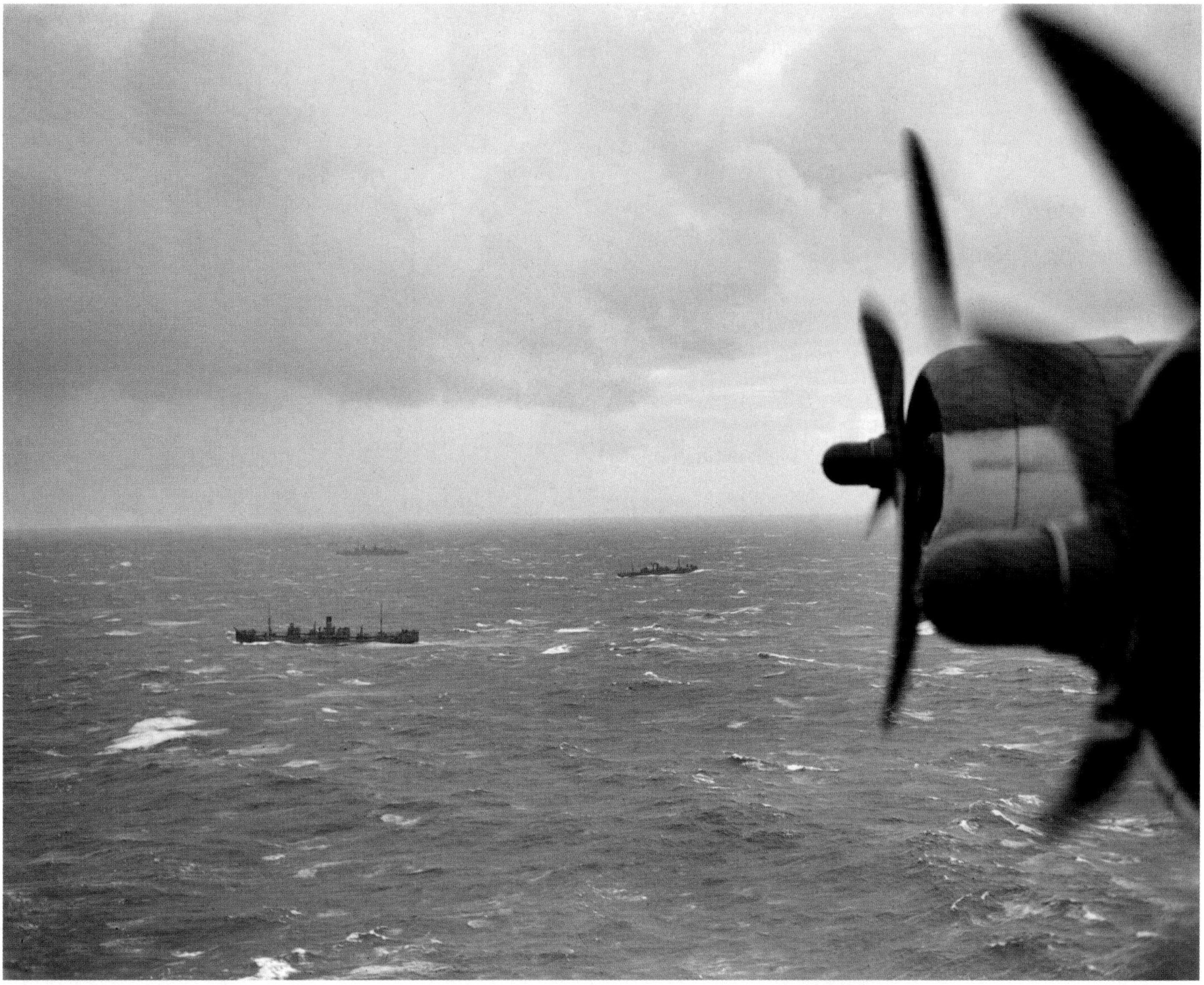

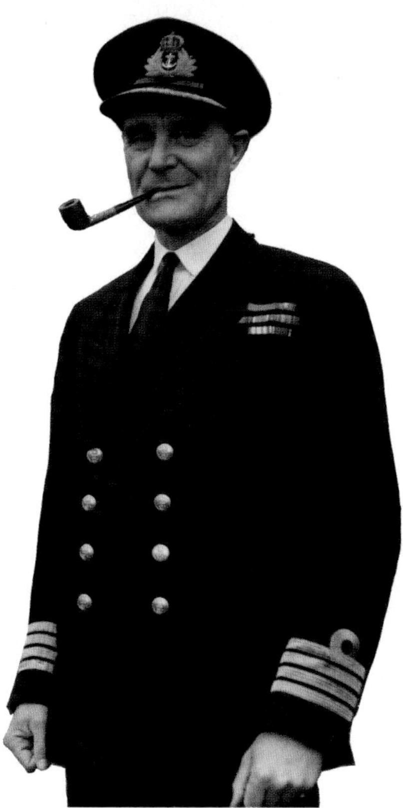

U-boats managed to pick off two more merchant ships.

Despite the presence of air cover on March 17, the U-boats tried to press home their attacks on the convoys, but the escorts were now able to take the fight to the enemy, forcing several U-boats to break off their surface attacks and dive. One U-boat captain launched an underwater attack on HX-229 and managed to penetrate the escort screen to sink two merchant vessels.

This cat and mouse game continued for two more days as the wolf packs harried the convoys and attempted to dodge past the escort screen and allied air patrols. Two more ships were picked off, before the U-boats lost contact with the convoys. A week later the survivors of the two convoys arrived in British ports. It had been a brutal battle in which 22 merchant ships had been sunk and 300 seamen had died.

The attacking wolf packs had mustered 38 U-boats to engage SC-122 and HX-229 and inflicted carnage for minimal losses. Only one U-boat was sunk during the course of the running battle, when U-384 was found on the surface and sunk by a RAF B-17 Flying Fortress. Eight U-boats were engaged by escorts and RAF aircraft, suffering varying degrees of damage but they were all able to return to base for repair.

This was the low point of the Battle of the Atlantic, with a senior Royal Navy commander commenting: "It appeared possible that we should not be able to regard convoy as an effective system of defence".

Nine more merchant ships were lost in convoys during April but in May the tide turned against the U-boats. Convoy ONS 5 comprising 42 merchant ships and seven escorts sailed from Liverpool on April 21 and headed for North America to pick up war cargo. By early May, it had reached the centre of the Atlantic and Dönitz ordered 43 U-boats to concentrate their efforts against it. At first the U-boats attacked with impunity. Two merchant ships were sunk on May 4 and the following day 10 more went to the bottom.

ABOVE: RAF Coastal Command's Shorts Sunderland flying boats were in the forefront of the maritime patrol campaign in the North Atlantic shepherding convoys to safety. (IMPERIAL WAR MUSEUM)

LEFT: Captain FJ Walker was the Royal Navy's most successful U-boat hunters and was credited with destroying 20 German submarines. (IMPERIAL WAR MUSEUM)

Royal Navy officers stand watch on an Atlantic convoy. The brutal weather and sea conditions in the North Atlantic winters took a terrible toll on the crews of both the merchant vessels and the escorts. (IMPERIAL WAR MUSEUM)

Black May

The Admiralty now sent reinforcements to bolster the protection of ONS 5 and for the first time committed support groups to a convoy battle in the North Atlantic. After a rapid passage from Newfoundland the 3rd Support Group with four destroyers joined the convoy on May 3 and two days later, they were joined by the 1st Support Group with five frigates. RCAF Catalina flying boats were now within range of the convoy and could also aid the fight back.

These reinforcements soon turned the tables on the U-boats. Using their radio direction finding equipment, the support groups were able to mass ships to intercept U-boats as they approached the convoy, forcing them to submerge and then lay down barrages of depth charges. The British frigates were then able to stay on station to hunt down the U-boats, tracking them with sonar and then dropping more depth charges. These duels lasted several hours at a time and while the frigates attacked, the rest of the convoy was able to continue on its way.

On May 5, 1943, two U-boats were depth charged and destroyed. Four more were sunk the following day, including one which was rammed by a Royal Navy frigate. In the course of this battle, two more U-boats were spotted by British and Canadian patrol aircraft and sunk. A further seven U-boats were damaged in engagements with the frigates and patrol aircraft.

Following convoys saw similar losses for the U-boats, for negligible losses in merchant ships, with five U-boats being lost for the same number of merchant vessels. Then the next convoy made it across the Atlantic without losing any ships and the escorts, support groups and patrol aircraft sank five U-boats. This set the trend for the rest of the war.

On May 6 Dönitz sent a message to his U-boat captains to call off the attack on ONS-5, citing heavy losses and strong escort coverage. Soon the U-boat crews nicknamed May 1943 as

BELOW: Merchant shipping was organised into convoys so Royal Navy warships could be massed to protect them from both the U-boats and surface raiders. (US NATIONAL ARCHIVES)

'Black May' after 40 U-boats failed to return from war cruises in the Atlantic. On board one of those U-boats, U-*954*, was Doenitz's own son Peter who was lost along with the rest of the crew. By May 23, almost a third of the Atlantic U-boat fleet had been lost.

Remarkably, the code breakers in Bletchley Park were able to decode orders from Dönitz on May 24, calling an end to the wolf pack campaign in the North Atlantic. The Admiralty was able to read their foe's message to his U-boats long before many of them were able to decode the signals themselves.

Dönitz acknowledged that Allied advances in anti-submarine war had rendered the majority of his fleet obsolete. He withdrew his fleet from the North Atlantic convoy routes but promised they would be back when faster, better equipped U-boats were available. They never materialised. The following month 17 U-boats were sunk and 37 more were lost in July 1943, setting the irreversible decline of the U-boat fleet. In 1943, the Germans lost a total of 258 U-boats, out of which 90 were confirmed sunk by aircraft and a further 51 were damaged in air attacks.

In his memoirs, written 15 years later, Dönitz admitted that 'Black May' marked the German defeat in the battle of the Atlantic. While the war continued for another two years and both merchant and U-boat crews suffered losses, the U-boat was never again to enjoy the success it had achieved during the time of the wolf packs.

Allied shipping losses were starting to drop dramatically as well and, by the end of 1943 it was routine for convoys to cross the Atlantic without losses. D-Day was safe and went ahead as scheduled in June 1944.

During the spring and summer of 1943, allied naval and air forces turned the tide against German U-boats. More than 250 Nazi submarines were sunk and German efforts to strangle Allied supply lines to Britain were defeated. The battle came to a climax in May 1943 when the Germans lost as many U-boats as the allies lost cargo ships. The allies were also now building merchant ships at up to 10 times the rate the Germans were able to build submarines.

Okinawa

Defeating the kamikaze

RIGHT: On the morning of May 11, 1945, USS *Bunker Hill* was struck and severely damaged by two Japanese kamikaze planes. In the subsequent fire and explosions 393 sailors and airmen were killed, including 41 missing, and never found, and 264 wounded. (US NAVY/US NATIONAL ARCHIVES)

BELOW: Task Force 58 massed 13 carriers off Okinawa in March and April 1945 to support the invasion force. (US NAVY/US NATIONAL ARCHIVES)

Operation Iceberg was the most audacious US Navy operation of World War Two. Its aim was to capture the heavily defended island of Okinawa, just 500 kilometres south of the Japanese mainland. It was intended to use the island's airfields to support the final Allied offensive to land on the Japanese home islands, but the defenders were expected to put up fanatical resistance. The Japanese defensive concept was built around the doctrine of attrition, with the commander of the Okinawa garrison telling his troops they had to fight to the last man. "One plane for one warship, one boat for one ship, one man for ten enemy, one man for one tank," was his slogan.

The main challenge for the top US commander in the Pacific theatre of operations, Admiral Chester Nimitz was that Okinawa itself was out of the range of any land-based allied aircraft, except the Boeing B-29 Superfortress heavy bomber which were best suited to carpet bombing industrial targets rather than precision bombing of small island airfields and installations. To win air supremacy over Okinawa and open the way for more than 180,000 US Army soldiers and US Marines to storm ashore, Nimitz would have to rely on carrier-borne airpower. The assault on Okinawa saw the biggest concentration of carrier airpower in the Pacific war and culminated in the sinking of Japan's last effective naval force, including the world's biggest ever battleship, the *Yamato*.

Divine Wind

The air and naval battles around Okinawa featured the first mass use of suicide aircraft, known as kamikaze. The name derived from the Japanese word for 'divine winds', which had long been associated with the legend of the typhoons that had dispersed the Mongol invasion fleet, under Kublai Khan, in 1274 and 1281. The Japanese military leadership was

the first phase of Operation Iceberg to dominate the seas and skies around Okinawa in the run up to the first landings. Their aircraft then provided a protective ring around the US fleet as the invasion played out. Close protection of the landing ships was carried out by aircraft from the escort carriers, and they then switched to providing close air support as the land battle escalated.

The US Navy was supported by the five aircraft carriers of the British Pacific fleet. These were the advance guard of a large British air, land, and naval force that was gathering in Australia ahead of the proposed invasion of the Japanese home islands. The British aircraft carriers played an important role in the battle for Okinawa and their armoured metal flight decks

convinced they could repeat the trick in the 20th century and that swarms of suicide attacks by its Divine Wind Special Attack Unit would inflict grievous damage on the US Navy.

The logistics of Operation Iceberg were on a scale never before seen in the Pacific theatre and rivalled those needed to put the allied armies ashore in Normandy the previous June. Admiral Raymond Spruance was the overall commander of the operation, and his landing force was led by Vice Admiral Raymond Turner. Vice Admiral Marc Mitscher led the fast carrier force, which had the task of protecting the amphibious force as it approached Okinawa and then fought to capture the island.

Turner's landing force mustered 183,000 soldiers and marines, who were carried in 430 assault ships and large landing craft. More than 1,000 other US ships sailed to protect the landing force or carry its supplies. This armada was launched from 11 ports on the US west coast, Australia, and the Philippines. It gathered in the central Pacific, ahead of the invasion.

Air support came from 11 large fleet carriers, six light carriers and 22 escort carriers of the US Navy. The fleet carriers were massed under Mitscher's command and spearheaded

LEFT: USS Bunker Hill burning after being hit by a Japanese suicide attack off Okinawa on, May 11. (US NAVY/US NATIONAL ARCHIVE)

BELOW: The Yokosuka MXY-7 Ohka was a purpose designed, rocket-powered kamikaze aircraft, with a 2,600lb warhead. (MUSEUM OF SCIENCE AND INDUSTRY, MANCHESTER)

ABOVE: US Navy carrier borne aircraft unleashed relentless bombardments on Japanese positions on Okinawa. (US NAVY/US NATIONAL ARCHIVES)

BELOW: The doomed foray of the giant battleship *Yamato* on April 7 was the symbolic end of the battleship era. US Navy carriers launched hundreds of aircraft to devastate the Japanese battleship and send her to the bottom of the East China Sea, with most of her crew. (ANDY HAY FLYING ART)

ABOVE: US Army soldiers and Marines battled for 81 days on Okinawa to overcome fanatical Japanese resistance. (US NAVY/US NATIONAL ARCHIVES)

Okinawa 1945: Last Cruise of the Yamato

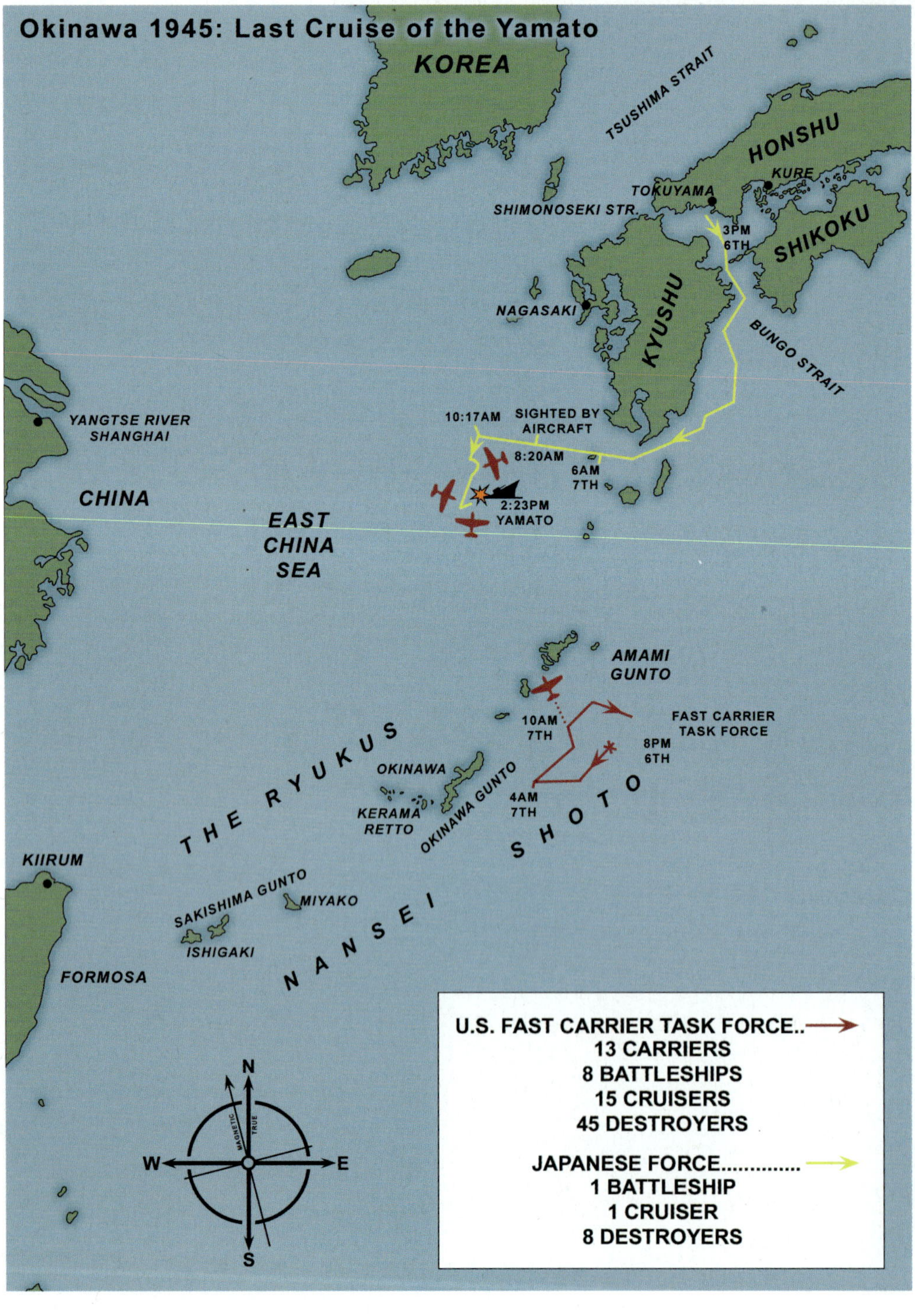

provided vital protection from kamikaze attacks. US Navy aircraft carriers had wooden flight decks that were easily penetrated by diving kamikaze aircraft and then quickly caught fire. This meant US carriers often had to withdraw back to port for repair after hits from kamikazes, the British carriers could return to action after a few hours of clearing debris from Japanese aircraft from their decks. The US Navy liaison officer on HMS *Indefatigable* commented: "When a kamikaze hits a US carrier it means six months of repair at Pearl [Harbor]. When a kamikaze hits a Limey [British] carrier it's just a case of 'Sweepers, man your brooms'."

Operations around Okinawa formally got underway in March 1945 and lasted until June when the final Japanese soldiers were killed or captured on the island. The main landings were scheduled for April 1 and in mid-March to prepare the way, Admiral Mitscher and his fast carrier force made a dash towards Okinawa to begin the campaign to win air supremacy. At the same time, the British Pacific Fleet launched a foray towards Formosa, now Taiwan, to launch air strikes to neutralise Japanese airbases that could be used to launch aircraft against the US fleet off Okinawa.

Mitscher's carriers began launching attacks against targets on Okinawa on March 18 and within hours, the Japanese struck back with waves of conventional and kamikaze aircraft against his fleet. After taking heavy losses in battles with the US Navy over the previous three years, Japan's war machine was reaching the end of the road. Almost all of its experienced aviators had been lost in battle and to compensate for this the Japanese resorted to suicide attacks. Barely trained pilots were ordered to fly their aircraft into US warships in the hope of setting off huge fires. The fanatical

LEFT: A huge logistic support network was needed to keep the US invasion force fighting on Okinawa and it was the job of the US and British fleets to protect them from Japanese air and sea attack. (US NAVY/US NATIONAL ARCHIVES)

Japanese pilots simply had to keep the aircraft pointing towards their targets and even if they were hit by anti-aircraft fire it was often not enough to stop them. In many cases, their forward momentum resulted in flaming debris engulfing the target ship, causing massive damage and heavy casualties. The battle for Okinawa was not the first time that the Japanese had used kamikaze tactics, but it was the largest use of these deadly tactics, with several hundred kamikaze aircraft being launched against the US and British fleets. For the first time, the Japanese also used their purpose-built Ohka, or Cherry Blossom manned flying bombs which featured 2,600lb of explosive packed into the human-piloted, rocket powered aircraft.

On the first day of the Okinawa operation, two of Mitscher's carriers were hit and badly damaged. The USS *Franklin* took a series of rocket hits on her flight deck, setting the ship on fire and listing badly. Almost 800 sailors were killed, and hundreds injured. Later on, the same day, the USS *Wasp* was hit, and 302 sailors killed.

Targeting the Beaches

The US fleet remained on station over the next two weeks launching airstrikes, while battleships and cruisers bombarded the invasion beaches. They put 13,000 shells on target, while under relentless kamikaze attacks that hit 10 more US warships. On schedule, on the morning of April 1, 1945, the first assault troops went ashore to confront 110,000 Japanese defenders, who were expected to fight to the last man, woman, and child.

It took nearly three months of brutal fighting to clear Okinawa of Japanese troops. In the final stages of the battle, the surviving defenders were cornered in a series of caves. In last eight days of the battle more than ➤

BELOW: The USS *Essex* off Okinawa in April 1945. (US NAVY/US NATIONAL ARCHIVES)

ABOVE: USS *Missouri* (BB-63) about to be hit by a Japanese A6M Zero *kamikaze* while operating off Okinawa on April 11, 1945. The plane hit the ship's side below the main deck, causing minor damage and no casualties on board the battleship. (US NAVY/US NATIONAL ARCHIVES)

8,000 Japanese soldiers and civilians committed suicide rather than surrender. Out of the original garrison only 2,902 were taken prisoner - the rest were either killed in battle or committed suicide - when fighting ceased on June 22.

As this horror was unfolding on Okinawa, the US Navy was locked in an equally bitter struggle to keep Japanese air and naval forces at bay. Mitscher deployed his fleet in a series of rings to protect his aircraft carriers and the supply ships supporting the troops ashore. The outer ring was held by a picket line of radar-equipped destroyers, whose job was to detect in-bound formations of Japanese aircraft and provide early warning to the rest of the fleet. Combat air patrols of US Navy and British fighters was the next line of defence. Radar operators on the destroyers had an important role to play, vectoring fighters to intercept in-bound Japanese aircraft. Heavily armed cruisers and battleships provided close protection with huge anti-aircraft batteries.

After the initial American landings on Okinawa at the beginning of April it took the Japanese several days to organise their first mass air attacks. On April 6 and 7, the Japanese launched more than 700 aircraft against the US fleet. Just over half, 355, were kamikaze aircraft, whose pilots were determined to make the Americans pay a heavy price.

Swirling air battles filled the sky between the Japanese mainland

RIGHT: US Navy warships put up a wall of flak when kamikaze planes dived to attack. (US NAVY/US NATIONAL ARCHIVES)

and Okinawa, as US fighters tried to intercept the enemy aircraft before they could get close to the main force. The Japanese lost more than 300 aircraft, including 50 falling to US fighters. Despite this heroic defence, 28 kamikaze aircraft got through and slammed into US warships, sinking three vessels.

In between these mass attacks, the Japanese staged a series of smaller strikes to keep the pressure up on Mitscher's fleet. The unrelenting tempo of operations meant that the US and British carriers could only spend a week or so on station off Okinawa before they had to be pulled off the line to refuel, rearm and repair any battle damage. Ammunition consumption rates were phenomenal because of the intensity of the fighting. In logistic zones, hundreds of miles to the southeast of Okinawa, the US 'fleet train' was standing by to transfer all the supplies the carriers needed to get back into the fight.

The Imperial Japanese Navy now made one last attempt to bring the US fleet to battle. As Japanese pilots were battling the Americans in the skies

around Okinawa, the last sizeable group of Japanese warships made a foray into the region. The 64,170-ton battleship *Yamato* was ordered to lead a flotilla of one cruiser and eight destroyers south from the port of Tokuyama on the afternoon on April 6. The battleship was to make a one-way journey to Okinawa, where

it was to be run aground to serve as a static gun platform against American warships off shore. This was a suicide mission in all but name, and the crew knew the ship only had enough fuel for a one-way journey to Okinawa.

After dawn on April 7, the Japanese warship entered open water south of the island of Kyushu. She was

ABOVE: The aircraft carrier HMS *Formidable* on fire after being struck by a kamikaze. A large steel splinter speared down through the hangar deck and the centre boiler-room, where it ruptured a steam line, and came to rest in a fuel tank, starting a major fire in the aircraft park. Eight crew members were killed and 47 were wounded. One Vought Corsair and ten Grumman Avengers were destroyed.
(IMPERIAL WAR MUSEUM)

LEFT: Royal Navy carriers boasted air groups of Avenger torpedo-bombers and the Seafire fighter, which were superior to the Japanese aircraft sent against the Okinawa carrier force.
(IMPERIAL WAR MUSEUM)

ABOVE: The *Yamato* photographed during the battle by an aircraft from USS *Yorktown* (CV-10). The Japanese battleship is on fire and visibly listing to port. (US NAVY/US NATIONAL ARCHIVES)

soon spotted by American patrol planes and submarines, and Mitscher began preparing his carriers to launch a devastating response. Just after midday two waves of American dive- and torpedo-bombers protected by waves of fighters struck at the Japanese ships. In total 383 American planes joined the attack. The Japanese air force was told to keep away to keep the skies clear for the warship's anti aircraft guns to fire without worrying about hitting their own aircraft, but this left the *Yamato* and her escort's undefended against American airpower.

The *Yamato* was the focus of the attacks with 131 US torpedo-bombers striking her from multiple directions. Then 75 dive-bombers swooped to finish her off. Ten torpedoes and six bombs were confirmed as hitting and penetrating the battleship's armour. In less than two hours of unrelenting attacks, the battleship was ravaged by explosions and fire. At 2.23pm, she capsized and then her magazines exploded. The mushroom cloud could be seen 160km away in Kyushu. An estimated 3,055 of her 3,332 crew, including fleet commander Vice-Admiral Seiichi Ito, went to the bottom with her.

During the afternoon, the Japanese cruiser and four destroyers were hit and sunk, ending the last opportunity for the Japanese navy to intervene in the battle. The US reported the loss of 10 aircraft in this hopelessly one-sided engagement. The foray of the *Yamato* did briefly distract Mitscher's aircraft carriers from confronting the airborne kamikaze attacks and

they managed to penetrate the US fleet's defences and badly damage the aircraft carrier, the USS *Hancock*.

Final Throw

A week later, the Japanese launched another maximum effort, sending 185 aircraft over on April 12 and 14. The kamikaze aircraft hit 14 US ships.

These attacks saw the first mass use of the Model 11 Ohka kamikaze rocket planes, which were dropped from the bomb bay of a large twin-engined bomber some 20 miles from the US fleet. Between 40 and 50 were launched on April 12. The destroyer picket line was particularly exposed and suffered heavily to the Ohka

attack, with one being sunk and another badly damaged.

By the end of June, the land battle was over. Mitscher and his aircraft carriers had successfully held the Japanese air force and navy at bay, but the US Navy and Royal Navy paid a heavy price. The Japanese launched 1,900 kamikaze aircraft during the battle and just under 15% hit their targets. This resulted in 25 warships being sunk and 157 were seriously damaged. A further 97 other ships suffered minor damage. Although several aircraft carriers were hit and damaged, none were sunk. The largest vessels to be lost were destroyers. Nearly 10,000 allied sailors became

RIGHT: US planes landed a close miss on *Yamato's* port side. The battleship is already burning and emitting white smoke from the rear. (US NAVY/US NATIONAL ARCHIVES)

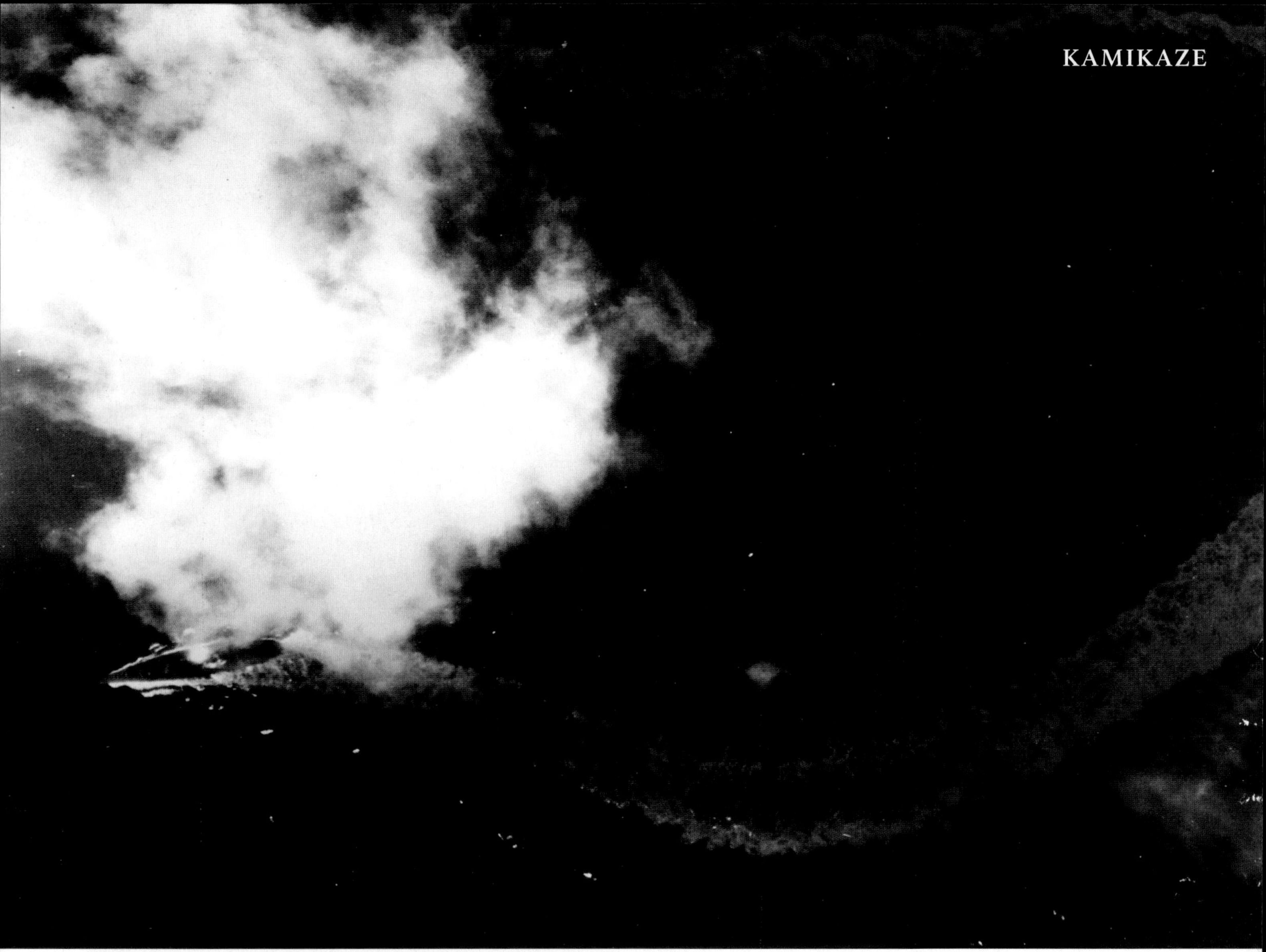

casualties, including 4,907 dead, during the kamikaze attacks.

At the peak of the kamikaze attacks in April, several senior US navy officers started to worry that the losses would become unsustainable if the intensity of attacks continued. However. Mitscher's carrier aviators held the line, and it was the Japanese who proved unable to sustain the fight.

Within days of the capture of Okinawa, Mitscher's carrier and their British allies were re-tasked to begin the opening phase of Operation Downfall, as the invasion of the Japanese home islands was code-named. The carrier strike groups cruised along the Japanese coast and launched their aircraft to attack targets in a bid to first win air supremacy and then degrade defences ahead of the landing by ground troops. The invasion was tentatively scheduled to start in November 1945. As on Okinawa, allied commanders were expecting fanatical Japanese resistance and were predicting up to one million allied casualties. Operation Downfall was cancelled after the Japanese surrendered in August 1945 following the devastation of the cities of Hiroshima and Nagasaki by US atomic bombs.

ABOVE: The Yamato desperately zig-zagged as it tried to avoid relentless US air attacks, but the battleship was doomed. (US NAVY/US NATIONAL ARCHIVES)

LEFT: Eventually the fires and explosions spread to the *Yamato*'s magazines, and she exploded. The mushroom cloud could be seen 160km away. (US NAVY/US NATIONAL ARCHIVES)

TODAY

Airforces Monthly is devoted entirely to modern military aircraft and their air arms.

shop.keypublishing.com/afmsubs

Combat Aircraft Journal is renowned for being America's best-selling military aviation magazine.

shop.keypublishing.com/casubs

ing.com

Aircraft Carrier Strike Suez

Operation Musketeer, 1956

When Britain launched a military expedition to regain control of Egypt's Suez Canal in 1956 it was spearheaded by three of the first generation of 'super' aircraft carriers. These new designs were fitted with angled flight decks that could accommodate high performance combat jets. This opened a new era in naval warfare. The first mass combat use of helicopters from warships also took place during the brief Suez conflict, which showed the potential of rotary wing naval aviation.

When the Egyptian leader Gamal Nasser announced in July 1956 that the British and French owned Suez Canal was to be nationalised, it lit the fuse that would lead to war.

The British and French governments were furious at the threat to the international waterway and colluded to launch an effort to attempt to overthrow Nasser and regain their influence in Egypt. The two colonial powers were locked in several bloody struggles against what was left of their empires and were determined to stamp down quickly on Nasser's defiance.

Nasser's move threw British Prime Minister Anthony Eden into a rage, and he immediately ordered an invasion force to be mobilised from British bases on Malta and Cyprus. Royal Marines of 3 Commando Brigade were massed on Malta as part of a large naval flotilla and the British Army's 16 Independent Parachute Brigade was sent to Cyprus. The French dispatched their own parachute contingent to join the British brigade on Cyprus and an amphibious force sailed from Algeria. To support the assault, strong air and naval forces were concentrated in the eastern Mediterranean, including three British and two French aircraft carriers, with more than 200 aircraft and helicopters embarked.

This was the biggest concentration of British aircraft carriers since World War Two and comprised three of the Royal Navy's most modern aircraft carriers: HMS *Albion,* HMS *Bulwark,* and HMS *Eagle.*

HMS *Albion* and *Bulwark* were both World War Two-era Centaur-class carriers while the 36,800 ton Audacious-class carrier, HMS *Eagle,* was one of the newest ships in the Royal Navy.

In the years before the Suez crisis, the three British carriers had been modified to operate fast jet aircraft, including the installation of arrestor gear, mirror landing systems and 5°

angled flight decks. This allowed all the ships to operate the Hawker Sea Hawk strike jets. HMS *Albion* and HMS *Eagle* also operated De Havilland Sea Venom FAW21 radar-equipped jet fighters and the bigger HMS *Eagle* additionally boasted a squadron of Westland Wyvern turboprop strike aircraft.

HMS *Albion* and HMS *Eagle* also boasted ship's flights of Douglas Skyraider Airborne Early Warning, or AEW, aircraft to provide long range radar coverage of the carrier task force.

The three British carriers gathered in the central Mediterranean, close to Malta, during late September and early October 1956 as the Anglo-French armada gathered ahead of Operation Musketeer. They were grouped under the command of Flag Officer Aircraft Carriers, Vice Admiral Manley Power, who was embarked with the staff of Task Group 345.4.1 on HMS *Eagle*.

Also sent to support the Suez operation were the carriers HMS *Ocean* and HMS *Theseus,* but they were re-configured to embark Westland Whirlwind and Bristol Sycamore transport helicopters and the Royal Marines of 45 Commando. They were destined to carry out the first helicopter-borne combat air assault. The operation was carried out by 845 Naval Air Squadron (NAS), which had 10 Westland Whirlwind HAS22s, and the combined British Army and RAF Joint Helicopter Unit, which flew

six Whirlwind HAR2s and six Bristol Sycamore HC14s. These were first generation helicopters, with limited range and load carrying capacity. The Whirlwind was built under licence from the US company Sikorsky by the UK-based Westland while HMS *Ocean* and HMS *Theseus* were both World War Two era carriers that had been rapidly converted to operate helicopters in the run-up to the Suez operation.

Two French Navy aircraft carriers provided the final naval airpower component of Operation Musketeer. The 13,600-ton FS *Arromanches* was an ex-Royal Navy Colossus-class carrier, and the FS *La Fayette* was an 11,000-ton surplus US Navy Independence-class carrier.

Neither of the French carriers was capable of operating modern jets so they had to make do with ex-US Navy F4U-7 Corsair ground attack aircraft from Aéronavale's 14F and 15F Flotillas (squadrons).

The five carriers would have a key role in the upcoming operation because the main targets in the Nile delta and Suez Canal zone were out of range of tactical aircraft, operating from British airbases in Cyprus, as well as French aircraft based in Israel. Fighter cover for the invasion would depend on aircraft launched from the carriers. So, if troops needed rapid air support, they were dependent on the flat tops for it.

To provide a legal and political pretext for the invasion, London and Paris hatched a secret plot with the

Israelis, which would see the Jewish state launch an unprovoked attack on Egypt. In response Britain and France would issue an ultimatum to both sides to 'withdraw' from the Suez Canal and allow their troops to arrive to 'protect' it from any accidental damage. The Israelis had already agreed to immediately abide by the ultimatum and give the British and French the excuse they needed to invade Egypt to retake the canal. In a secret meeting at Sèvres outside Paris on October 22-24, the attack plan was finalised. Within a week Egypt would be under attack.

ABOVE: Egyptian leader Gamal Nasser was determined to end British and French control of the Suez Canal and relished the confrontation as way to mobilise nationalist spirit across his country. (BELGRADE MUSEUM OF AFRICAN ART)

BELOW: British Prime Minister Anthony Eden was equally determined to deal Nasser a blow and nip in the bud any further challenges to British Imperial dominance across the Middle East. (HARRY S TRUMAN PRESIDENTIAL LIBRARY)

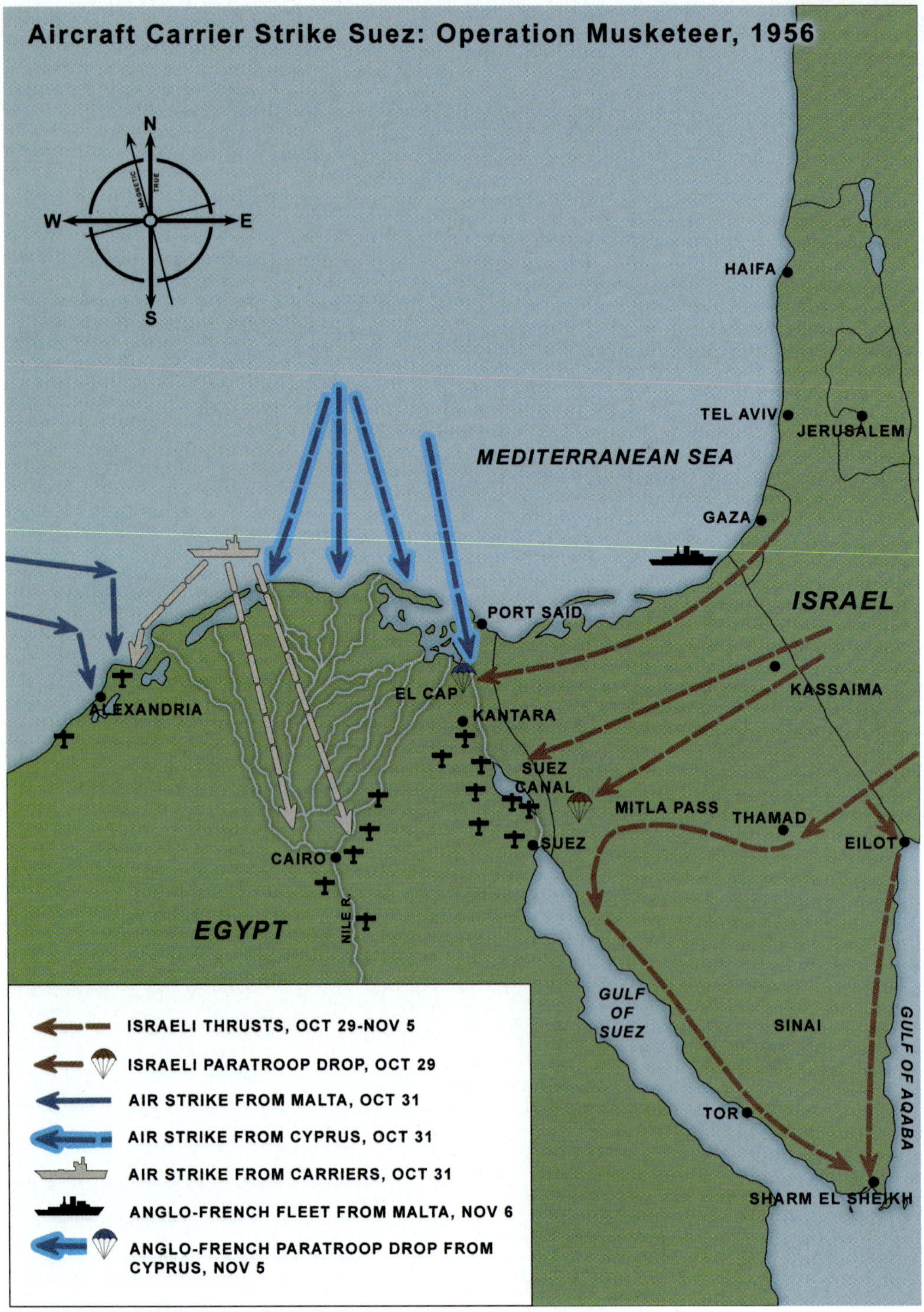

Aircraft Carrier Strike Suez: Operation Musketeer, 1956

ABOVE RIGHT: HMS *Albion* had been modified to incorporate one of the first angled flight decks to allow far more efficient flying cycles, dramatically increasing the number of strike sorties that her jets could fly. (ROYAL NAVY)

ABOVE LEFT: The Hawker Sea Hawk was the Fleet Air Arms main ground attack jet during the Suez crisis. It proved a robust and versatile jet. (RONNIE MACDONALD)

LEFT: Five British and two French aircraft carriers gathered off Egypt to provide air support for the Anglo-French-Israeli intervention to regain control of the Suez Canal. Although British and French carrier aviation soon dominated the skies, the war did not end well as international opinion turned against London and Paris. (ANDY HAY FLYING ART)

Israeli Offensive

The plot against Egypt unfolded on October 29, with the launching of an Israeli offensive into the Sinai peninsula. This kicked off with a parachute drop onto the Mitla Pass to block the Egyptian lines of communications. London and Paris then issued their pre-planned ultimatum. Nasser refused to play along so on the evening of October 31, British and French aircraft began bombing Egyptian airfields. Carrier-borne aircraft joined the air offensive on November 1, and the bombardment continued for another four days until the combined British and French military command considered Egyptian defences suitably degraded. The invasion could begin on the morning of November 5.

The Anglo-French air offensive had the aim of achieving air supremacy by devastating the Egyptian air bases and then shooting down any Egyptian aircraft that did manage to get airborne.

Sea Venoms from HMS *Eagle* began operations on November 1, with a surprise attack on the Egyptian airfields in the canal zone. 893 NAS was responsible for the destruction of many of the Soviet supplied Mikoyan MiG-15s on Almaza airfield near Cairo while the other Sea Venom squadrons shot up airfields nearby. Alongside attacking ground targets,

LEFT: France dispatched two aircraft carriers, including the FS *Arromanches* – a former Royal Navy carrier - but they only had prop-aircraft, not jets. (US NAVY)

the Sea Venoms also supplied Combat Air Patrols(CAP) over the fleet against possible retaliation that never materialised. Continued operations by the Sea Venoms were carried out against various ground targets using both cannon and rocket fire.

In the early hours of November 1, RAF bombers based in Malta and Cyprus attacked Egyptian airfields with the task of destroying the Egyptian Air Force.

Soon afterwards, the Sea Hawks of HMS *Eagle* began their briefed objective of destroying the Egyptian air assets either on the ground or in the air. Surprisingly, the Egyptian Air Force did manage to get a patrol of MiG15s airborne, although, given the lack of training in combat techniques and a lack of ammunition, this meant they did not engage British aircraft in combat.

As the Sea Hawks closed in on Almaza Air Base the pilots were astonished to see the shiny silver MiG-15s parked in long rows on

BELOW: When she entered service in 1952, HMS *Eagle* was the biggest aircraft carrier ever built for the Royal Navy. Two years later she was modified with an angled flight deck to allow her to embark jets. (ROYAL NAVY)

RIGHT: A Sea Hawk launches from HMS *Eagle*. (ROYAL NAVY)

the airfield hard standing. Although the local defence gunners did their best to shoot down their attackers, the Sea Hawks swept in, firing their cannons at the parked aircraft before leaving a shambles of exploding MiGs behind them.

The successful first day attacks on the Egyptian airfields had the desired effect of giving the attackers air superiority, however, the anti-aircraft gunners obviously caused problems because, by day five of the attacks, many of the Sea Hawks were sporting minor repairs after being hit sometime during the campaign.

During its part in Operation Musketeer the *Bulwark* aircraft flew over 600 sorties in support of the various segments of the Anglo-French

landings before departing the area for a much-needed refit in Portsmouth.

When offensive operations began on November 1, the Wyverns of 830 NAS were assigned to attack the airfield at Dekheila, once a home to the Fleet Air Arm. Eighteen sorties were flown by the squadron, their remit was to strafe and bomb the airfield and its aircraft during which 18 1,000lb bombs were dropped and 420 rounds of 20 mm were fired. During this attack, some light flak was encountered although none of the Wyverns were hit.

The second day of operations saw the number of aircraft missions drop to 15 during which Dekheila was attacked again and military vehicles south of Cairo were attacked. On November 3, 830 NAS suffered its first casualty when a Wyvern was hit

by anti-aircraft fire while attacking the bridge at El Gamil near Port Said. Fortunately, the aircraft was still controllable, and the pilot was able to glide his aircraft towards HMS *Eagle* before ejecting and was quickly picked up by the rescue helicopter.

In the first two days of the operation, the Corsairs embarked on the French carriershad been tasked with destroying Egyptian Navy ships at Alexandria, but adjacently moored US Navy vessels prevented the successful completion of the mission. Then, on November 3, six F4U-7s from the FS *Arromanches* and 12 from the FS *La Fayette*, attacked airfields in the Nile delta during which one aircraft was shot down and the pilot killed by anti-aircraft fire. Two Corsairs were also damaged when landing back on

BELOW: The De Havilland Sea Venom was the Fleet Air Arm's first all weather and night capable, jet-powered air supremacy fighter and it dominated the skies over Suez in 1956. (RUTH AS)

LEFT: The3rd Parachute Battalion's drop on Gamil airfield was opening phase of the Anglo-French operation to seize the Suez Canal. (IMPERIAL WAR MUSEUM)

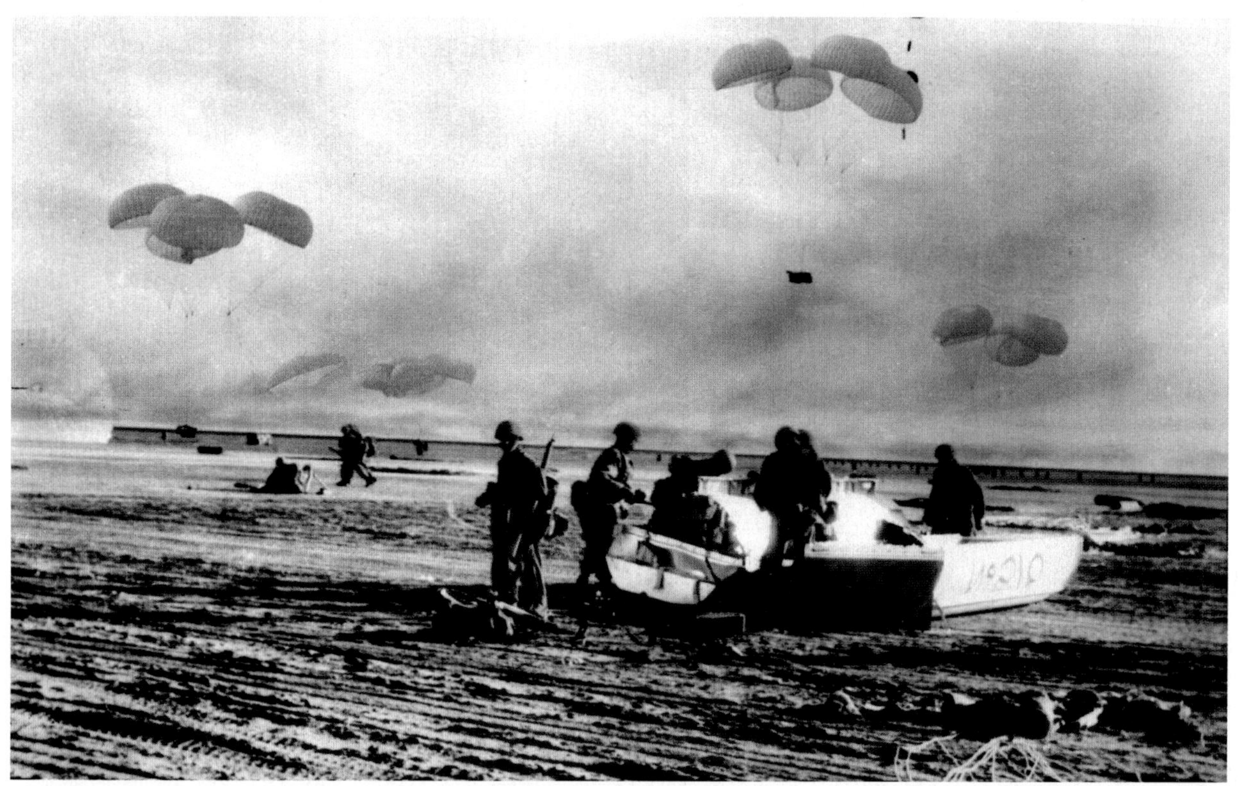

their carriers. The Corsairs engaged in Operation Musketeer dropped a total of 25 tons of bombs and fired more than 500 rockets and 16,000 20mm rounds.

On November 3, the focus of the air campaign switched to striking ground and naval targets of opportunity in the vicinity of the landing beaches. It was during one of these attacks that a Sea Venom of 893 NAS, attacked and sank an Egyptian 'T' boat that was attempting to close in on the Anglo-French fleet.

More than 1,000 British and French paratroopers began loading and emplaning into their aircraft on Nicosia and Tymbou airfields on Cyprus just before dawn on November 5 and then headed south. The plan was for the airborne troops to neutralise the Egyptian defences around the landing beaches of the main amphibious force.

November 3, 1956

The 3rdParachute Battalion group and 16 Parachute Brigade'stactical headquarters began their jump on to Gamil Airfield to the west of

BELOW: The first wave of British helicopters heads to Port Said. (ROYAL NAVY)

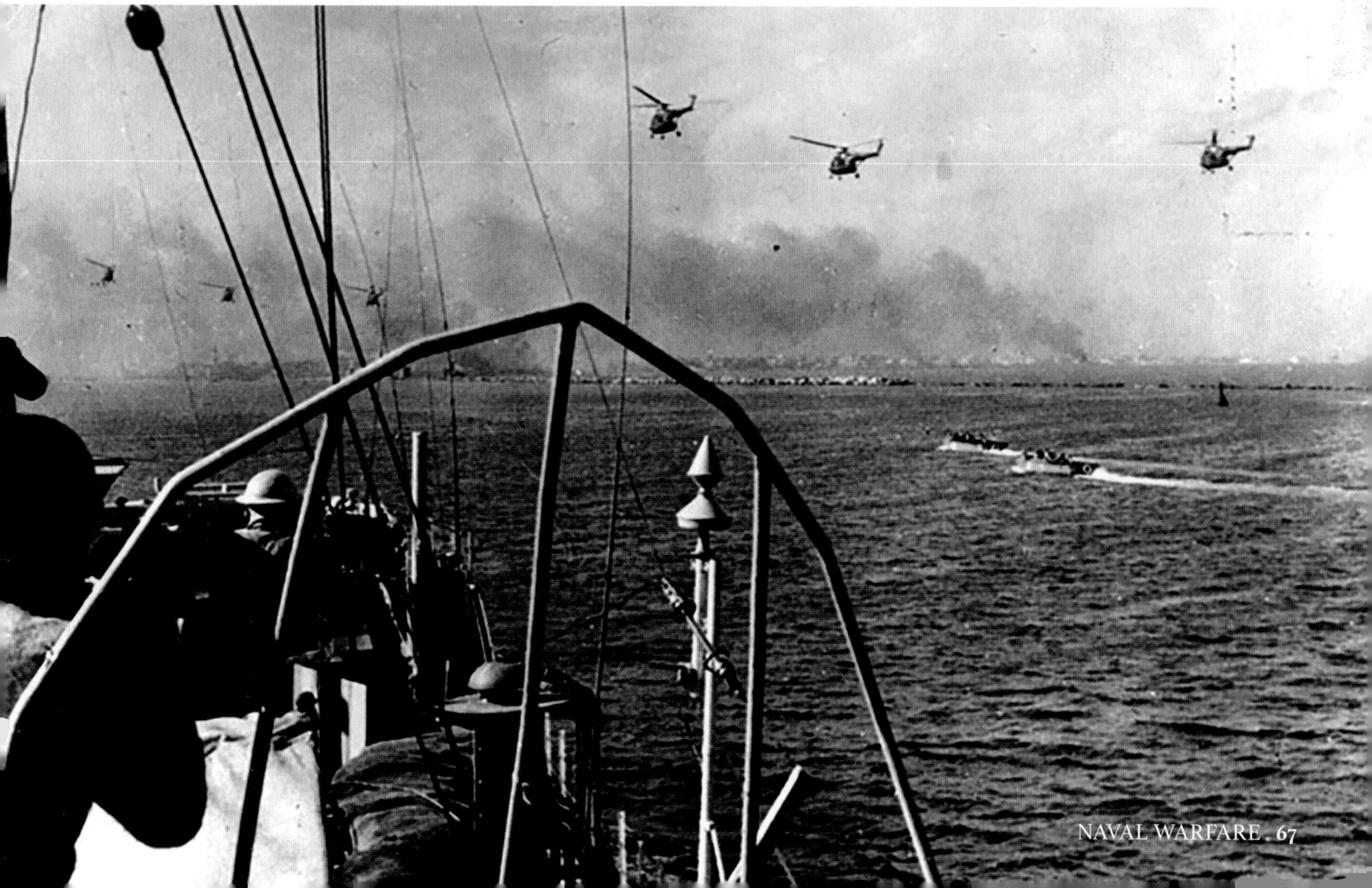

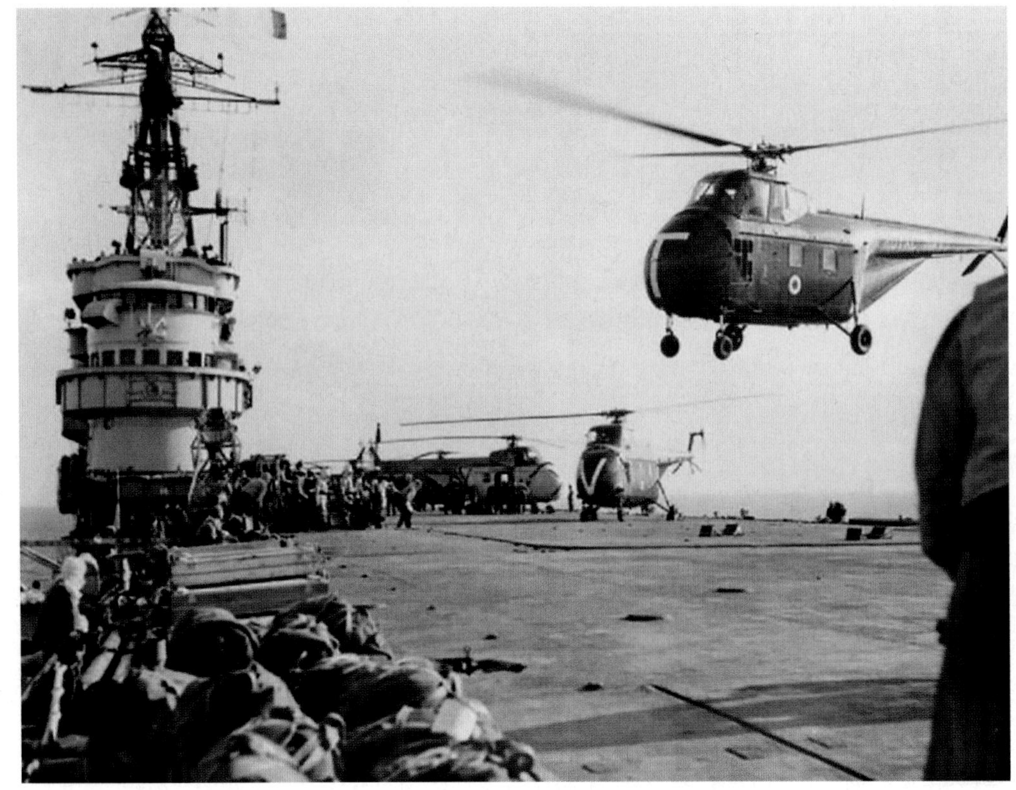

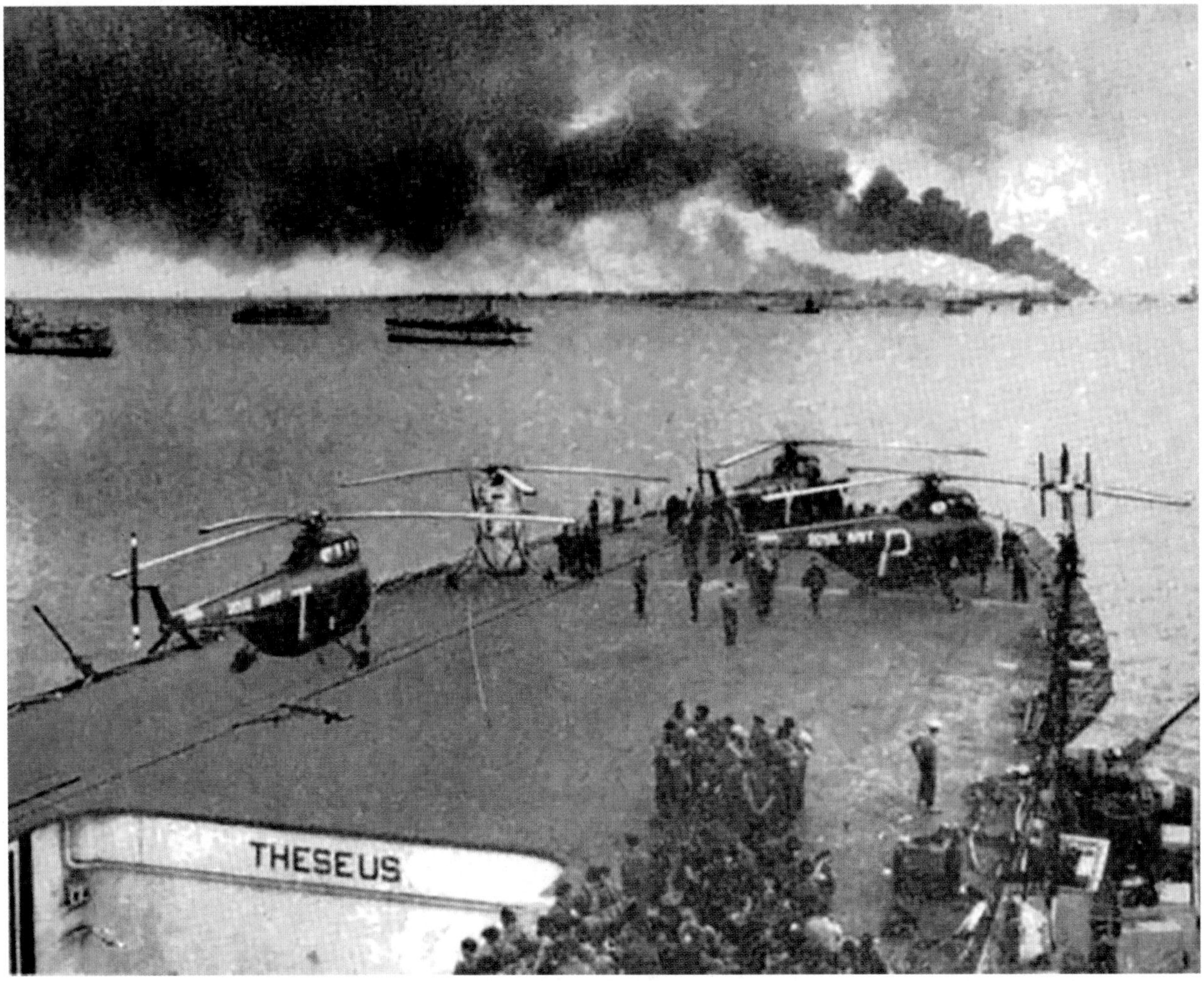

RIGHT: HMS *Theseus* approaches Port Said before launching 45 Commando into action. (ROYAL NAVY)

the town of the same name. A few minutes later 500 men from the French 2e Regiment Parachutistes Coloniaux (2RPC) dropped near the waterworks to the south of Port Said city.

Escorting fighter bombers from the carriers neutralised Egyptian anti-aircraft guns as the troop transports approached the drop zones and by 9am, the British Paratroopers had cleared their objectives of defenders and shortly afterwards a Royal Navy helicopter was able to fly into pick up several casualties. The battalion was then ordered to advanceeast towards the town of Port Said to link up with its French allies.

A rear guard of Egyptians in the Coastguard Barracks were neutralised by an accurate air strike by Fleet Air Arm Wyverns and Sea Hawks strike aircraft called down by the paratroopers.

One of the features of this operation was the continuous support provided by the aircraft from the carrier force. Continuous missions were flown throughout the day and there was always a 'cab rank' of British and French aircraft overhead waiting to be called down on targets by the troops on the ground.

On day five, the Wyverns of HMS *Eagle* were assigned to the support of army units. A total of 16 individual sorties were flown, during which rockets and bombs were dispensed as needed. Overall, three strikes were launched from HMS *Eagle* during which the squadron dropped seventeen 1,000lb bombs, fired 176 rockets with 60lb warheads, and 2,250 rounds of 20mm cannon ammunition, all being used during that day's 473 sorties. During Operation Musketeer, 830 NAS lost

BELOW: Royal Marines on the deck of HMS *Theseus* preparing to embark on Whirlwind helicopters to fly ashore. (ROYAL NAVY)

two aircraft while others suffered minor damage to their tailplanes and engine installations.

The British advanceinto Port Said was stalled on the outskirts of the city by Egyptian artillery and rocket fire. This meant the British Paratroopers spent an uncomfortable night trading fire with the city's defenders.

In the early hours of November 6, 3 Commando Brigade started to put its troops ashore on landing beaches around Port Said. As the British landing craft were approaching the shore, the Royal Marines of 45 Commando were on the deck of the converted aircraft carrier, HMS *Ocean*, preparing to fly ashore in Westland Whirlwind and Bristol Sycamore helicopters.

Helicopter Raids

The commanding officer of 45 Commando led the way, taking-off from HMS *Ocean* in a helicopter to overfly the landing zone his unit was due to capture in a few hours. In the smoke and haze the helicopter pilot lost his way and landed temporarily in a football stadium held by Egyptian troops. They opened fire on the Royal Marines, and they rapidly re-embarked on the helicopter to make their escape. Despite the bullet holes, the helicopter was safely able to return to *HMS Ocean* so final orders could be issued for the air assault.

45 Commando took off from HMS *Ocean* and HMS *Theseus* in 22 British helicopters and 90 minutes later, 400 Royal Marines and 23 tons of stores were ashore near the Casino Pier. They met no resistance but had proved that it was possible to move a large body of troops into battle by helicopter. As the battle developed, the Royal Navy helicopters then began shuttling supplies to shore and bringing back wounded for

medical treatment. The British invasion force eventually suffered 96 wounded while the French had 33, the majority of which were flown by helicopter to a hospital ship. HMS *Albion's* Skyraiders also undertook relief missions into theGamil Airfield taking in vital supplies and flying out the wounded.

For the rest of the day, 3 Commando Brigade and its supporting tanks started to clear the main areas of Port Said in a bid to link up with the British and French paratroopers in the east and south of the city. Streets had to be cleared house by house and sometimes room by room. This took time and required a considerable expenditure of small arms ammunition and grenades by the Royal Marines. When stubborn pockets of resistance were encountered, Fleet Air Strike aircraft were called up to neutralise them.

However, the British and French intervention met with furious international reaction. Most importantly, the United States government made its disapproval known by threatening financial sanctions against London and Paris. Later, on November 7, the United Nations called a ceasefire,and the invasion force was ordered to stop its advance. An uneasy ceasefire settled over the battlefield. Thousands of Egyptian troops and armed civilians remained in pockets around Port Said and they continued to open occasional fire on British and French troops over the days to come.

Within a matter of days, the British and French had to agree to a humiliating withdrawal and the handing over of Port Said to a United Nations monitoring force which had arrived later in November. Then a full-scale withdrawal was ordered, with the last British and French troops leaving on December 22, 1956.

Although British and French forces, backed by strong carrier aviation and helicopter-borne troops, had completely outmatched their Egyptian opponents, Operation Musketeer was a strategic disaster for the British and French. Their key ally, the United States had turned on them just as the operation was reaching its climax. The display of British and French military power had not cowed the Egyptians. Across the Middle East and North Africa anti-imperialist forces staged coup d'étatand uprisings. The British government soon announced a retreat from its empire, citing a 'wind change'. Rebels in Algeria fought a bloody war against French colonial forces but by 1962 Paris too had thrown in the towel.

LEFT: French paratroopers dropped around the Port Said's waterworks in a bid to secure the southern approaches to the city. (FRENCH ARMY)

BELOW: Royal Marines move into Port Said to link up with the British and French airborne forces. (IMPERIAL WAR MUSEUM)

Gulf of Tonkin 1964-65

First shots in America's conflict in Vietnam

RIGHT: Aircraft carrier crews nicknamed themselves the 'Gulf of Tonkin Yacht Club' to boost morale during their long cruises off the coast of Vietnam. (US NAVY/US NATIONAL ARCHIVES)

America's long and bloody conflict in Vietnam 'officially' started on August 2, 1964, when a US Navy destroyer and North Vietnamese gunboats traded fire in the Gulf of Tonkin. This brief and confused naval skirmish was a small affair, with only a handful killed and wounded on both sides, but it set off a chain of events that led to the commitment of more than 500,000 American military personnel to war in southeast Asia. By the time the US embassy and civilian personnel were evacuated from Saigon 11 years later, some 58,000 Americans had been killed. Over three million Vietnamese died in the war.

The Gulf of Tonkin incident was the most consequential engagement of the Vietnam conflict, and the US Navy was central to events that unfolded over three days in August 1964.

For a decade, Washington had been supporting the pro-US

BELOW: US Navy aircraft carried out the first strikes against North Vietnam, leading to 11 more years of American military involvement in South East Asian conflicts. (US NAVY/US NATIONAL ARCHIVES)

government in South Vietnam against a communist insurgency, directed by North Vietnam. It was the era of the 'Domino Theory', which said Moscow and Peking were set on a drive for global communist revolution and if more countries in southeast Asia fell under their control it would lead to others rapidly falling, like a line of dominos. Washington drew a line around North Vietnam and was determined to prop up its pro-US

neighbours, Laos, South Vietnam, and Cambodia. A team of military advisors were sent to South Vietnam to bolster its armed forces but US President John F Kennedy and his successor, Lyndon B Johnson, promised the American people and Congress, that they were only there in a 'non-combat' role. At the same time, the US Central Intelligence Agency (CIA) began a covert campaign of sabotage and subversion against North Vietnam, which involved small fast patrol boats dropping off groups of South Vietnamese and anti-communist Chinese agents in remote coastal locations. This was a 'black' or deniable' programme.

Yankee Station

In the spring of 1964, the USS *Kitty Hawk* was dispatched to the Gulf of Tonkin as a result of rising tension over Laos and this resulted in the US Navy establishing a near permanent presence off the coast of North Vietnam. It soon nicknamed the

operational area, Yankee Station, and for the next decade at least one US Navy carrier and its supporting warships were continuously cruising the Gulf of Tonkin. The US and North Vietnamese were backing rival sides in the country, despite international agreements that were supposed to secure its neutrality. Photographic reconnaissance jets from the USS *Kitty Hawk* started flying missions over Laos, looking for evidence of communist interference. US Navy chiefs were increasingly convinced that they needed to prepare for an escalation of tension with the North Vietnamese and they sought permission to begin a secret intelligence programme to monitor communist radio communications. Starting in February 1964, the US sent destroyers fitted with eavesdropping equipment to patrol along the edge of North Vietnamese territorial waters. These missions became known as DESOTO (DeHaven Special Operations off TsingtaO) patrols. Although they were not officially linked to the CIA's secret missions to land its agents in North Vietnam, the US Navy coincided its DESOTO patrols with CIA operations so sailors listening to communist radio networks could listen in to their reactions and gain intelligence on their defences.

On July 28, 1964, the USS *Maddox* started its DESOTO patrol and two days later a CIA-led South

Vietnamese commando team launched a seaborne attack on a radar site on the island of Hòn Mê island. The North Vietnamese Navy began sending out patrol boats to head off any further attacks. During the afternoon of August 2, three North Vietnamese Navy torpedo boats of the 135th Torpedo Squadron approached the USS *Maddox*. A sea battle resulted, in which USS *Maddox* expended over 280 three-inch and five-inch shells. Four US Navy Vought F-8E Crusader jet fighter-bombers were scrambled

off the aircraft carrier, USS *Ticonderoga,* to support the destroyer, and they swooped down to strafe the torpedo boats. One US aircraft was damaged, one 14.5mm round hit the destroyer, three North Vietnamese torpedo boats were damaged, and four North Vietnamese sailors were killed and six were wounded. There were no US casualties.

Controversy continues over who fired the first shot. Investigators subsequently found US military records showing that the captain

Flying Fish

By day break, no one was any the wiser. None of the pilots or any of the destroyer crews were able to confirm a visual identification of North Vietnam attackers. The destroyers claimed to have sunk two torpedo boats, but no wreckage, survivors, or bodies of crew were ever recovered. Even President Johnson had his doubts, commenting a few days later, "Hell, those damn, stupid sailors were just shooting at flying fish". But the US President was determined to use the incident to his advantage and went on television to accuse the North Vietnamese of aggression on the high seas. He ordered the US Navy to begin planning for a retaliatory attack the following day.

On August 5, US Navy jets off the USS *Ticonderoga* and USS *Constellation* struck at four communist torpedo boat bases and an oil storage depot along the North Vietnamese coast. More than 60 aircraft – F-8Es, McDonnell F-4B Phantoms, Douglas A-4C Skyhawks, and Douglas A-1H Skyraiders - were involved, including 34 from the USS *Ticonderoga*. The

TOP: The USS *Maddox* and US Navy fighter jets drove off the attack of North Vietnamese craft, but a subsequent incident two days later has never really been satisfactorily explained. (US NAVY/US NATIONAL ARCHIVES)

ABOVE: US President Lyndon B Johnson used the August 4, 1964, incident to push the infamous Gulf of Tonkin resolution through the US Congress. This granted him wide authority to conduct war across southeast Asia. (US NATIONAL ARCHIVES)

RIGHT: Minor naval skirmishes off the coast of North Vietnam in 1964 proved decisive in drawing America into the conflict in southeast Asia. US Navy carrier-borne aircraft then struck back against communist bases in North Vietnam, beginning America's decade long involvement in the conflict. (ANDY HAY FLYING ART)

carriers were launched to provide top cover and the destroyers directed them to investigate the radar returns. The pilots could not find anything to attack and returned to their carriers, saying they received confusing orders and information from the destroyers.

of the USS *Maddox* ordered warning shots when the North Vietnamese boats approached, indicating that the Americans fired first. However, that was unclear at the time and President Johnson was in no mood to give the communists the benefit of the doubt. The White House announced the communists had launched an unprovoked attack and Johnson ordered the USS *Maddox* to continue to probe into the 12-mile territorial limit of North Vietnam. Another destroyer, the USS *Turner Joy*, was sent to join the USS *Maddox* on more daylight DESOTO patrols. The carriers, USS *Ticonderoga*, and *USS Constellation* stood ready on Yankee Station to provide air support if the situation escalated.

During the early hours of August 4, the two US destroyers were 11 miles off the coast when they picked up radar contacts of approaching patrol boats. The ship's sonar operators said they heard the sound of torpedo boat propellers and the eavesdropping experts heard communist radio traffic indicating an attack was underway. The weather was terrible, so the US ships started firing flares in a bid to get a visual identification of the attacks. The ships then opened fire against the radar contacts. Aircraft from the

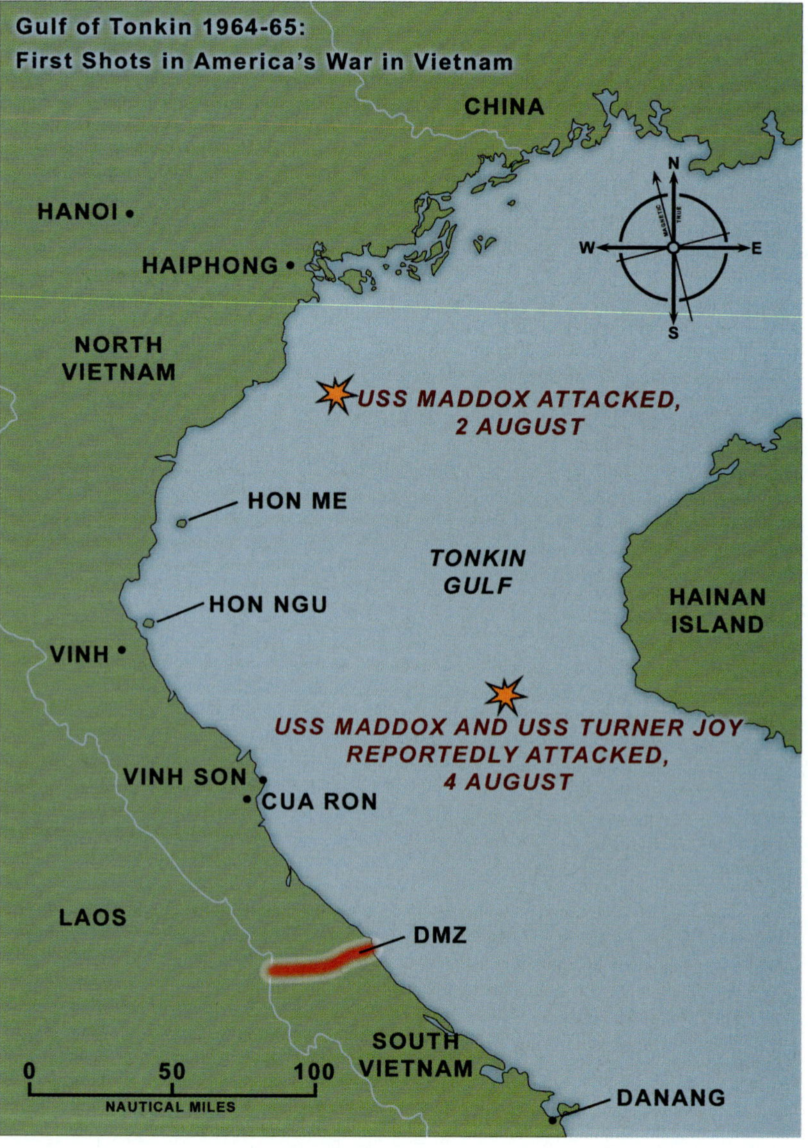

carrier's pilots hit naval sites at Quang Khe and claimed the destruction of eight patrol boats and the damage of 21. The USS *Constellation's* aircraft hit the oil depot at Vinh, resulting in its storage tanks being set on fire and causing a huge plume of smoke to rise over the city.

North Vietnamese air defences were thick around the targets and two of the USS *Constellation's* aircraft were shot down. One of its Skyraider pilots, Lieutenant Richard A. Sather, became the first US Navy pilot to be killed in Vietnam, and the pilot of the downed A-4E Skyhawk, Lieutenant Everett Alvarez, became the first US Navy prisoner of war in Vietnam. He spent over eight years in captivity, enduring brutal conditions in the notorious Hanoi Hilton prison camp.

President Johnson now turned to the US Congress to secure war powers to allow him to expand the war against North Vietnam. On August 10, Congress passed the infamous Gulf of Tonkin resolution. The House of Representatives voted 416 to 0 and only two senators voted against the resolution. It stated, "Congress approves and supports the determination of the President, as Commander in Chief, to take all necessary measures to repel any armed attack against the forces of the United States and to prevent

RIGHT: US Navy fighter pilots flew the F-8 Crusader into action over North Vietnam in 1964 and 1965, flying fighter sweeps, strafing, and photographic reconnaissance missions.
(US NAVY/US NATIONAL ARCHIVES)

BELOW: Bridges and other lines of communications were high priority targets of US Navy strikes during Operation Rolling Thunder in a bid to interrupt communist military supplies and reinforcements heading into South Vietnam.
(US NAVY/US NATIONAL ARCHIVES)

further aggression"…"to protect peace and security in southeast Asia."

Ground Operations

By the early spring of 1965, President Johnson had committed to sending US combat troops to fight on the ground in South Vietnam and his military chiefs were preparing for an air offensive against North Vietnam. In the Pentagon, planners were expecting the war to escalate quickly, even before the US Army and US Air Force had managed to establish themselves in strength in South Vietnam.

The US Navy mustered three carriers - the USS Coral Sea, USS *Hancock,* and USS *Ranger* – in Yankee station under the command of Task Force 77, ready to react to events. A series of retaliatory options were planned. Meanwhile in the Pentagon, US Navy and US Air Force chiefs proposed an all-out air offensive aimed at crippling the North Vietnamese strategic infrastructure – railway lines, power stations, oil refineries, ports, arms factories, ammunition dumps, truck parks and bridges - that allowed the communist state to support its forces fighting in the south. President Johnson and his advisors were not keen on a rapid escalation in the war, out of fear of prompting Soviet or Chinese intervention, as had happened during the Korean war in 1950.

President Johnson signed off on a 'trip wire' strategy. If the communists escalated their attacks on American bases in South Vietnam, then a series of limited air raids would be launched from Task Force 77 to signal to the North Vietnamese that they would

LEFT: The classic F-4 Phantom progressively took on more roles in the US Navy campaign in Vietnam as later variants started to field improved radars, weapons, and other systems. (US NAVY/US NATIONAL ARCHIVES)

pay a price for sending more troops into South Vietnam.

In February 1965, two communist mortar attacks on US bases in South Vietnam left 23 GIs dead and more than 100 wounded. It was time to react. Operation Flaming Dart was launched on February 7, 1965.

US Navy aircraft carriers launched aircraft for strikes on the barracks at Vit Thu Lu and Đồng Hới, both just north of the border with the south. A 29-plane strike formation from USS *Coral Sea* approached Đồng Hới, home of the People's Army of Vietnam (PAVN) 325th Infantry Division under a low cloud ceiling at 500kts. The A-4 Skyhawks, of attack squadrons VA-153 and VA-155, hit the barracks with rockets and 250lb bombs. North Vietnamese anti-aircraft gunners threw up a curtain of fire from 37mm guns, automatic weapons and small arms based ashore and from Swatow gunboats in a nearby river. Some of this fire hit Lieutenant Edward A. Dickson's A-4 but he continued his attack before ejecting from his crippled plane. However, his parachute failed to open, and he plunged to his death. Right behind USS *Coral Sea's* formation came 17 A-4s, of attack squadrons VA-212 and VA-216, from the USS *Hancock,* which dropped their ordnance on already burning and smoking camp facilities, as F-8 put down suppression fire on the anti-aircraft sites. Completing the mission, RF-8ACrusader reconnaissance jets rolled in to photograph the scene for naval intelligence analysis. The results were unimpressive. The attack had destroyed or damaged only 22 of the 275 buildings in the camp.

In reaction to Flaming Dart, the communist Vietcong fighters in South Vietnam attacked a hotel billeting US personnel in Qui Nhơn,

LEFT: Tight rules of engagement controlled the actions of US Navy pilots during the Vietnam war, limiting targets, weapon loads, attack routes and responses to enemy fire. Many US naval aviators felt they were fighting the war with one arm tied behind their backs. (US NAVY/US NATIONAL ARCHIVES)

BELOW: USS *Bon Homme Richard* undertook five combat tours off Vietnam, making it one of the most heavily committed aircraft carriers during the conflict. (US NAVY/US NATIONAL ARCHIVES)

RIGHT: Soviet supplied SA-2 surface-to-air missiles and anti-aircraft guns inflicted heavy losses on US Navy aircraft over North Vietnam. (US NATIONAL ARCHIVES)

Enemy Antiaircraft Weapons. North Vietnam used 57-mm (above), 85-mm (right), and 100-mm (below) weapons, as well as surface-to-air missiles (bottom) to combat U.S. aircraft in Laos.

BELOW: Mikoyan MiG-21 fighters made well orchestrated interventions against US air raids over North Vietnam as part of communist efforts to disrupt American bombing raids and drive attack aircraft into surface-to-air missile engagement zones. (US NAVY/ US NATIONAL ARCHIVES)

prompting Operation Flaming Dart II. The US Navy launched 99 fighter-bombers from the three carrierson Yankee Station. The A-1s and A-4s from the carriers delivered tons of bombs and rockets to the target area at Chanh Hoa as F-8Es and F-4Bs rocketed and strafed anti-aircraft positions. A total of 33 F-8s, F-4s and A-1s protected the attack force by deterring North Vietnamese MiGs based near Hanoi from challenging the mission. Although MiGs did not interfere with the operation, anti-aircraft gunners damaged a USS *Coral Sea* A-4C, forcing the pilot to make an emergency landing at Da Nang Air Base, in South Vietnam.

However, these limited demonstrations of US military power did not convince the North Vietnamese leadership that they faced certain defeat and the communist leadership had not been cowed by American airpower. There were no peace overtures from Hanoi.

Escalation

Washington now decided to escalate the war, with the first US combat troops in South Vietnam taking the offensive. The US Air Force was now ready to attack North Vietnam from bases in Thailand and the US Navy aircraft struck from the Gulf of Tonkin. The bombing campaign was code-named Operation Rolling Thunder, and the navy played a leading role. Between 1965 and 1968, there were usually three or four carriers on Yankee Station.

For just over nine years from April 1964 US Navy aircraft maintained a near continuous presence off the coast of Vietnam, launching daily air strikes across southeast Asia.

The US naval aviators and sailors on the carriers were members of an exclusive group known as the

LEFT: From April 1966, US Navy A-6 Intruders carried out night time strikes on North Vietnam using their revolutionary terrain-following radar to avoid enemy air defences and then drop their bombs on targets with pin point accuracy. (US NAVY/US NATIONAL ARCHIVES)

'Gulf of Tonkin Yacht Club'. They flew classic aircraft – the F-4 Phantom, A-4 Skyhawk, A-1 Skyraider, A-6 Intruder, A-7 Corsairs, F-8 Crusader, and the mighty A-5 Vigilante – into action against what was then the most heavily defended airspace on the planet. The North Vietnamese had ringed their cities and strategic targets with thousands of anti-aircraft guns and Soviet supplied surface-to-air missiles, backed up by MiG-21 fighters, and were soon locked in daily duels with US air power. In 1968, President Johnson ordered a pause in air strikes on North Vietnam in a bid to kick-start peace talks with the communists. Then, his successor, President Richard Nixon, ordered US ground troops to be pulled out of the south after he took office in January 1969. However, US Navy aircraft carriers remained on station in the South China Sea over the next four years flying air support for the South Vietnamese army as it tried to expand to fill the vacuum left by withdrawing US ground troops.

A major North Vietnamese ground offensive was launched into South Vietnam in the spring of 1972 and President Nixon ordered a massive build up of US airpower to turn the back the communist tide. Eventually, the USS *Kitty Hawk*, USS *Constellation*, USS *Midway*, USS *America*, USS *Saratoga*, USS *Coral Sea*, USS *Hancock*, and USS *Oriskany* operated off the coast of Vietnam during Operation Linebacker as the air offensive was code-named.

The last US Navy aircraft lost in combat in Vietnam was shot down on January 27, 1973, just days before the Paris peace accords came into effect to end the US combat involvement in southeast Asia.

During the conflict, 17 US aircraft carriers spent just over 9,000 days in total cruising on Yankee Station off the coast of Vietnam. Some 532 US Navy aircraft were lost in combat and 329 in accidents. In total, 401 US Navy aircrew were lost, 64 reported missing in action and 179 ended up as prisoners of war.

The cruises of the 'Gulf of Tonkin Yacht Club' did not win the war in Vietnam, but the US Navy played a critical role in the actions that formally brought America into combat. Up until the infamous Gulf of Tonkin incident, American military had been advising their South Vietnamese allies. From August 1964, Americans were in the frontline. US Navy aircraft carriers were President Johnson's weapon of choice until the main American force was ready for action in South Vietnam and Thailand. From now on, whenever there is a crisis anywhere in the world, the call from the White House has always been "where are the carriers?" US Naval airpower proved its worth off North Vietnam, as a way to project combat power into crisis regions.

BELOW: After nearly nine years of bombing North Vietnam, the US Navy missions against the country ceased in January 1973. (US NAVY/US NATIONAL ARCHIVES)

The evacuation from Saigon saw Air America UH-1 Hueys airlift thousands of civilians from around the city in a desperate attempt help South Vietnamese civilians flee the communist advance. (USAF/US NATIONAL ARCHIVES)

Leaving Saigon

America's Dunkirk in southeast Asia

ABOVE: Dozens of South Vietnamese air force helicopters were pushed off US Navy warships after their flight decks became full. The evacuation flights kept coming all through April 29, 1975. (US NAVY/US NATIONAL ARCHIVES)

By 1975 America had tired of its war in southeast Asia and US allies across the region were being supported with arms and money only. When the North Vietnamese offensive surged across South Vietnam in the spring of 1975, the US Congress refused requests by US President Gerald Ford for additional military aid to keep the communists at bay. It seemed only a matter of time before Saigon fell. The situation in neighbouring Cambodia was little better, with Khmer Rouge forces occupying most of the country and laying siege to the capital, Phnom Penh.

The Vietnamese capital, Saigon, was home to around 10,000 American diplomats, military advisors, intelligence operatives and civilians. No one was quite sure about the exact number. America's ambassador in Saigon, Graham Martin, also estimated that more than 100,000 Vietnamese – politicians, army officers, intelligence agents, business leaders and their families – would flee because of fears they would be killed or imprisoned after a communist takeover.

In March 1975, the situation looked grim. The nearest US forces were in Thailand and the North Vietnamese were moving SA-2 Guideline heavy surface-to-air missiles (SAMs) to within range of Saigon, threatening to close down airspace over the city. In the Pentagon, the order came to mobilise a naval task force to head to the South China Sea to prepare to rescue the remaining US personnel in Vietnam and Cambodia, as well as salvage some of America's honour by evacuating as many of its local allies as possible. This was to be America's 'Dunkirk in southeast Asia'. The commander of Task Force 76, Admiral Don Whitmire, had to rapidly draw up plans to rescue thousands of people from the middle of a war, yet no one was sure by what means.

Option IV

Operation Frequent Wind, as the mission was named, saw nearly 30 US Navy warships and more than a dozen civilian transport ships arrive in the South China Sea in early April 1975 as part of Task Force 76. US planners hoped the South Vietnamese army

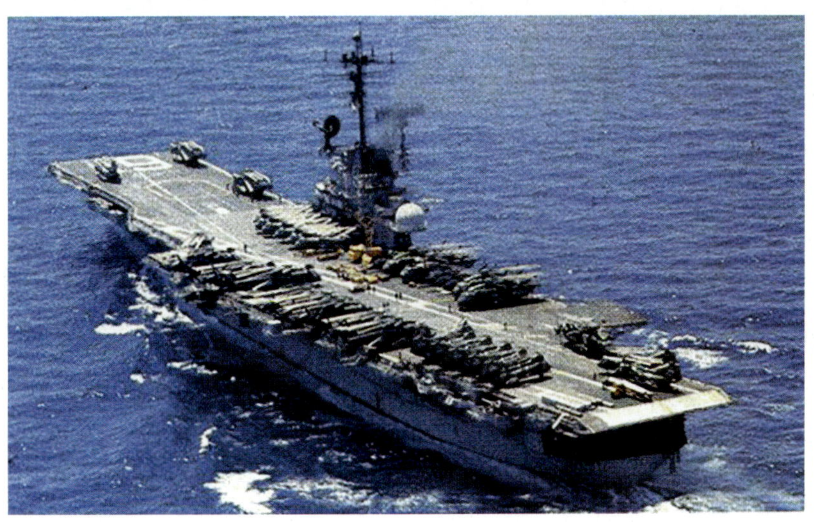

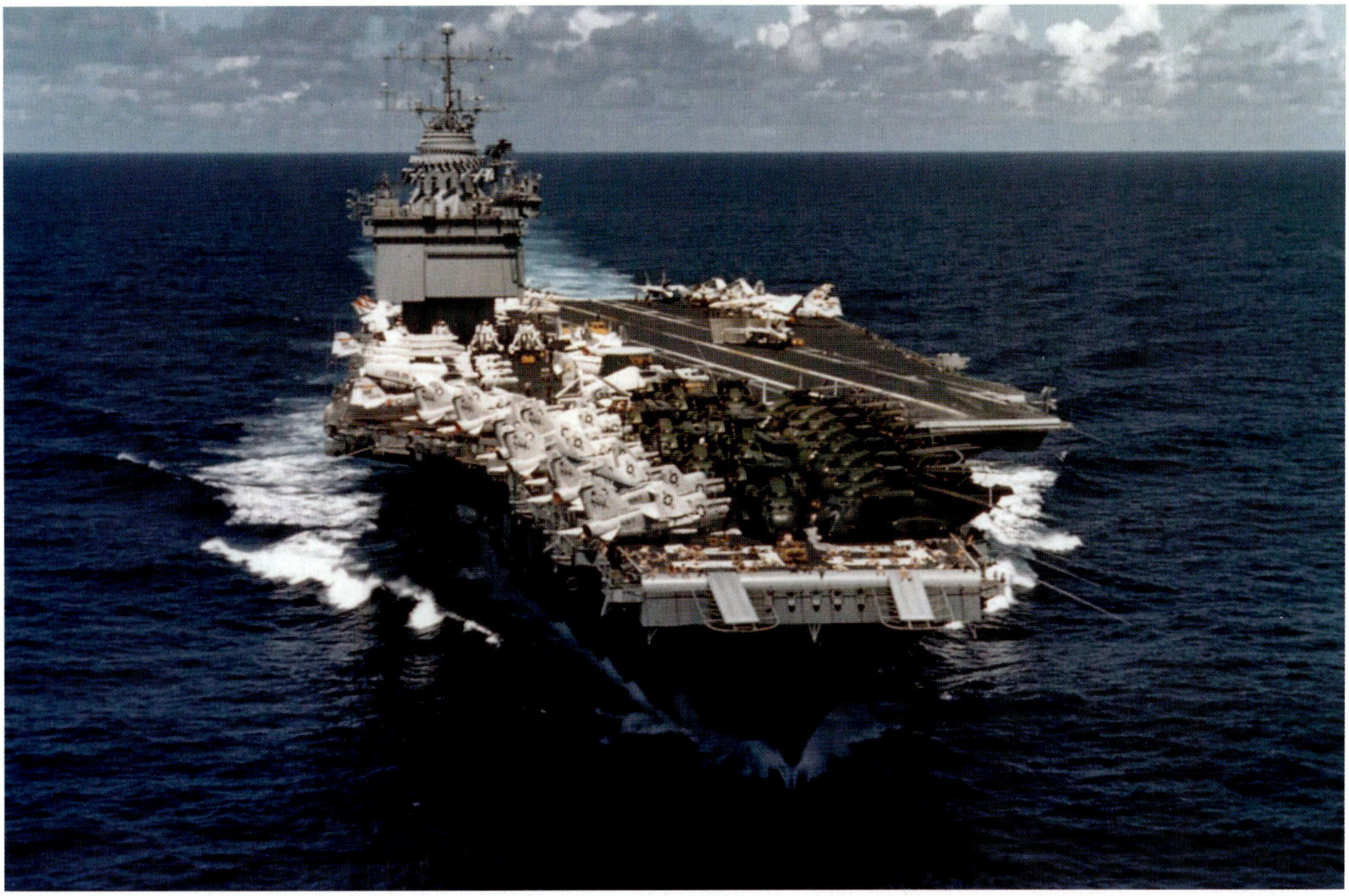

would hold off the communists long enough to allow civilian airliners and US Air Force military transports to lift the majority of the refugees out of Saigon. If the situation deteriorated, then Admiral Whitmire proposed landing his brigade of US Marines to seize a port or bridgehead to bring the refugees out by landing craft and transport ship. As a last resort, it was proposed to use helicopters to fly out refugees from downtown Saigon. This was known as Option IV.

Ambassador Martin was convinced that all was not lost and tried to stall the evacuation plan. He claimed if it became public knowledge that the Americans were going, the South Vietnamese army would collapse. The ambassador kept pushing for the US Congress to increase military aid so the South Vietnamese could turn back the communists. It was a forlorn hope and within weeks the North Vietnamese would be at the gates of Saigon.

At the start of April, Task Force 76 was on station and ready for action. The three battalions of US Marines from the 9th Marine Amphibious Brigade, were ready to go ashore aboard their Boeing CH-46D Sea Knight and Sikorsky CH-53D helicopters embarked in the amphibious ships, USS *Dubuque,* and USS *Okinawa.* Two aircraft carriers, the USS *Hancock,* and USS *Midway,* were pressed into service as additional helicopter platforms, with the former carrying US Marine Corps machines and then later embarking US Air Force Sikorsky HH-53/CH-53 Jolly Green Giant helicopters. In total, Admiral Whitmire had 32 CH-46Ds and 46 H-53 variants available, as well six Bell UH-1E Huey utility helicopters and eight Bell AH-1J Cobra gunships.

The task force also boasted eight dock ships and landing ships, which could launch dozens of landing craft or come alongside in ports and embark thousands of refugees. A small team of US Navy officers were also sent ashore to link up with the South Vietnamese navy and co-ordinate using their warships to bring out thousands of refugees, as well as organising the requisition of giant civilian barges from Saigon's commercial harbour to also carry passengers.

The first domino to fall was Cambodia, when Khmer Rouge fighters closed in on the city's airport, effectively cutting it off from the outside world. President Ford gave the order to execute Operation Eagle Pull on April 12 to lift out the last US embassy staff and civilians from Phnom Penh. The first helicopters over the city were three rescue USAF HH-53Cs flying from Thailand. They delivered a team

ABOVE: Air cover for Operation Frequent Wind was provided by the nuclear-powered aircraft carrier, USS *Enterprise.* (US NAVY/US NATIONAL ARCHIVES)

LEFT: The USS *Hancock* was repurposed into a helicopter carrier for Operation Frequent Wind, with US Marine squadron HMH-463 embarked. (US NAVY/US NATIONAL ARCHIVES)

ABOVE: Operation Eagle Pull was launched on USS *Okinawa* to evacuate the staff of the US Embassy in the Cambodian capital, Phnom Penh, on April 12. US Marines lifted off from the USS *Okinawa* for the mission. (US NAVY/US NATIONAL ARCHIVES)

of combat air controllers into the embassy compound to co-ordinate the inbound US Marine Corps CH-53Ds which had flown from the USS *Okinawa* off-shore. A USAF Lockheed HC-130P command post aircraft orbited over the city, relaying communications to all the players in the operation. After the Marines' Sea Stallions had moved the bulk of the 276 evacuees, a final pair of rescue HH-53Cs landed to recover the control team and the last Marines of the security force. The operation went without a hitch but the situation in Saigon would be very different.

Saigon

Seventeen days later, Option IV of Operation Frequent Wind would be launched to evacuate the US embassy in Saigon. Admiral Whitmire's rescue armada was supported by Task Force 77, which had the combat jets of aircraft carriers,

RIGHT: The mission to Phnom Penh went without a hitch and evacuated US diplomats, American civilians, and citizens of several allied countries. (US NAVY/US NATIONAL ARCHIVES)

USS *Enterprise,* and USS *Coral Sea* on hand to provide air support should the US Marines have to fight their way ashore and evacuate the refuges under fire. USAF jets and Lockheed AC-130 Spectre gunships in Thailand were also on call. The biggest fear was that the North Vietnamese would install a ring of SA-2 missiles around Saigon and effectively hold the Americans still in Saigon hostage. On April 24, a secret mission was flown by US Navy and USAF jets to bomb a convoy of SA-2 missiles moving towards the city. The raid was not announced at the time, but the intention was to send a signal to the North Vietnamese not to build up their air defences.

On April 18, the USAF formally began its fixed wing airlift out of Tan Son Nhut airport outside Saigon but over 4,000 refugees had already boarded US aircraft ahead of this public announcement. Three days later, Admiral Whitmire ordered his task force to concentrate off the Vung Tua peninsula, just outside Vietnamese territorial waters. He sent a command team of US Marines to the US Defense Attache Office base at Tan Son Nhut to co-ordinate with the US Embassy and Central Intelligence Agency (CIA), which operated a fleet of 22 Bell UH-1H/205 Huey helicopters under the cover name, Air America. The small Air America Hueys and a fleet of buses were mobilised to pick up refugees in Saigon and move to the docks to board ships, or to Tan Son Nhut in case Option IV was activated for a helicopter lift.

ABOVE: US Air Force HH-53 'Jolly Green Giant' rescue helicopters were embarked on the USS *Midway* to boost the size of the helicopter force for Operation Frequent Wind. (US NAVY/US NATIONAL ARCHIVES)

LEFT: The US Embassy in Saigon was built in the 1960s and by 1975, was the largest US diplomatic mission in the world. (US STATE DEPARTMENT)

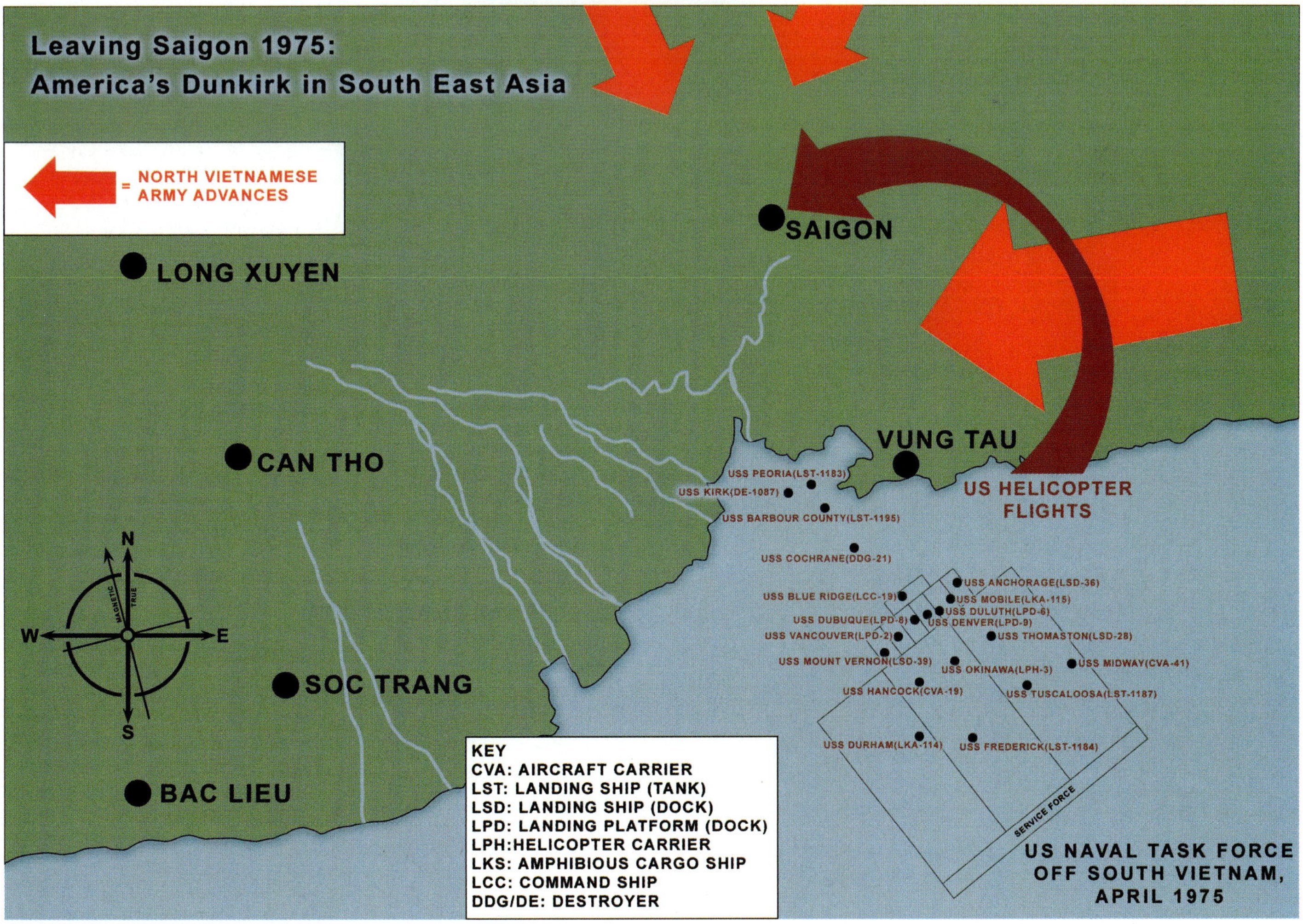

BELOW: A huge US Navy flotilla gathering off South Vietnam in April 1975 to evacuate US citizens and local people escaping the communist advance on Saigon. In a dramatic 24 hours the US Navy managed to extract more than 80,000 people. (ANDY HAY FLYING ART)

Tightening Noose

As the clock ticked down, North Vietnamese troops got closer to Saigon. By April 28, they were well within artillery range of the city and evacuations from Tan Son Nhut were being conducted only with Lockheed C-130E Hercules tactical airlifters. Civilian aircraft would no longer risk landing there. More than 7,000 had been shuttled out to Clark Airbase in the Philippines the day before and another 6,000 would be lifted out during the day. There were now less than 1,500 Americans in Saigon.

Just after dawn on April 29, a flight of three C-130Es landed at Tan Son Nhut to pick up the first batch of refugees when communist artillery and rockets started to explode all over the airfield. For several hours, Ambassador Martin pressed for the airlift to be resumed with fighter escorts. Out on Task Force 76, Admiral Whitmire started to prepare for Option IV.

Two landing ships, the USS *Peoria*, and USS *Barbour County*, were sent close to Vung Tua peninsula to provide emergency landing pads for the evacuation helicopters and the destroyer USS *Cochrane* was close by for protection. She also acted as a forward air traffic control point for the airborne armada. A Military Sealift Command (MSC) ship, the SS *Pioneer Commander,* joined them to take on board any refugees that escaped by ship. However, the option of putting US ships into Vung Tua's port was closed off after North Vietnamese troops closed the road to the peninsula from Saigon. Eventually, more than 6,000 refugees were carried out of Saigon harbour on the barges during the day.

White Christmas

By 10.51am, Ambassador Martin had relented, and Option IV was authorised. At noon, the prearranged evacuation signal was broadcast over American Forces Radio in Saigon. "It is 105 degrees and rising," followed by Bing Crosby singing *White Christmas*. When they heard it, American officials, businessmen and journalists dropped everything and made for their pick-up points, knowing they now had only hours to get out. Lucky South Vietnamese were told to report to the embassy and be grouped for evacuation.

The US Air Force launched a package of fighter jets from Thailand to provide air cover for the evacuation helicopters flying from

The Sea Stallions, Sea Knights, and Jolly Green Giants joined the shuttle from the embassy and Tan Son Nhut out to the fleet loaded with scores of Vietnamese civilians at a time. On the ground, the US Marines organised the refugees into groups and then rapidly bundled them onto helicopters. Other marines formed security perimeters to stop the embassy and Tan Son Nhut being overrun by desperate South Vietnamese.

As the helicopter shuttle gained momentum, US Navy and USAF jets patrolled overhead to deter attacks on the evacuation. Cobra gunships provided close protection for the transport helicopters. Disgruntled South Vietnamese troops repeatedly hit American helicopters with small arms fire throughout the evacuation, without causing serious damage.

LEFT: Tan Son Nhut airport came under North Vietnamese artillery and rocket fire on the morning of April 29, prompting US Ambassador Graham Martin to authorise Option IV, the helicopter evacuation. (US NATIONAL ARCHIVES)

the fleet but there was confusion over the timings and it was not until 12.30pm that the first wave of 36 CH-46Ds and CH-53Ds from USS *Hancock* lifted off carrying the security force of more than 800 US Marines to the DAO compound at Tan Son Nhut and the US Embassy in downtown Saigon. They landed at Tan Son Nhut just in time to prevent it being overrun by a group of rogue South Vietnamese paratroopers. Saigon was descending into chaos as the communist columns pushed forward.

Fittingly, it fell to the covert aviators of Air America to fly their UH-1s around the city picking up groups of evacuees and deliver them to collection points or out to the fleet.

LEFT: US Marine security contingents protected the waves of evacuation helicopters at landing zones around Saigon, including at the DAO compound at Tan Son Nhut airport. (US NAVY/US NATIONAL ARCHIVES)

BELOW: US Navy F-14A Tomcat swing-wing fighter received their combat debut during Operation Frequent Wind, flying off the USS *Enterprise*. (US NAVY/US NATIONAL ARCHIVES)

RIGHT: Once Option IV was called, the South Vietnamese air force started its own evacuation effort with aircrew flying themselves and their families out to US ships in the South China Sea or to Thailand. One Cessna O-1E observation plane even put down on the flight deck of USS *Midway*. (US NAVY/US NATIONAL ARCHIVES)

RIGHT: Thousands of South Vietnamese civilians and military personnel escaped to the US fleet onboard US helicopters. (US NAVY/US NATIONAL ARCHIVES)

BELOW: The flight decks of US ships were soon full of South Vietnamese helicopters and many were pushed overboard to make room for in-bound US helicopters. (US NAVY/US NATIONAL ARCHIVES)

on the big flat tops. A Cessna O-1E observation plane even put down on the flight deck of USS *Midway*.

At just before midnight, the last US Marines left the DAO compound and by 5am on April 30 Ambassador Martin had been lifted from the helipad on the roof of the embassy. The final group of US Marines were flown out at 7.51am. Elsewhere in Saigon, North Vietnamese tank columns were approaching the presidential palace to take the surrender of the South Vietnamese government.

Flotilla

The evacuation drama was not over yet. At Saigon's naval base, the final act of the great escape was underway. Thirty ships of the South Vietnam Navy cast off and headed out to sea, with more than 20,000 sailors and their families on board. By the early hours of May 1, they had safely navigated the Saigon River past communist guns and were in the South China Sea. The destroyer, the USS *Kirk*, was waiting to greet the armada and escort it to the safety of the fleet. US Navy officers, medics and engineers went aboard the South Vietnamese ships to help them on their way, while the USS *Kirk* scanned the sea and skies to make sure the communists did not attempt to interfere.

Admiral Whitmire's sailors, marines and airmen had pulled off

Helicopter door gunners regularly returned fire. There was one incident when a communist radar illuminated USAF jets patrolling near Tan Son Nhut, prompting the American airmen to engage a 57mm anti-aircraft gun that opened fire on the jets. An anti-radiation missile and cluster bomb silenced the threat.

As the US helicopters were heading out to the fleet, South Vietnamese air force helicopter crews also sensed this was the time to make a dash for freedom. Scores of helicopters landed on the ships off Vang Tua or

LEFT: The USS *Kirk* was dispatched close to the mouth of the Saigon river to escort the remains of the escaping South Vietnamese navy and bring more than 20,000 refugees to safety. (US NAVY/US NATIONAL ARCHIVES)

a miracle. The show of force by the US Navy and US Air Force had kept the communist army at bay during the final day. In 638 US military helicopter sorties on April 29, more than 7,000 people were lifted out of the city, including 978 Americans, 1,220 Vietnamese and others rescued from the US Embassy in the heart of Saigon. This followed on from 44,000 refugees airlifted by fixed wing aircraft during April from Tan Son Nhut. A further 30,000 eventually made their way out to the fleet on South Vietnamese helicopters, planes, boats, or barges. America's Dunkirk in southeast Asia rescued more than 80,000 people. It remained the largest US evacuation operation until the August 2021 mission to rescue Afghans from Kabul. The helicopter phase of Operation Frequent Wind on April 29 was the largest ever movement of people by rotary wing aircraft in a single day and was the first time a naval force had relied on helicopters for such a dangerous and difficult mission.

LEFT: For several years after the fall of Saigon, thousands of Vietnamese tried to escape their country by setting sail to try to find a better life in the neighbouring countries. They become known as the 'Vietnamese Boat People' and many eventually found their way to the United States. (US NAVY/US NATIONAL ARCHIVES)

BELOW: As the last US helicopter took off from Tan Son Nhut airport just before midnight on April 29, demolition charges destroyed the Defense Attache Office compound. This had been the US military headquarters in South Vietnam for more than decade and symbolised the end of American presence in the country. (US NAVY/US NATIONAL ARCHIVES)

ABOVE: South Vietnamese pilots flew out to the US fleet with family members crammed into their helicopters. They were all relieved to have made it to safety, but they still faced an uncertain future. (US NAVY/US NATIONAL ARCHIVES)

The Falklands 1982

Fleet Action in the Missile Age

The 1982 conflict between Britain and Argentina over the Falkland Islands was the only occasion after World War Two when opposing aircraft carriers have found themselves locked in combat on the high seas. It also saw the first and, to date, only sinking of an enemy vessel in time of war by a nuclear-powered attack submarine.

Argentine forces captured the disputed islands in a surprise assault on April 2, 1982, setting in motion a series of events leading Prime Minister Margaret Thatcher to order the dispatch of a naval task force, led by the carriers, HMS *Hermes* and HMS *Invincible*, to retake the British territory.

As the Royal Navy task force approached the Falklands at the end of April to enforce a 200-mile maritime exclusion zone, the Argentine Navy put to sea to counter the British move.

Some 13,000 Argentine troops were garrisoned in the Falklands and the British hoped to isolate them from their home bases by threatening to sink any ships that tried to enter the exclusion zone. In addition to the maritime blockade, in the early hours of May 1, HMS *Hermes* and HMS *Invincible* launched their Hawker Siddeley Sea Harrier FRS1 jump jets to attack Port Stanley airport in a bid to crater its runway and stop re-supply flights from the Argentine mainland. They hit the runway a few hours after a Royal Air Force Vulcan bomber had hit the same target.

ARA *Veinticinco de Mayo*

This was the cue for the Argentine aircraft carrier, the ARA *Veinticinco de Mayo* to launch its counter-attack. The carrier was probing along the northern edge of the exclusion zone later on May 1 and it launched an S-3 Tracker maritime patrol aircraft to try to find the British carriers so they could be attacked. Eight A-4 Skyhawks were armed and readied to launch from the carrier when the Trackers found their targets. Meanwhile, land-based Argentine air force aircraft were launched from their home bases.

Royal Navy Sea Harriers launched to intercept the attackers and two Argentine aircraft were shot down in dogfights.

By the evening of May 1, the Argentinian Junta had worked out that they had been tricked and that there was no British invasion to recapture the Falklands, just incursions to drop off small reconnaissance teams. There was no need launch an immediate attack, so the ARA *General Belgrano* and ARA *Veinticinco de Mayo* task groups were ordered to head back towards the Argentine coast. Both groups of warships were ordered to be ready to re-engage should the British attempt an invasion. On the ARA *Veinticinco de Mayo,* the Argentine task group commander Rear Admiral Jorge Allara still thought there was an opportunity to attack the British fleet, so he turned his task group

BELOW: The iconic image of the ARA *General Belgrano* sinking on the May 2, 1982, taken by an Argentine navy officer from a life raft.
(MARTÍN SGUT)

around and headed east. His carrier was within range of the British force at dawn on May 2, but unusually low winds saved the British. As the Argentine carrier arrived on station, the wind dropped, and it proved impossible to launch her eight Skyhawks with a full fuel and bomb load. She turned around and headed back towards Argentina.

Britain's GCHQ signals intelligence organisation intercepted and decoded the Argentine Junta's commands to their fleet and soon, the British task force commander, Rear Admiral Sandy Woodward, was alerted to the looming threat. Royal Navy nuclear attack submarines were already moving to intercept the Argentine task groups in the run up to the May 1 strikes on Port Stanley. HMS *Conqueror* had picked up the ARA *General Belgrano* on that day but HMS *Splendid* had yet to find the Argentine aircraft carrier.

Admiral Woodward was unaware of the Argentine fleet movements during the early hours of May 2, and he was working out his options to neutralise the threats to his fleet. HMS *Conqueror* still had the ARA *General Belgrano* in her sights but did not yet have permission from London to engage the ship. The submarine was also not under Woodward's command but was controlled directly from the task force headquarters at Northwood, outside London, by Vice Admiral Peter Herbert, who held the post of Flag Officer Submarines. Communications via this intermediary route were normally a long, drawn-out process,

but Woodward did not think he had time to go through this. Instead, he issued a direct order to its captain, Commander Chris Wreford-Brown, to attack the Argentine ship. Woodward was fully aware that the satellite radio message would be routed through Herbert's office, and

RIGHT: The ARA *General Belgrano* survived the Japanese attack on Pearl Harbor in 1943 as the USS *Phoenix* and was sold to Argentina in 1951.
(ARGENTINE NAVY)

RIGHT: British and Argentine fleets manoeuvred for advantage on the fringes of the Total Exclusion Zone around the Falkland Islands in the early days of May 1982. The Royal Navy caught and sunk the Argentine battleship, ARA *General Belgrano*, on May 2, but the Argentine Navy struck back two days later to sink HMS *Sheffield*.
(ANDY HAY FLYING ART)

BELOW: HMS *Splendid* arrived off the Falklands in mid April, allowing the British to activate their maritime exclusion zone around the islands.
(ROYAL NAVY)

he would intercept the command. This, hopefully, would kick-start Herbert and his boss, the Operation Corporate overall commander, Admiral John Fieldhouse, to rapidly get the War Cabinet into agreeing to ordering HMS *Conqueror* to attack the cruiser.

Rules of Engagement

Woodward's move had the desired effect and, by mid morning, on May 2 Fieldhouse was heading to the prime minister's country residence, Chequers, to brief the War Cabinet. There was little discussion and Margaret Thatcher, and her ministers quickly approved the new rules of engagement, or ROE, for Wreford-Brown. It took a few hours for the message to be successfully passed to HMS *Conqueror,* which needed to break off trailing the ARA

LEFT: HMS *Sheffield* burns after being hit by an Argentine Exocet missile. (ROYAL NAVY)

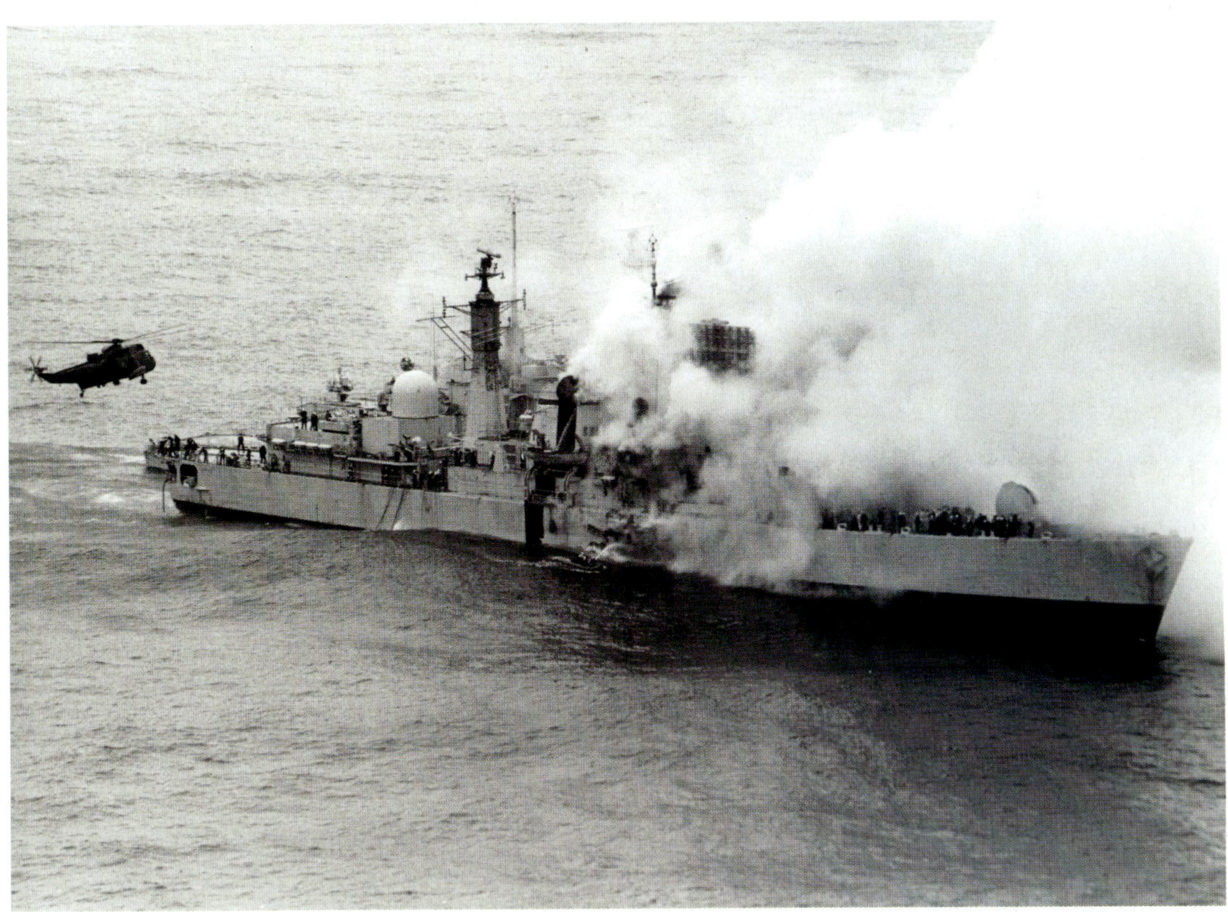

General Belgrano to re-establish radio contact with the satellite to download their new orders. At the first attempt the message was garbled, and a second attempt had to be made to re-establish communications.

Wreford-Brown sent his own update back to Northwood, reporting that the Argentine cruiser had changed course and was now heading westwards away from the Falklands. Admiral Herbert did not think it changed the situation and did not countermand Wreford-Brown's new orders or pass this new information up to Fieldhouse.

In the South Atlantic, Wreford-Brown now moved to attack. It took

BELOW: HMS *Sheffield* was the first Type 42 air defence destroyer to enter service in 1975. Her first captain was Sandy Woodward, who in May 1982 was commander of the British naval task group. (US NAVY)

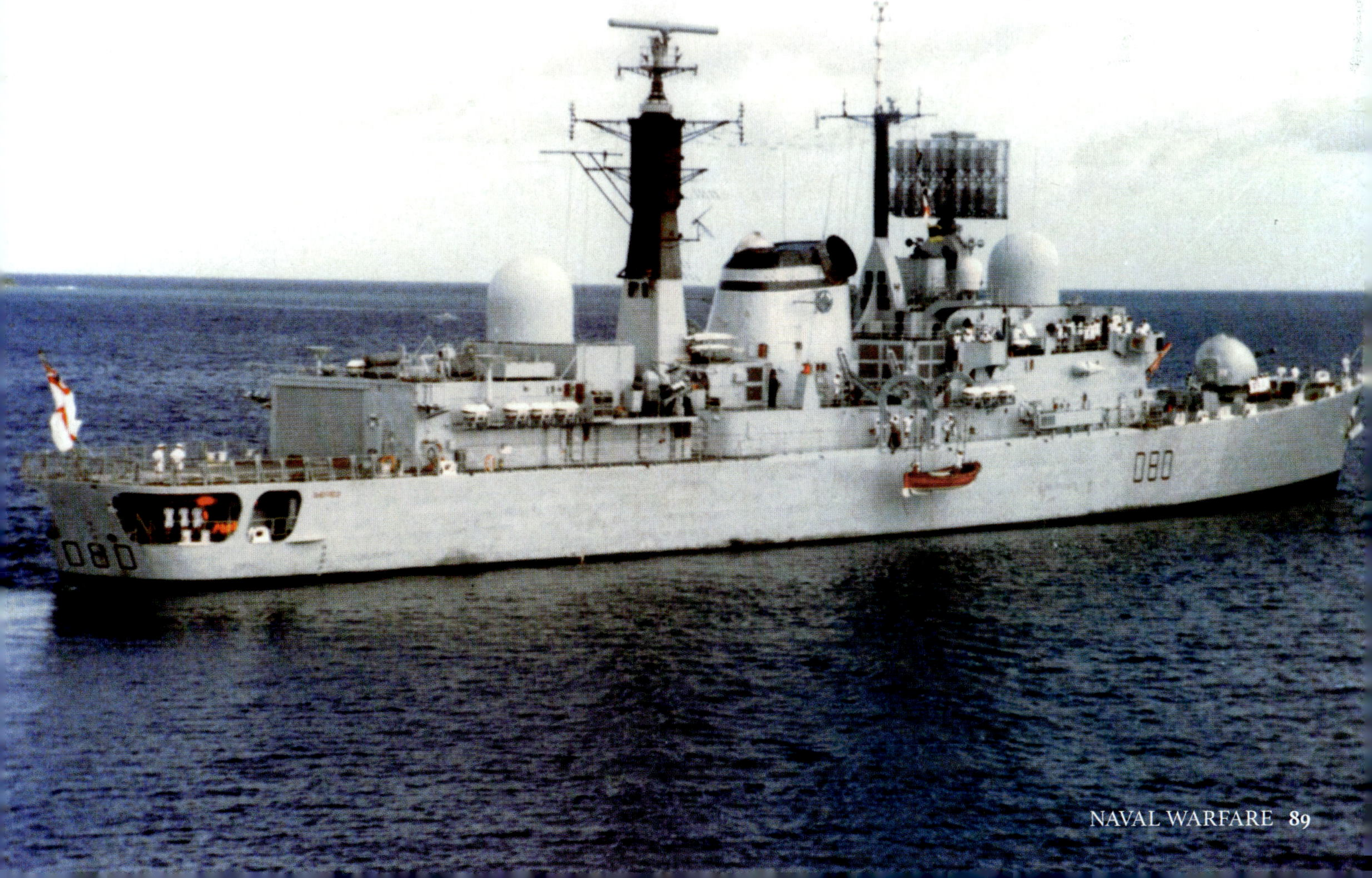

ABOVE: An Argentine naval aviation P-2 Neptune flew ahead of two Super Étendard strike jets to find the British task group. (ARGENTINE NAVY)

BELOW: Air-to-air refuelling from Argentine air force KC-130 tanker aircraft was essential to allowing the Super Étendards to reach their missile launch position to the southeast of the Falkland Islands. (MARTÍN OTERO)

some time to re-acquire the Argentine cruiser and her escorts. He had to manoeuvre his submarine to within 1,400 yards of his target to fire three Mark 8 torpedoes. These were World War Two era unguided weapons, but they were far more reliable than the wire-guided Tigerfish torpedoes that were also in HMS *Conqueror's* weapons store.

In his log, released by the British Ministry of Defence in 2012, Wreford-Brown wrote: "At 4.25pm, traffic now received. COR177 [message from submarine command in Northwood] gives me permission to attack."

An entry at 6.56pm reads "FIRE Order of firing [torpedo tubes] 6, 1, 2". Wreford-Brown watched alone through a periscope as the torpedoes he had ordered to be fired at the 600ft Argentine cruiser closed on their target.

"Orange fireball seen just aft of the centre of target, in line with the aft mast, shortly after the first explosion was heard," he added.

"Second explosion heard about five seconds later after I think I saw a spurt of water aft, but it may have been smoke from the first. Third explosion heard but not seen — I was not looking!"

Two of the three torpedoes hit the ARA *General Belgrano*, one of them hitting amidships and exploding in the engine compartment. The ship quickly started to take on water. The crew had left open many of the ship's watertight doors and within minutes smoke, flames, and water were engulfing the ship. Her captain, Hector Bonzo, ordered his crew to abandon ship. Many of the crew then spent two days afloat in life rafts as Argentine and Chilean rescue ships scoured the South Atlantic looking for survivors. In the end 772 of her 1,042 crew were rescued.

Blockade

Since the major Argentine forays on May 1, the Junta had pulled their air and naval forces back to their home waters and bases, leaving the British free to operate in the 200 nautical mile total exclusion zone. Admiral Woodward was now focusing on tightening the air and naval blockade

around the islands to prevent supplies and reinforcements reaching the Argentine garrison.

The British task group took up station astride the eastern fringe of the exclusion zone, which was close enough to the Falklands to allow night time dashes by helicopters to land the covert special forces surveillance teams, and for Sea Harriers to patrol around Port Stanley to deter daytime air traffic using the airport.

Admiral Woodward deployed his ships in layers to provide defence in depth against air attack. The outer crust of his defence was a picket line of his three Type 42 air defence destroyers – running north to south, HMS *Coventry*, HMS *Glasgow*, and HMS *Sheffield*. They had long range radars to give early warning of Argentine air and missile attacks, electronic surveillance equipment to detect and identify hostile radars, and the Sea Dart air defence missile. Sea Dart was designed to engage Russian bombers at medium and high altitude out to 40 nautical miles range.

Behind this picket line of Type 42s were the two carriers, HMS *Hermes* and HMS *Invincible,* and they were each protected by one of the latest Type 22 frigates armed with the short-range Sea Wolf air defence missiles. The frigates were nicknamed 'goalkeepers' because they were considered the carriers' last line of defence.

Late on the morning of May 4 the British task group was on station in its operational area. There were intermittent radar contacts, and many were dismissed as false alarms by radar operators. The air defence of the task group was being co-ordinated by the battle staff in the operations room of HMS *Invincible*.

Since the sinking of the ARA *General Belgrano* the Argentine navy had been preparing to strike back. That task fell to its naval aviation, or *Comando de Aviación Naval (COAN)*, detachment at Rio Grande air base in the far south of the country. A P-2 Neptune maritime patrol aircraft launched from the base on the morning of May 4. It was followed by a pair of Super Étendard jets of the 2nd Fighter and Attack Squadron and an air force C-130 Hercules refuelling tanker. The Neptune found the British fleet and passed on their co-ordinates to the Super Étendards. After taking on extra fuel from the tanker, the two jets dropped down to low level to pass around the southern coastline of the Falklands to line up for their attack.

Exocet Threat

The jets were armed with two of Argentina's five Exocet missiles. They had only been delivered to the country earlier in the year. French technicians had not yet completed the integration of the missiles onto the Super Étendards at the beginning of April and they had left for home after the European Community (EC) imposed its arms embargo on Argentina. The Argentine navy had to complete the integration work itself.

As they made their final approach, the jets had to momentarily pop-up to allow the Exocet's internal radar to acquire their targets. Then they dropped down to low level again and released the two weapons, before turning for home. This took a matter of minutes to execute, and the British fleet would have even less time to react.

The first British ship to react was HMS *Glasgow*. Its electronic warfare operators picked up the emission of the Exocet's radar as they popped up to acquire their target. It called out a warning over the task group radio net. The ships went to action stations to be ready for the incoming missiles and orders were issued to start firing chaff to decoy the weapons. Controllers on HMS *Invincible* could not see the radar signal themselves and were sceptical, saying it was just a false alarm. There had already been several false alarms over the previous four days. Nothing to worry about, they said.

ABOVE: Argentine airmen were convinced they hit many British warships and their aircraft, including this Dagger, sported kill markings. Their kill claims subsequently proved to be inaccurate. (CARLOS AY)

ABOVE: The Type 22 frigate HMS *Broadsword* alongside the task force flagship, HMS *Hermes*. (ROYAL NAVY)

On HMS *Sheffield,* the nearest British ship to the threat, their own electronic warning equipment was off-line because a satellite communications systems that used the same frequencies was transmitting. Her commanding officer, Captain Sam Salt, was off duty in his cabin and the next most senior officers who should have been in the operations room co-ordinating the defence of the ship were elsewhere.

Seconds after the missiles were released HMS *Glasgow* picked them up on radar and the crew started to issue desperate radio warnings to the task group. On HMS *Invincible,* the warnings were still not taken seriously, and Sea Harriers were not launched to intercept the Super Étendards.

There was little sign of reaction on HMS *Sheffield.* The first warnings were only raised when officers on the ship's bridge saw the smoke trails from a missile on the horizon. They shouted a warning over the ship's public address system, calling on the crew to 'hit the deck'. It was too little, too late. No chaff was fired

and seconds later the missile hit square amidships, just below the bridge. There is still uncertainty about whether the missile's warhead actually exploded but the impact of the weapon was enough the shake the ship. As the weapon penetrated the hull it ripped apart several compartments, cutting power and water lines as well as starting fires as it went. Within seconds the ship was full of acrid smoke and pandemonium ensued.

The centre of the ship was soon a blazing inferno, forcing Captain Salt and his senior officers to vacate the bridge and operations room. Damage control teams fought a losing battle to keep fire away from the ship's fuel tanks and Sea Dart missile magazines. The frigates HMS *Arrow* and HMS *Yarmouth* closed in on the destroyer to take off wounded and help fight the fires. Helicopters from HMS *Hermes* arrived to shuttle the wounded to safety.

After a few hours, Captain Salt realised his vessel was doomed and gave the order to abandon ship. Out of a crew of 281, 20 were dead and 26 injured, many of whom were seriously

burned. Fire now consumed the ship, and she was left to burn herself out. HMS *Yarmouth* eventually took the hulk under tow to frustrate any Argentine attempt to seize her but on May 10 water surged through the hole in the hull, causing the ship to roll over and sink.

Reality Strikes

HMS *Sheffield* was the first major British warship to be lost to enemy action since World War Two. The sense of shock in the Royal Navy, British government, media, and public after news was released of her fate late on May 4 was palpable. The Argentine military had graphically demonstrated that they had the weapons and wherewithal to use them to deadly effect. The campaign to recapture the Falklands was clearly not going to be a walkover.

A second Étendard attack with Exocets took place on May 25, the intended targets were HMS *Hermes* and HMS *Invincible,* but the Argentine reconnaissance mistook a civilian container ship the MV *Atlantic Conveyor,* for one of the British carriers. The ship had been converted

LEFT: HMS *Hermes* eventually embarked Royal Navy Sea Harrier fighters and Royal Air Force Harrier GR3 strike jump jets. (ROYAL NAVY)

into an improvised flat top, carrying Harriers and helicopters to the South Atlantic to reinforce the task force. Her cargo of Harriers had already been flown off, but several helicopters were still being prepared for flight when she was hit by two Exocets.

The Argentine Navy made one last foray to fire its final Exocet on May 30, but the British had improved their defensive tactics, so they were able to detect the in-bound missile and a frigate was able to shoot down the weapon. With all their Exocets fired, there was now little the Argentines could do resist the final British offensive that captured Port Stanley on June 14, thanks to the air support provided from HMS *Hermes* and HMS *Invincible*.

The Falklands War was the first naval conflict of the guided missile age, and the power of these weapons was brutally demonstrated by the devastation of HMS *Sheffield* by the French-made Exocet sea skimming missile. While the Argentines achieved an impressive hit rate with their Exocets - five air and one ground launched, hitting four targets – the British air defence missiles proved less impressive. Analysis of British missile engagements from ships revealed that the fundamental problem was a lack of reliability that meant at critical moments, control switches did not work because of corrosion, software crashed, or missiles refused to fire.

BELOW: HMS *Arrow* pulled alongside HMS *Sheffield* to help fight the fires on the ship and evacuate her wounded crewmen. (ROYAL NAVY)

Gulf War 1991

Precision Strike from the Sea

At the height of the Cold War in the 1980s, US President Ronald Reagan and his supporters boasted that America would win the standoff simply by spending more money on building military hardware than the Soviet Union could or would. He ordered the expansion of the US Navy to a target of 600 warships and submarines. As part of this expansion, four World War Two-era Iowa-class battleships were brought back into service and turned into floating missile batteries to fire the new BGM-109 Tomahawk Land Attack Missiles (TLAMs). This was a revolutionary weapon that was intended to allow the US Navy to hit targets deep inside the Soviet Union.

The Iowa-class battleships were 57,540-ton leviathans that had been built back in the early 1940s and the USS *Missouri* had famously been the venue for the Japanese surrender in Tokyo Bay in September 1945. Reagan's dynamic navy secretary, John Lehman, enthusiastically backed the increase in firepower on the battleships and ordered the installation of launchers for 32 TLAMs on each ship. Scores of missiles could be stowed in the battleship's magazines, allowing them to keep up an impressive rate of fire. US Navy destroyers, cruisers, and

nuclear-powered attack submarines were also soon equipped with the Tomahawk. The missile had a range of 1,500 nautical miles (2,778km) and was guided to its targets by Terrain Contour Matching (TERCOM) and terminal Digital Scene Matching Area Correlator (DSMAC) technology. This compared digital maps with radar scans of the terrain ahead of the missile, which meant a missile could hit within a few metres of its intended target.

The US Navy fielded several versions of the TLAM. The BGM-109A Tomahawk Land Attack Missile-Nuclear (TLAM-N) was armed with a W80 nuclear warhead and the RGM/UGM-109B was the anti-ship variant. For conventional strikes, the BGM-109C (TLAM-C) was fitted with a 1,000lb warhead and the BGM-109D (the TLAM-D-I) was fitted with sub-munitions to dispense up to 166 bomblets in 24 packages. There was a specialist version, dubbed the TLAM D-IIs, which was fitted with reels of thin metal cables for use against electricity sub-stations, causing short circuits and fires.

In November 1989, crowds stormed the Berlin Wall and when East German border guards declined to open fire, it was clear that the Cold War was over. Within months, East Germany collapsed, and the Warsaw Pact was dissolved. The Soviet Union itself soon followed. President Reagan's ambition to bankrupt the Soviet Union appeared to have been achieved.

No Enemy?

For the US Navy, this meant that for the first time in 50 years it lacked an opponent. However, in August 1990, the Iraqi dictator Saddam Hussein invaded the oil rich emirate of Kuwait and the world changed, again. US President George H Bush ordered more than 100,000 US troops to Saudi Arabia to stop the advance of Saddam's tanks.

US Navy aircraft carriers and their supporting battlegroups were quickly on the scene to bolster the firepower available to defend Saudi Arabia and by the end of 1990,

President Bush ordered an additional wave of reinforcements to enable an offensive to be launched to liberate Kuwait. Ahead of the land invasion, US commanders were preparing a massive air offensive to win air supremacy, defeat Iraq's suspected weapons of mass destruction, and paralyse Saddam Hussein's high command. The US commanders were all veterans of the Vietnam war and were determined not to repeat the mistakes of that conflict. They didn't follow the Vietnam strategy of gradual escalation. The plan for Operation Desert Storm was built around the concept of hitting the Iraqis with every weapon in the US arsenal, as quickly as possible. It was the doctrine of overwhelming force.

America's Middle East commander, General 'Stormin' Norman Schwarzkopf, ordered his air commander, US Air Force Lieutenant General Chuck Horner, to strike deep into Iraq in the opening hours of the war and relentlessly pound Saddam Hussein's most vital strategic assets.

General Horner mustered more than 2,400 combat aircraft, including 400 on six US Navy aircraft carriers, around the Middle East but to reach their targets they would have to battle past Iraq's thick air defences, made up of hundreds of surface-to-air missiles and thousands of anti-aircraft guns. To avoid putting his pilots at risk, Horner turned to the US Navy and its arsenal of Tomahawk cruise missiles. USAF and US Navy planners built up a detailed plan to neutralise Iraq's air defences around the country's capital, Baghdad, in opening hours of the war. They would then relentlessly strike at more targets in the city to keep the Iraqi leadership on the run. To borrow a phrase from the Vietnam war, the intention was to 'go downtown' from

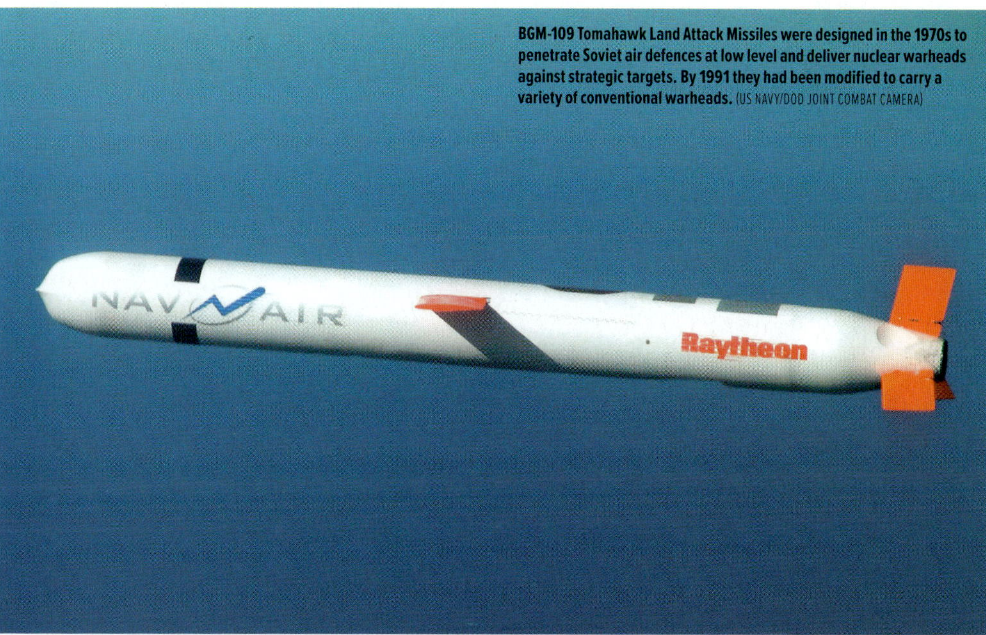

BGM-109 Tomahawk Land Attack Missiles were designed in the 1970s to penetrate Soviet air defences at low level and deliver nuclear warheads against strategic targets. By 1991 they had been modified to carry a variety of conventional warheads. (US NAVY/DOD JOINT COMBAT CAMERA)

the start of the strike on Iraq. The US Navy and its Tomahawks were to be instrumental in this plan and Operation Desert Storm would be the first time a navy had struck deep into enemy territory with precision guided weapons. Naval warfare would never be the same again.

To peel open the Iraqi air defence, the USAF planned to send its secret Lockheed F-117 Nighthawk 'stealth' fighters in first. These black painted jets were designed to be invisible to enemy radar by being shaped to reflect radar signals in an unpredictable way, so the aircraft would appear on radar scopes looking like flocks of birds or rain showers.

Desert Storm

The plan for Operation Desert Storm called for it to open with a wave of F-117s penetrating the skies above downtown Baghdad to hit the command posts of the Iraqi

air defences and their supporting communications links. Behind them a wave of Tomahawks would take out more headquarters, communications nodes, and power distribution facilities. This in turn would open the way for a massive wave of hundreds of manned strike aircraft to attack Iraqi airfields, ammunition dumps, naval headquarters, and army garrisons. This was not to be the end. General Horner and his airmen, backed by US Navy missile crews, were to keep up a constant tempo of attacks and the Iraqi occupation army in Kuwait would be weakened by 50%. The US and coalition ground troops would surge forward to take on Saddam Hussein's army in what the Iraqi

ABOVE: USS *Wisconsin* served as the **TLAM** strike commander for the Arabian Gulf, directing the sequence of launches that marked the opening of Operation Desert Storm. (US NAVY/DOD JOINT COMBAT CAMERA)

LEFT: Four World War Two Iowa-class battleships were modified with four quad-TLAM launchers during the 1980s. (US NAVY/ DOD JOINT COMBAT CAMERA)

Just over 90 minutes later the first F-117s were striking at targets around Baghdad and within minutes television images of the Iraqi air defences lighting up the sky over the city were broadcast around the world. At 3.11am, the first wave of TLAMs started impacting. As dawn broke, there was no let up in the American attacks. Two more waves of missiles struck the city during the first 24 hours of Operation Desert Storm. A total of 114 missiles were fired from nine warships during these attacks and another 102 TLAMs were fired on the second day of the war.

RIGHT: US Navy nuclear-powered attack submarines opened a new front against Iraq from the Red Sea firing TLAMs at strategic targets. (US NAVY/DOD JOINT COMBAT CAMERA)

MIDDLE: The US Navy Tomahawks did not have penetrating warheads to strike at buried or hardened targets so were saved for targets in the open, such as parked aircraft and electricity facilities. This is imagery from a pre-war test. (US NAVY/DOD JOINT COMBAT CAMERA)

BELOW: A new era of naval warfare began in January 1991 when the US Navy began bombarding the Iraqi capital Baghdad with precision guided Tomahawk cruise missiles. In any subsequent crisis, US presidents would turn to the Tomahawk as 'America's weapon of choice'. (ANDY HAY FLYING ART)

dictator dubbed, "the Mother of All Battles."

The barrage of Tomahawks began at 1.30am on January 17, 1991, even before the F-117s were over Baghdad, when the Aegis cruiser, USS *San Jacinto* cruising in the Red Sea launched the first ever TLAM fired in anger. Eleven minutes later, the destroyer USS *Paul F. Foster* and the cruiser USS *Bunker Hill* commenced launching from the Arabian Gulf. Accounts vary as to which one launched first. Within minutes, the first salvo of 48 TLAMS was en route to targets in Iraq. The battleships, USS *Missouri* and USS *Wisconsin* also launched TLAMs in the first salvo.

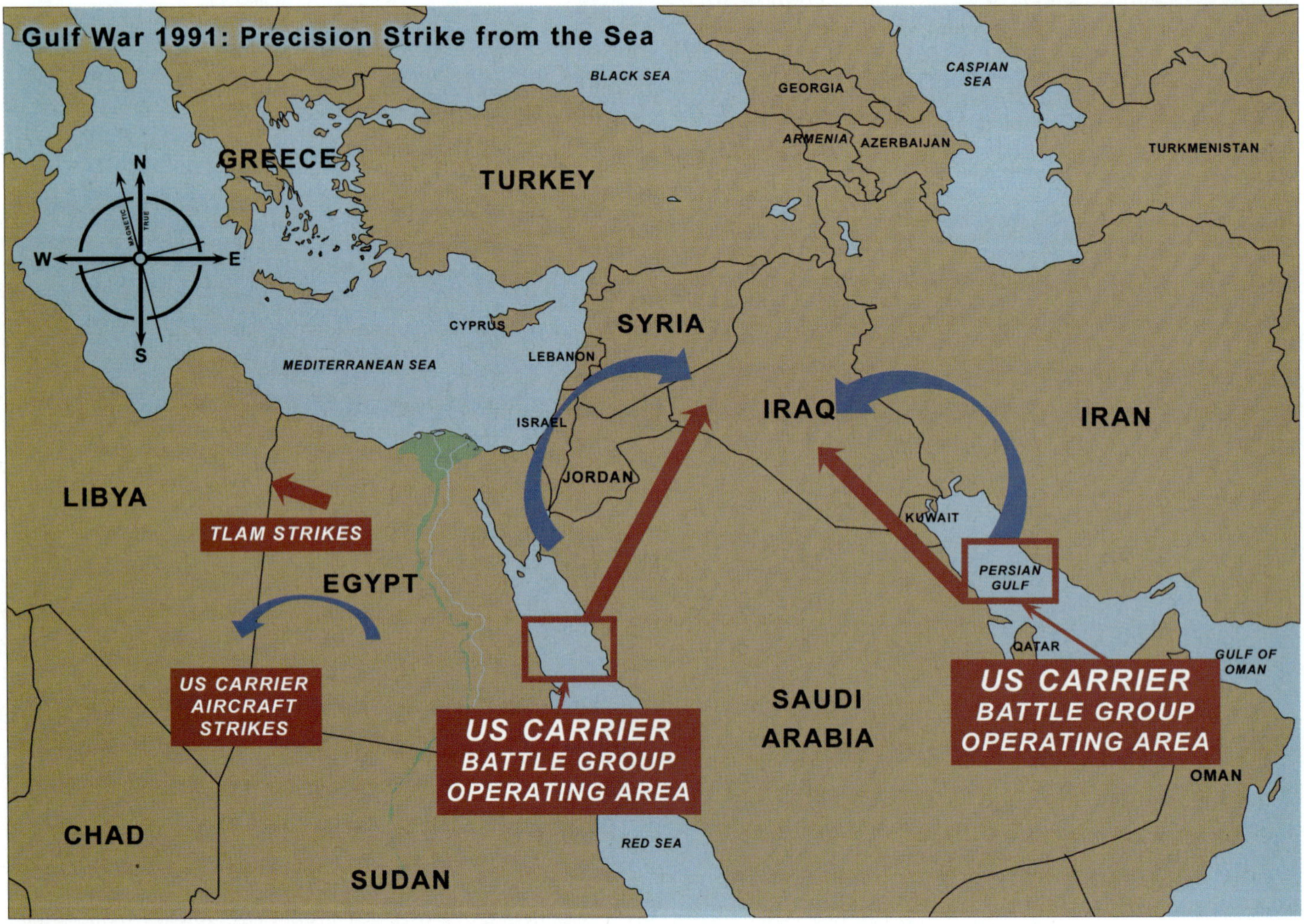

Gulf War 1991: Precision Strike from the Sea

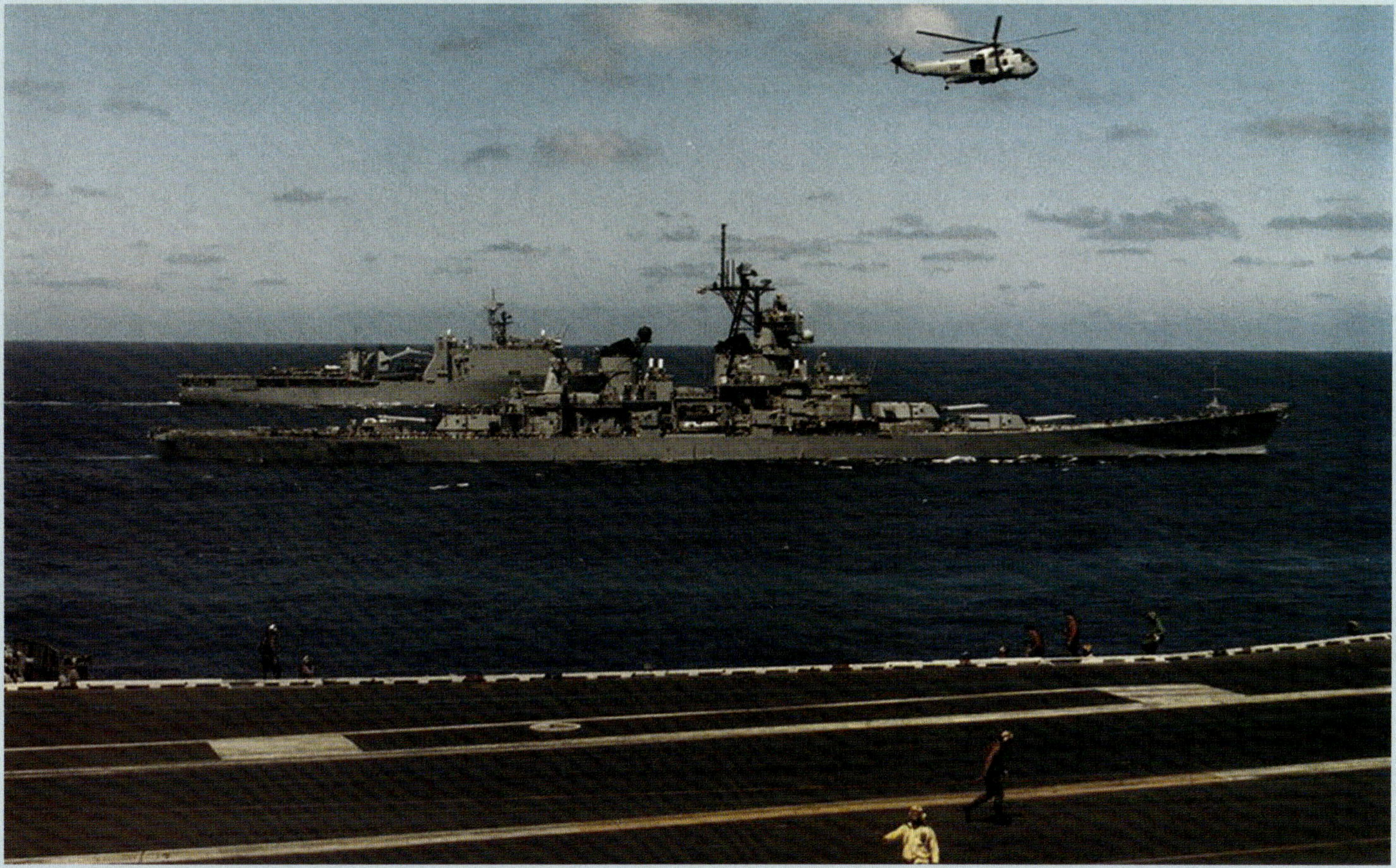

War in the Media

The Iraqis let international journalists remain in the city to report on the US strikes and during the first day of the war the first images of TLAMs appeared in news broadcasts. Images of Tomahawks - sometimes flying high, sometimes low over Baghdad - became one of the spectacles of that televised war. Around the world, viewers in homes as well as workplaces and bars, watched real-time scenes of combat. "The skies over Baghdad have been illuminated," Bernard Shaw reported on CNN as viewers saw on their TV screens "bright flashes going off all over the sky." The few fleeting images of Tomahawks were taken from the ground as they flew by at high subsonic speeds. One famous video clip appeared to show a TLAM making a sharp turn over the city, leading a journalist to say the missile was turning around a street corner.

Despite the efforts of the F-117s to neutralise the Iraqi air defences, General Horner was never convinced that it was safe to fly manned non-stealth aircraft over downtown Baghdad in daylight. For the rest of the war TLAMs would also be the only other weapons to strike the Iraqi capital during daylight hours. This allowed the US to keep the Iraqi leadership under pressure and not give them a chance to regain their composure.

Launches were conducted from both the Red Sea and the Arabian Gulf from nine cruisers, five destroyers, two battleships, and two nuclear powered attack submarines. The top shooter was the destroyer, USS *Fife*, which fired 58 missiles, out of a total of 297 TLAMs fired in the war.

The USS *Wisconsin* served as the TLAM strike commander for the Arabian Gulf, directing the sequence of launches that marked the opening of Operation Desert Storm and firing a total of 24 TLAMs during the first two days of the campaign. Within sight of the USS *Wisconsin*, missile after missile rose from other ships in the area, including her sister ship USS *Missouri,* which fired 28 TLAMs in total. USS *San Jacinto*

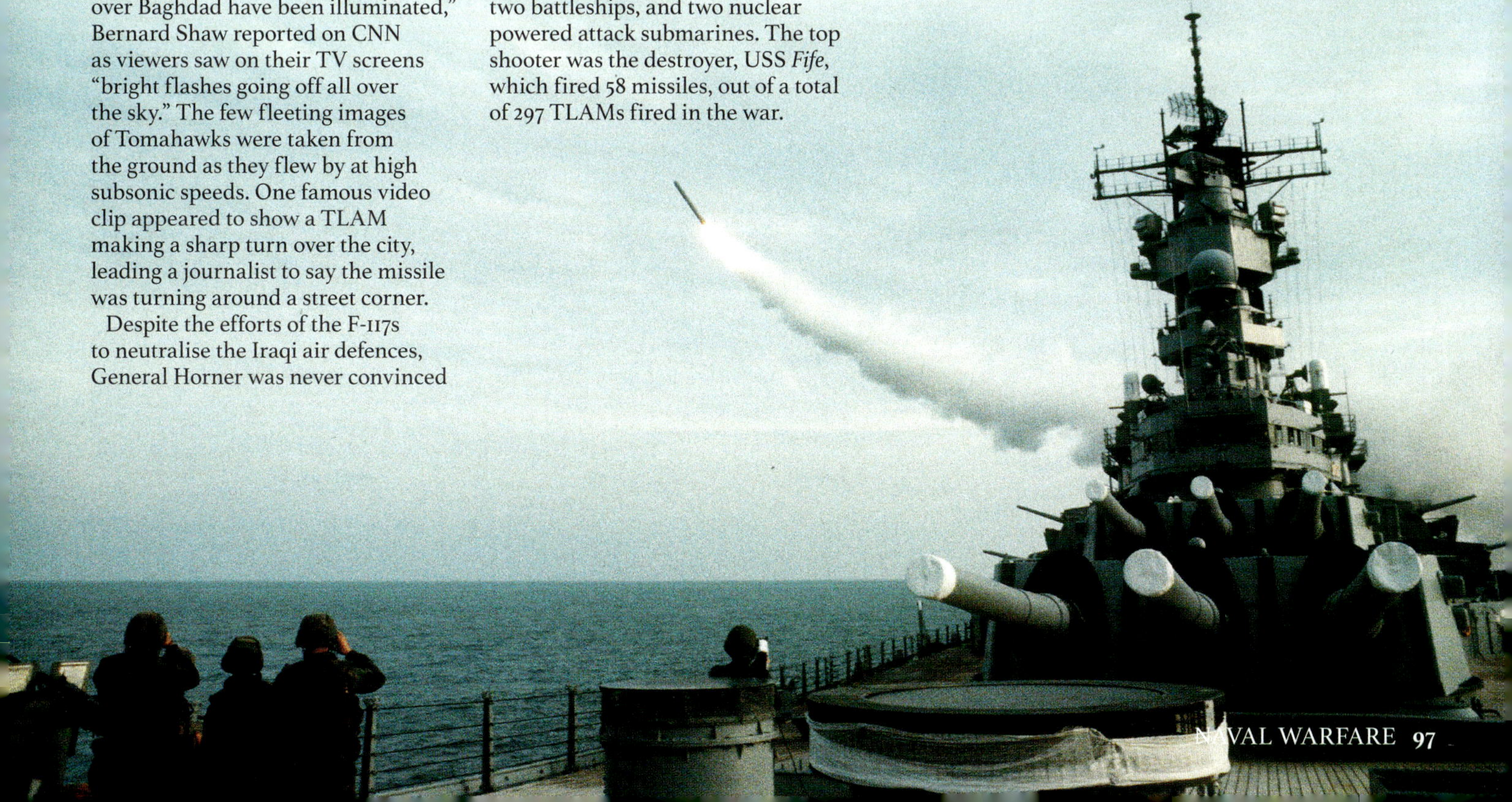

RIGHT: TLAMs were fired from hull mounted launchers on US Navy cruisers to ease their re-loading. (US NAVY/DOD JOINT COMBAT CAMERA)

kept up the barrage from the Red Sea, firing 16 cruise missiles during the 42-day war.

The US Navy achieved another first on January 19, when the attack submarine USS *Louisville* conducted the first ever combat launch of a TLAM while submerged in the Red Sea. Soon afterwards the USS *Pittsburgh* joined the underwater barrage, which totalled 12 submarine TLAM launches by the end of the war.

The First Three Days

TLAM launches occurred overwhelmingly in the first three days of the war. Out of the 260 TLAM Cs and D-Is that transitioned to cruise phase, more than 39% were fired in the first 24 hours; 62% were launched during the first 48 hours; just over 73% in the first 72 hours; and no TLAMs of any kind were launched after February 1, 1991, just two weeks after the war started.

The last TLAM strike occurred on February 1, when six TLAMs were fired in a 'stream raid', all aimed at the Rasheed airfield, south of Baghdad. They arrived in the target area about 11am, when they were fired upon, and four were believed shot down. The high cost and low return of this strike prompted a re-think of US strategy.

General Schwarzkopf did not approve any additional TLAM strikes

BELOW: Up to 61 TLAMs could be fired from the Mk 41 vertical launcher cells installed on Spruance-class destroyers, such as the USS *Fife*. (US NAVY/DOD JOINT COMBAT CAMERA)

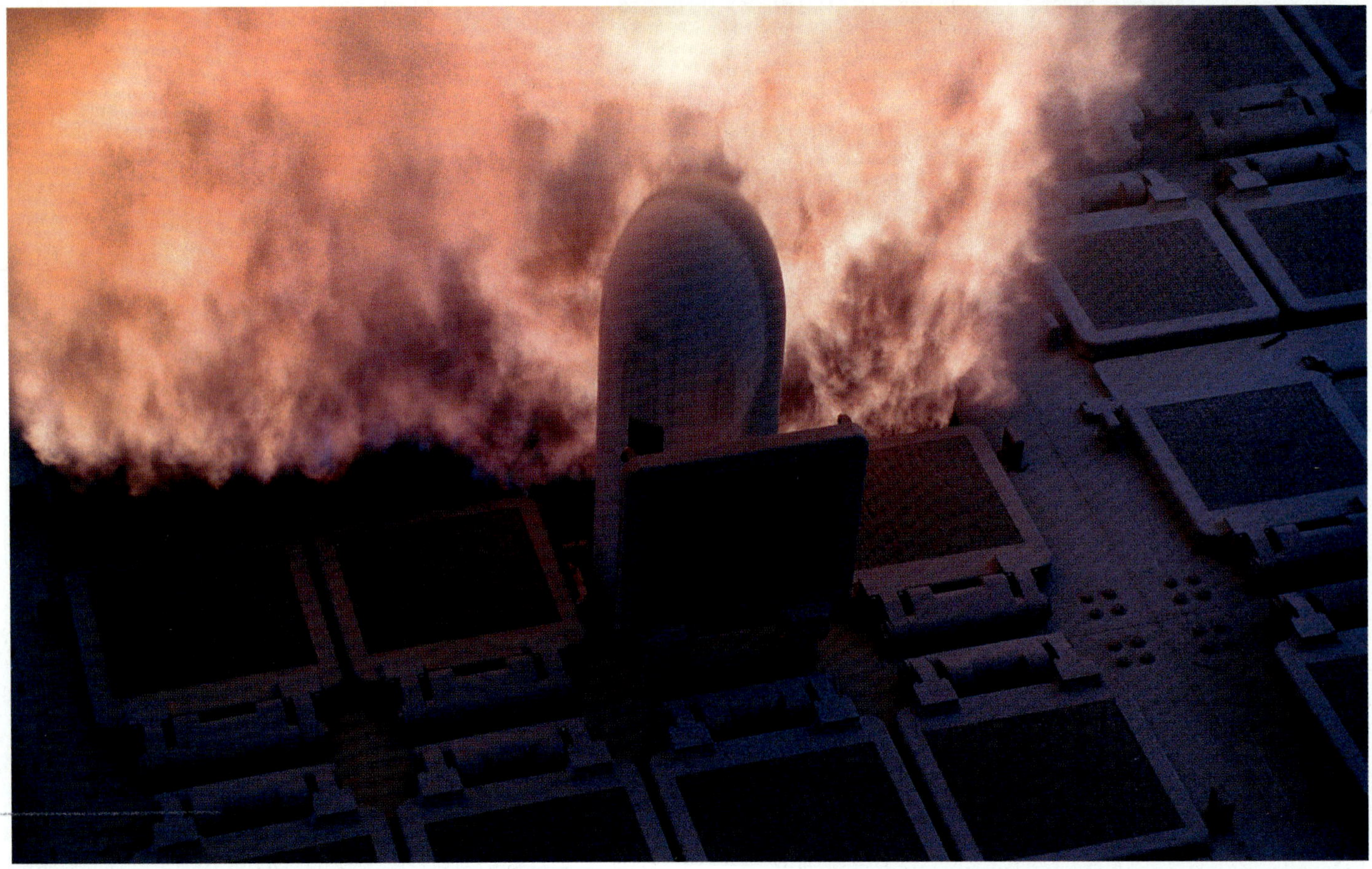

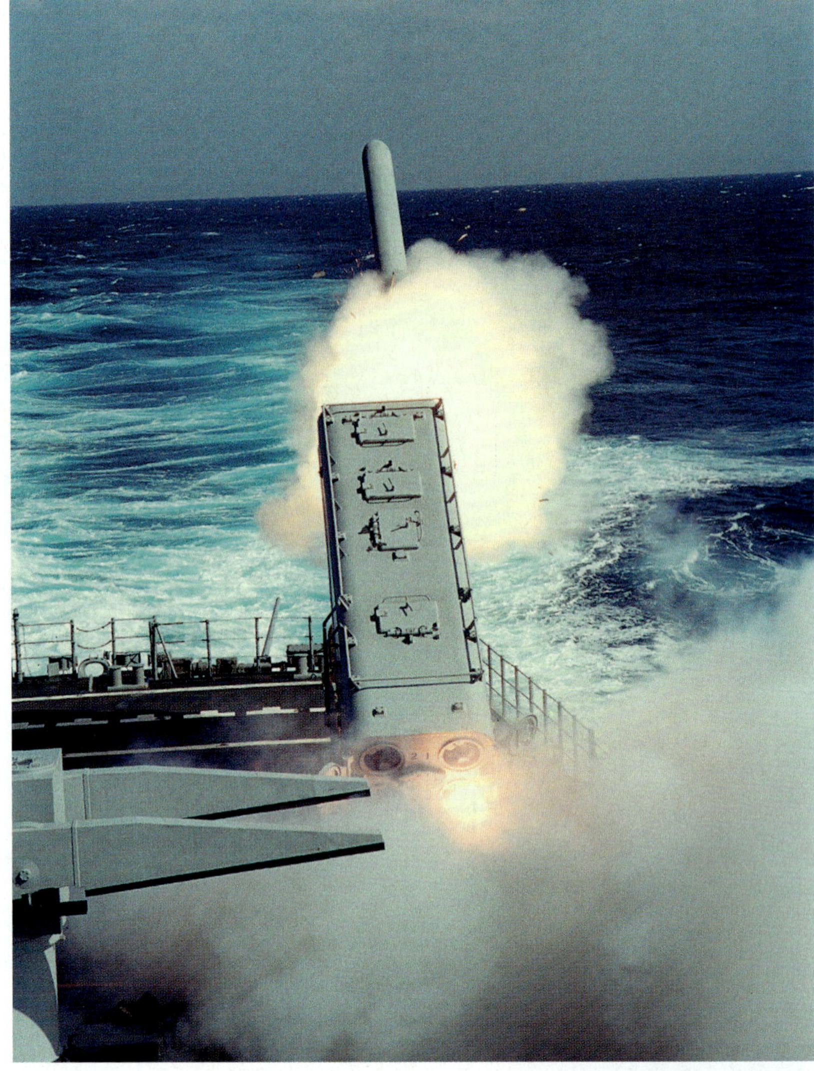

either because television coverage of daylight strikes in downtown Baghdad proved unacceptable in Washington or their use was deemed too expensive given its relatively small warhead and high cost, at $2.8m per missile.

During that war, 297 TLAMs were launched, of which 288 successfully transitioned to flight. Iraqi forces probably shot down between two and six Tomahawks.

During Operation Desert Storm, 307 TLAMs were loaded for launch from US Navy ships or submarines. Out of those 307, 19 experienced pre-launch problems. Ten of the 19 problems were only temporary; thus, these missiles were either launched at a later time or returned to inventory. Of the 288 actual launches, six suffered boost failures and did not transition to cruise. Of the 282 missiles that did transition to cruise, 22 were TLAM D-IIs and 260 were TLAM Cs and D-Is.

In total, 38 different targets were attacked by TLAMs, 37 were attacked by the 260 TLAM Cs and D-Is. These 37 targets had a total of 173 individual aim points, which includes ten leadership targets, six communications targets, three air defence targets, eight electric power targets, four oil-related targets, four chemical weapon and missile targets, and two airfield targets. The 38th target was an electrical site, which was attacked by TLAM D-IIs alone. According to the US Navy, about 80 to 85% of the missiles hit their targets.

However, TLAMs were limited in the type of target to which they could be aimed, since they did not have anywhere near the 'hard target' penetrating capability of an air-dropped 2,000lb laser guided bomb. The US Defence Intelligence Agency later reported that although two TLAMs hit the Baghdad air defence operations centre, they made only "small craters on the roof" of the 11ft-thick reinforced concrete bunker.

The only weapons sent against the heavily defended but critical targets in downtown Baghdad were TLAMs and F-117 'stealth' fighter-bombers. This allowed the US to strike at key targets without putting the lives of pilots at risk.

LEFT: Once their TLAMs were in the air, there was little the crews of US Navy warships and submarines could do. It took up to two hours for the missiles to reach their targets in Iraq. (US NAVY/DOD JOINT COMBAT CAMERA)

BELOW: After the ceasefire on 28 February, US experts headed to Kuwait and southern Iraq to study the performance of weapons, such as the TLAM. (US NAVY/DOD JOINT COMBAT CAMERA)

BGM-109C TOMAHAWK
Length (with booster): 20ft 6in
Wingspan: 8ft 7in
Diameter: 21in
Range: Approx 1,000 miles
Cruise speed: 375 to 560mph
Warhead: 1,000lb high-explosive

Cutting Their Losses

Before the war, US Navy commanders feared their manned aircraft would take heavy losses. A 5% loss rate on each strike was projected as reducing the carrier air wings to 60 aircraft in ten days - seriously degrading their offensive capabilities. Even a 1% attrition rate would have reduced the air wings to 70 aircraft each in 35 days.

By using TLAMs, the US Navy and USAF avoided this attrition. US Navy combat losses in Operation Desert Storm included three McDonnell Douglas F/A-18 Hornets, five Grumman A-6 Intruders (one returned but was damaged beyond repair), and one Grumman F-14 Tomcat. The F-14 was hit by a surface-to-air missile; the remainder were probably hit by anti-aircraft artillery fire or lost in accidents. These losses represent an overall campaign attrition rate of just under 2% of the 430 or so US Navy aircraft involved in the campaign. Losses were expected to be higher, and probably would have been, had TLAMs not been available. An F/A-18 cost about $31m in 1991, and an F-14 had a price tag of almost $72m.

ABOVE: The last TLAMs were fired at an Iraqi airfield near Baghdad on February 1, 1991. (US NAVY/ DOD JOINT COMBAT CAMERA)

RIGHT: US Navy radar controllers had to deconflict manned aircraft away from TLAM routes and also alert friendly forces not to engage the US missiles as they headed to their targets. (US NAVY/DOD JOINT COMBAT CAMERA)

This was significantly more than the $2.8m cost of a Tomahawk.

TLAMs were used in Operation Desert Storm to both destroy important targets and save Allied aircraft by attacking defensive positions in advance of the initial air assault. "It costs a lot of money," said veteran US Senator Sam Nunn, chairman of the US Senate Armed Services Committee at the time, "but when you look at the precious savings of lives, I think the dollars are well invested."

US Presidents of all political persuasions learnt this lesson and in every subsequent conflict over the following 30 or so years America's armed forces have made extensive use of the sea-launched weapons. The Tomahawk cruise missile has become the de facto weapon of choice for American presidents in time of crisis. This has transformed naval warfare and many other nations have sought to acquire the capability to strike from the sea with pinpoint accuracy. In Moscow, they took notice and by 2015 Russia's warships and submarines were equipped with their equivalent, the Kalibr cruise. It would be used in large numbers in Syria in 2015 and then in Ukraine from 2022.

OPERATION DESERT STORM TOMAHAWK SHOOTERS - JANUARY-FEBRUARY 1991		
Name Ship/Submarine	**Launch Area**	**Missiles Fired**
Battleships		
USS Missouri	Arabian Gulf	24
USS Wisconsion	Arabian Gulf	28
Cruisers		
USS San Jacinto	Red Sea	17
USS Bunker Hill	Arabian Gulf	28
USS Mobile Bay	Arabian Gulf	22
USS Missippi	Red Sea	5
USS Normandy	Red Sea	26
USS Princeton	Arabian Gulf	3
USS Philippine Sea	Red Sea	10
USS Leyte Gulf	Arabian Gulf	7?
USS Virginia	Mediterranean	2
Destroyers		
USS Fife	Arabian Gulf	58
USS Paul F Foster	Arabian Gulf	40
USS Spruance	Red Sea	2?
Nuclear Attack Submarines		12
USS Louisville	Red Sea	
USS Pittsburgh	Red Sea	
	Confirmed Total	284

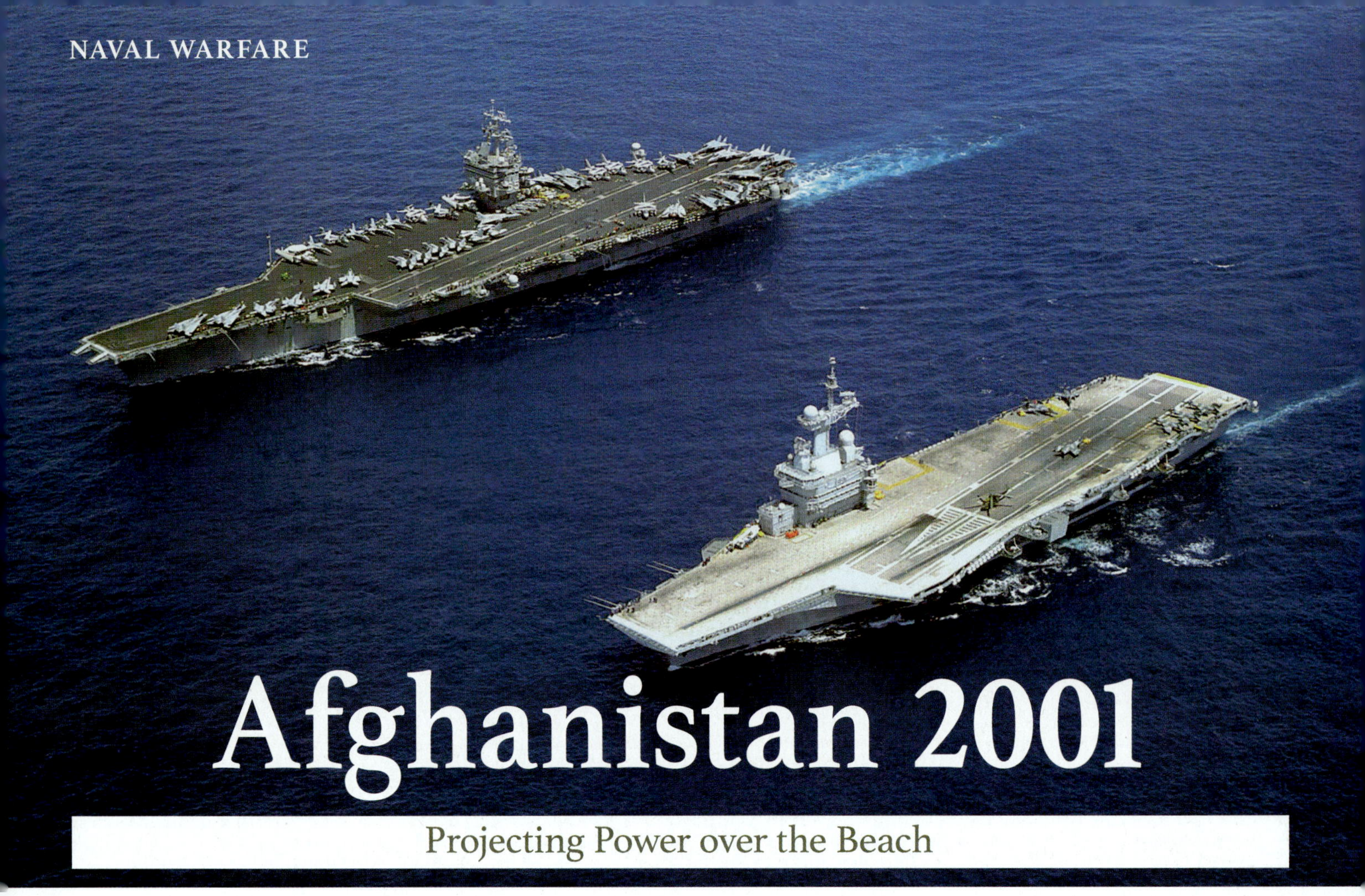

Afghanistan 2001

Projecting Power over the Beach

ABOVE: French carrier FS Charles de Gaulle, USS *Enterprise* (top), seen here with the French carrier FS *Charles de Gaulle*, had just finished a six-month long cruise in the Arabian Gulf region when she turned around to spearhead the US response to the 9/11 attacks. (US NAVY/DOD JOINT COMBAT CAMERA)

As hijacked airliners flew into the twin towers of the World Trade Centre in New York and Pentagon in Washington DC on the morning of September 11, 2001, Captain James 'Sandy' Winnefeld was working in his office onboard the nuclear-powered aircraft carrier, USS *Enterprise*. When the first airliner hit the Twin Towers, one of his staff alerted him to what was going on and suggested he turn on the television.

The aircraft carrier had just completed a six-month long cruise in the Arabian Gulf and was heading south through the Indian Ocean, with the 5,500-strong crew looking forward to shore leave in South Africa as a reward for their hard work. Winnefeld's ship was pulling more than 30kts, or close to her top speed.

As he watched images of the second airliner explode in a huge fireball,

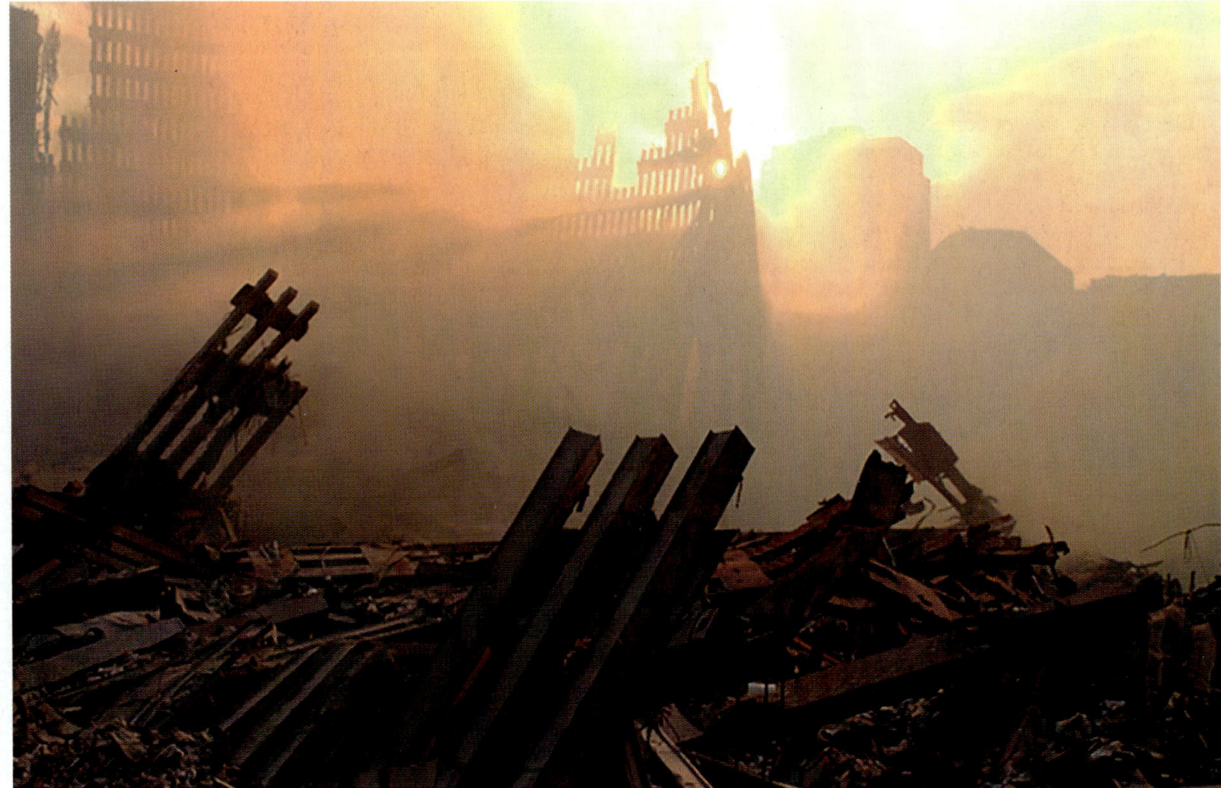

RIGHT: After the Twin Towers were brought down on 9/11, US President George W Bush ordered the US military to strike back against Osama bin Laden's hideouts in Afghanistan. (DOD JOINT COMBAT CAMERA)

LEFT: US Predator drones were sent over Afghanistan to hunt down al-Qaeda and Taliban strongholds in the days before American airpower was unleashed. (DOD JOINT COMBAT CAMERA)

Winnefeld realised his carrier and its air wing of 90 jets and helicopters would soon be at the centre of America's response.

"Well, we immediately slowed down, realising we probably were not going to be going to South Africa, after all," he recalled. "There was a lot of discussion among senior people in the theatre, including myself, my strike group commander, and the fleet commander in Bahrain. And it wasn't long before we were essentially directed to turn north towards the coast of Pakistan to be ready for combat operations the next morning, if need be."

Turning around a 90,000-ton aircraft carrier safely is not an easy business and if Winnefeld had not taken the decision to slow down USS *Enterprise* on his own initiative it might not have made its rendezvous with destiny on time. In Washington DC, chaos reigned, as US President George W Bush and his senior advisors tried to work out what had happened, organise rescue and recovery efforts, and then craft a response. Thanks to Winnefeld and the other US Navy commanders in the Middle East, key assets were in place and ready to go into action against al-Qaeda bases in Afghanistan ahead of senior decision makers in Washington DC getting organised. The US Navy provided useable options even before President Bush needed them.

Ultimatum

For American military planners, Afghanistan was a very difficult target.

Afghanistan's land-locked location and the relative lack of bases in neighbouring countries meant the fastest way to get tactical airpower into play was from US Navy aircraft carriers, positioned in the North Arabian Sea off the coast of Pakistan. The nuclear-powered carriers USS *Carl Vinson* and USS *Theodore Roosevelt* were ordered to make best speed for the war zone, with more than 150 tactical combat aircraft to augment the USS *Enterprise*, which had been on station since September 12.

During the build up to the conflict, US Navy Grumman F-14 Tomcats from the USS *Enterprise* flew reconnaissance missions over southern Afghanistan in the last two weeks of September 2001, taking high level images of airfields, surface-to-air missiles, anti-aircraft artillery sites, army barracks and training camps used by Osama bin Laden's al-Qaeda group.

As the US military build-up gained momentum, President Bush issued an ultimatum to the Taliban regime ➤

BELOW: US Navy and US Marine Corps F/A-18 Hornets flying off aircraft carriers in the North Arabian sea spearheaded the US air campaign over Afghanistan until bases could set up inside the central Asian country. (US NAVY/DOD JOINT COMBAT CAMERA)

ABOVE: By 2001, the veteran F-14 Tomcat fighter had been converted to carry laser guided bombs and they flew many long-range mission into the far north and west of Afghanistan. (US NAVY/DOD JOINT COMBAT CAMERA)

RIGHT: Without US Navy carrier airpower the American military campaign in Afghanistan would have taken longer and been more difficult to execute. (US NAVY/DOD JOINT COMBAT CAMERA)

that ruled Afghanistan to give up Osama bin Laden and his al-Qaeda network. US intelligence had quickly linked bin Laden to the 9/11 attacks and President Bush promised rapid retribution to any country or group that offered them sanctuary.

There was no reply from Kabul, so President Bush ordered his military commanders to strike. Operation Enduring Freedom began on October 7, 2001, with missile and air attacks on key targets across Afghanistan to defeat air defence and open the way for the insertion of US special forces teams to link up with rebel groups opposed to the Taliban and al-Qaeda.

A few minutes behind the Tomahawk cruise missile strike on Kabul in the early hours of October 7, was a package of Tomcats and McDonnell Douglas F/A-18C Hornets from the USS *Carl Vinson*. The Hornets used AGM-84-ER Stand-off Land Attack Missiles to mount a precision strike on the remains of the Afghan air defence network around the capital. This was followed up by a laser-guided bomb attack by Tomcats, who also bombed a barrack complex. The USS *Enterprise* launched a follow-up strike on Kabul's air defences later in the night.

Further south, Hornets from both the USS *Enterprise* and USS *Carl Vinson* pounded the airfield south of Kandahar city, hitting aircraft, SAMs, and radars. Nearby, a pair of Tomcats from the USS *Enterprise* were tasked to hit a suspected al-Qaeda cave complex with laser guided GBU-24 Paveway III penetrator bombs.

The long range of the Tomcats meant they were selected to join a strike by B-1Bs on Herat air base, near the Iranian border. Several Mikoyan MiG-21s were destroyed on the ground in the raid. Once the heavy bombers turned for home, the F-14s dropped more laser guided bombs on a Taliban communications site at Farah.

During the first wave of strikes, the Central Intelligence Agency (CIA) used a Predator unmanned aerial vehicle to monitor a group of suspected Taliban leaders leaving a compound in Kandahar and driving off in a convoy of vehicles. The Predator beamed video imagery

RIGHT: When the US military wanted to establish its first permanent military base in Afghanistan, the US Navy and US Marine Corps were ordered to launch a helicopter-borne assault from a fleet cruising in the North Arabian Sea. (ANDY HAY FLYING ART)

back to its headquarters in Virginia to allow a pair of US Navy Hornets to be directed to attack.

In the first five days of Operation Enduring Freedom, US Navy Hornets and Tomcats dropped 240 JDAMs, 1,000lb and 2,000lb laser guided bombs. The relatively modest amount of weaponry dropped illustrated the lack of large, fixed targets in Afghanistan and the difficulty of finding the elusive and fleeting high value targets linked to the leadership of al-Qaeda and the Taliban.

'Surrender'

Towards the end of November, Taliban forces were on the run, with

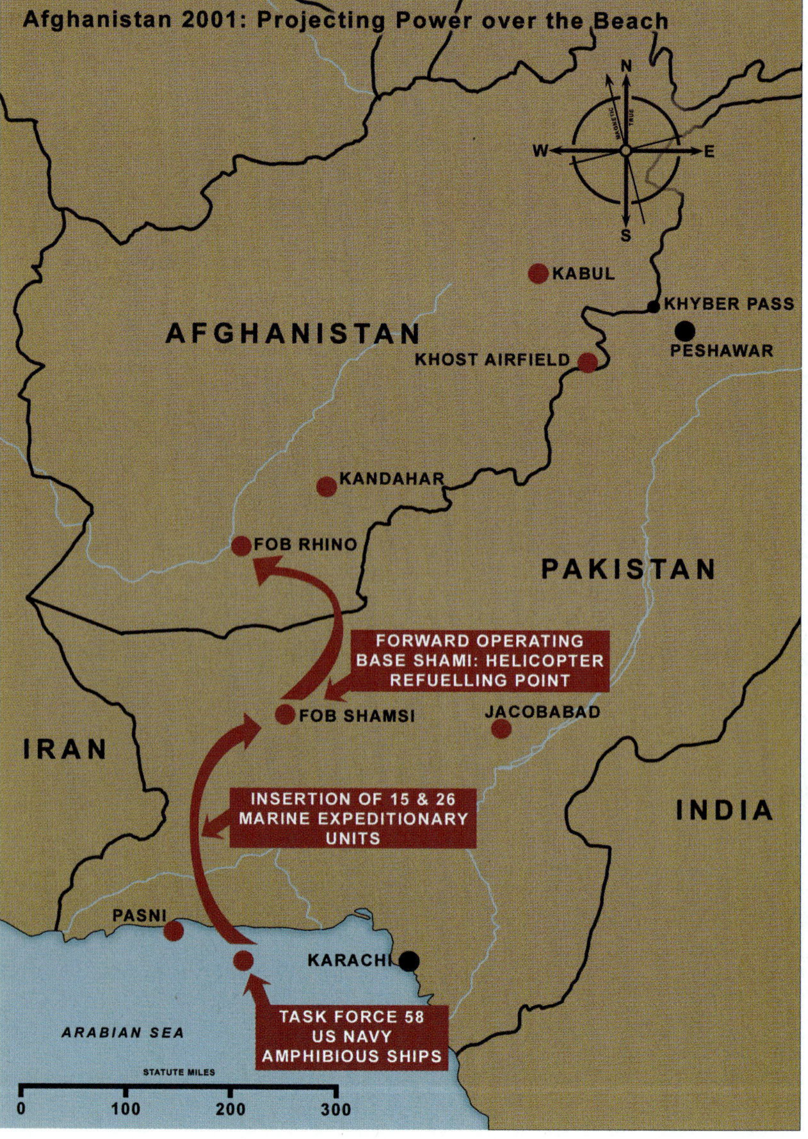

mass desertions and surrenders taking place to pro-US militia groups. Several hundred Taliban prisoners were corralled in the Qala-e-Jangi fortress outside Mazar-e-Sharif, but such was the volume of prisoners being processed that searches were often rudimentary and many 'surrendering' Taliban still intended to fight. The prisoners revolted and overpowered their guards, killing a CIA operative in the ensuing battle. US and British special forces teams arrived on the scene and began directing waves of US Navy jets and USAF AC-130 gunships to pound the escaped Taliban. It took several days for their resistance to be broken. Less than 100 Taliban fighters survived the battle.

As this battle was unfolding, in southern Afghanistan pro-US militia fighters and US special forces seized control of a provincial capital, Tarin Kwot. The Taliban assembled a large

column of troops, pick-up trucks, and tanks in Kandahar to strike back. The US Green Berets and 50 militia fighters took up positions dominating the main road through a pass that the Taliban column would have to take. On November 17, the Taliban troops approached the first US position and air strikes were called in to repel them. US Marine Corps F/A-18Cs and US Navy F-14s pounded the Taliban column for three hours until they were

in full retreat, leaving 30 destroyed vehicles and 300 dead behind.

US Central Command chief, General Tommy Franks, decided this was the moment to put "American boots on the ground," to establish a forward operating base near to Kandahar, in southern Afghanistan. This would allow ground troops to launch helicopter-borne raids against al-Qaeda hide outs and capture vital

ABOVE: Air-to-air refuelling was the essential enabler that allowed US Navy tactical jets to operate over Afghanistan for extended periods. (US NAVY/DOD JOINT COMBAT CAMERA)

BELOW: The US Navy maintained a continuous presence of aircraft carriers in the North Arabian Sea in 2001 and 2002 to ensure 24/7 air support for US troops in Afghanistan. This gave the US Air Force time to build up its network on in-country airbases that supported the US occupation force over the next 20 years. (US NAVY/DOD JOINT COMBAT CAMERA)

RIGHT: Ordnance crews on US Navy aircraft carriers set a relentless pace loading bombs and missiles onto jets bound for Afghanistan. (US NAVY/ DOD JOINT COMBAT CAMERA)

BELOW: The USS *Theodore Roosevelt* joined the US air campaign over Afghanistan in October 2001 and remained on station in the North Arabian Sea for the remainder of the year. (US NAVY/DOD JOINT COMBAT CAMERA)

intelligence material needed to track down bin Laden. For this purpose, since the start of Operation Enduring Freedom he had massed a contingent of US Marines, dubbed Naval Expeditionary Task Force 58, off the coast of Pakistan onboard the amphibious warships, USS *Peleliu* and USS *Bataan,* to be ready to pounce should an opportunity arise. The tough US Marine Corps officer, Brigadier General Jim Mattis, was placed in command of Task Force 58.

With the military situation in southern Afghanistan appearing to be moving more favourably in the last week of November, General Franks decided the time was right to introduce these forces. Task Force 58's mission commenced with operations to seize Objective Rhino, an old dirt airstrip in the desert to the east of the Taliban capital Kandahar. A small US Navy SEAL reconnaissance team was sent ahead to scout the site and guide in the assault force.

FOB Rhino

According to the USMC official history of the operation, the first flight lifted off from the USS *Peleliu* at around 4.15pm on November 25 and headed inland. Led by Major William Bufkin II, this escort force included four Bell AH-1W Cobra and three Bell UH-1N Huey helicopters. They were followed by six US Marine Corps CH-53E's, three each from the 15th and 26th Marine Expeditionary Units (MEUs) , carrying more than 200 US Marines.

LEFT: The 26th Marine Expeditionary Unit was embarked on the USS *Bataan* as she cruised off the coast of Pakistan in November 2001. (US NAVY/DOD JOINT COMBAT CAMERA)

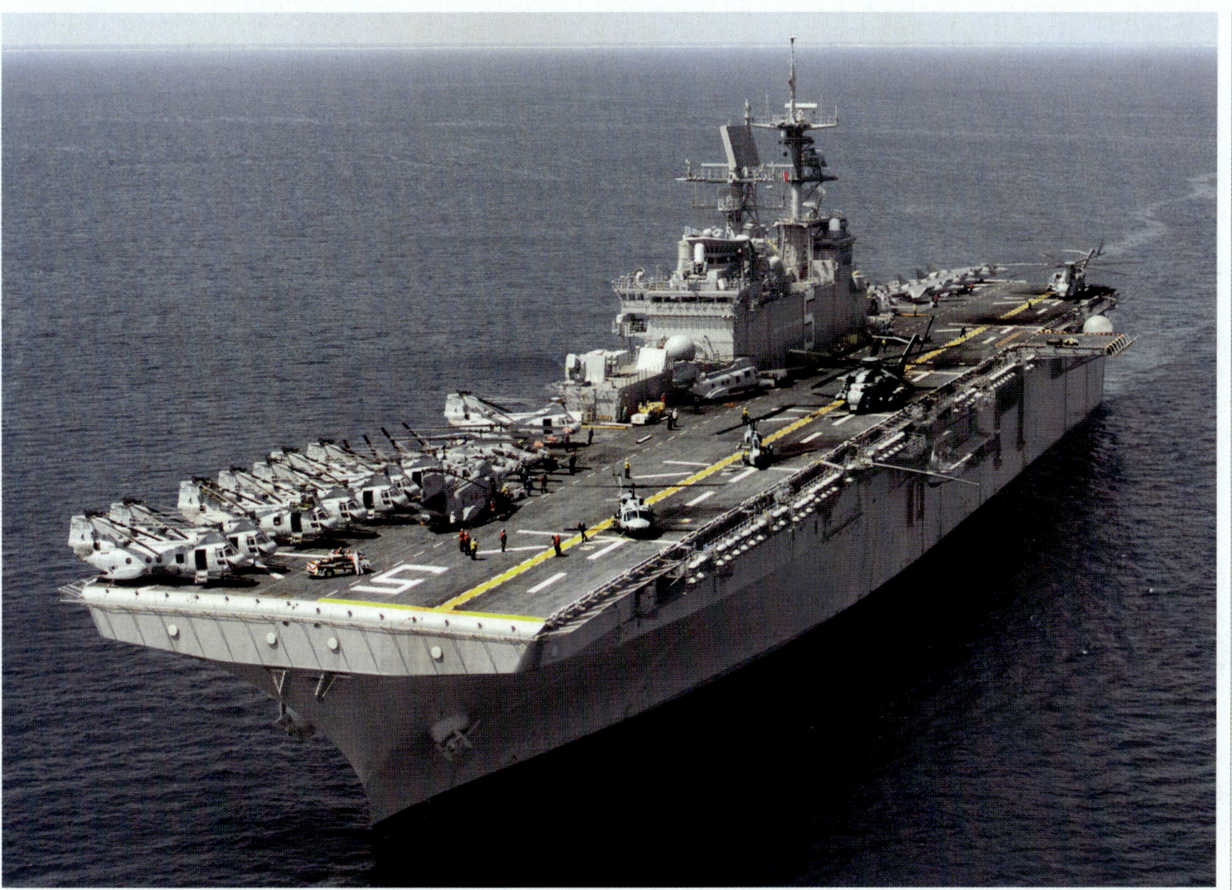

The escort force flew in staggered waves, two Cobras, three Hueys, and then two more Cobras, on their 92-mile mission to Objective Rhino. It first headed toward Shamsi in Pakistan to refuel at a US controlled airstrip before continuing toward the objective area.

The assault force of CH-53E's, flown by crews from Marine Medium Helicopter Squadron (HMM) 163, headed toward a 57-mile-long helicopter aerial refuelling track established just south of the Afghan border to take on fuel from USMC Lockheed KC-130K Hercules tankers, in the darkness. The three helicopters in the second wave had difficulty conducting aerial refuelling but pressed on.

As the assault force crossed the border behind the Cobras, the moonlit terrain shifted from low mountains to flat desert, and the speeding aircraft rose from 75 to 200ft above sea level to compensate for the decrease in visual contrast. The crews also conducted penetration checks, switching off unnecessary devices that produced illumination or emitted an electronic signature, to decrease the likelihood of premature detection during the final leg of their journey. As the assault element approached the abandoned airfield, visible two miles in the distance, the escort

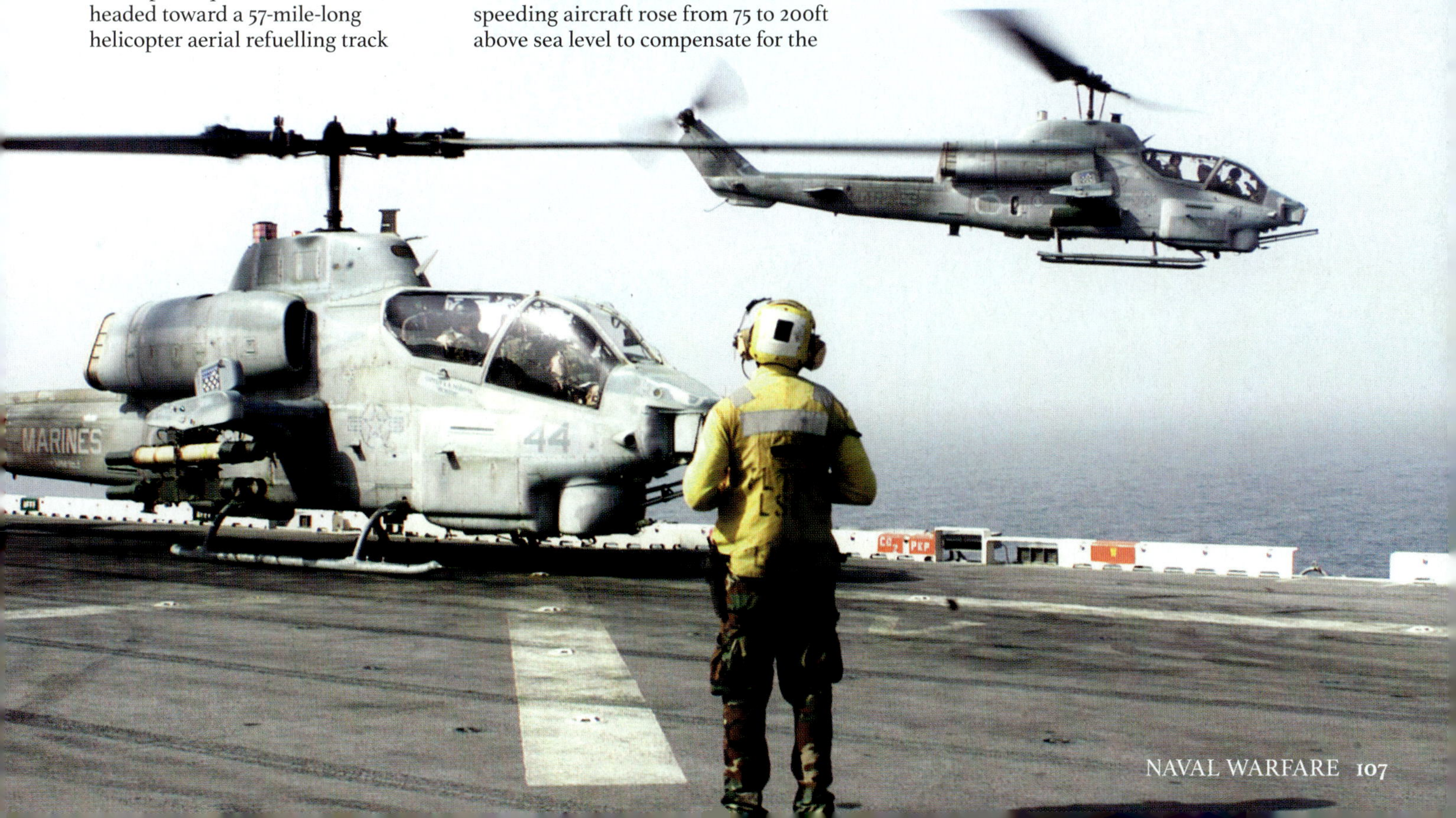

BELOW: Cobra gunships on board the USS *Peleliu* prepare to head for Afghanistan as Task Force 58 assembles in the North Arabian Sea. (US NAVY/DOD JOINT COMBAT CAMERA)

ABOVE: US Marine Corps CH-53E Sea Stallions used air-to-air refuelling to fly to FOB Rhino and deliver Task Force 58 to its objective. (US NAVY/DOD JOINT COMBAT CAMERA)

BELOW: Follow-up waves of CH-47E Sea Knight helicopters ensured a rapid build-up of US forces at FOB Rhino. (US NAVY/DOD JOINT COMBAT CAMERA)

flight leader relayed confirmation that the runway remained clear of hostile forces by passing the radio code word 'Winter'.

After more than four hours in the air, the first flight of CH-53 helicopters and their Cobra escorts began to descend toward the landing zone at 10-minute intervals, guided toward their destination by flashing infrared strobe lights that the SEALs had placed in the middle of the dirt runway. Due to severe brownout conditions, thick, towering dust clouds stirred up by the aircraft's spinning rotor blades, several of the pilots were forced to approach the runway several times before successfully landing. The Huey and Cobra helicopters began to land, taking up positions along the airfield where they remained on a 15-minute strip alert. In a classic case of understatement, Captain Fallon later remarked: "It was a fairly busy 30, 40 minutes until the second wave hit the deck."

They were met by the US Navy SEAL reconnaissance team and a US Navy Lockheed P-3C Orion AIP aircraft provided continual Intelligence, Surveillance and Reconnaissance (ISR) coverage around the US Marines throughout the night and on all subsequent nights. At the same time, a USAF Northrop Grumman E-8C Joint STARS surveillance aircraft provided wide area surveillance with their radars, which could detect vehicle movement over hundreds of square miles of desert.

Power Projection

The operation was the tour de force of power projection operations. Once Forward Operating Base Rhino's runway was surveyed by USAF Special Tactics Squadron (STS) personnel and declared KC-130 capable, additional troops flew in on Marine Corps' KC-130s from the US airbase at Jacobabad in Pakistan where they had been pre-positioned. The first KC-130 to land on the dirt airstrip was flown

by a VMGR-352 detachment aircrew, landing an hour and a half after the insertion of the assault force.

The following day, a E-8A JSTARS detected several Taliban armoured vehicles to the northwest of FOB Rhino. After airborne forward air controllers in F-14 Tomcats confirmed their identity, more F-14s from the USS *Theodore Roosevelt* and AH-1Ws, flying from the newly renamed FOB Rhino, were called in to attack the column.

The US Marine aircrews included Captains John Barranco and David Steele piloting the first aircraft, which had the call sign Evil Eye 34, and Captains Kristian Pfeiffer and Richard Lawson, piloting the second Cobra, callsign Evil Eye 35. The Cobras headed toward the convoy and - at the E-8A's request - helped coordinate the attack, watching as the Tomcats engaged the armoured personnel carriers. After the US Navy jets had completed their bombing run, striking just in front of the lead armoured personnel carrier, and disabling it, the Marines took their turn. Emerging from behind a nearby ridge, the Cobras used their 20mm cannon and rockets to engage the two armoured vehicles and eight to ten dismounted personnel.

Captain Barranco later described the attack, saying: "At least some of the Taliban were out of the vehicles. I'm guessing they thought they hit a mine since the F-14s were so high. They heard us and some of them started firing wildly in the air toward the sound of the Cobras—the rest started running. We made several passes, destroying the vehicles and killing the squad. Passing back over the convoy, the pilots used their night-vision goggles and infrared sensors to assess the battle damage but determined that nothing of military value was left."

The first wave of Boeing C-17 Globemaster aircraft arrived at FOB Rhino on November 28, transporting SEABEES from Naval Mobile Construction Battalion (NMCB) 133 to begin improving the conditions of the airstrip to allow it take sustained air operations. By this point over 1,000 US Marines were ashore in Afghanistan and ready to start offensive operations. Within days, the Taliban and al-Qaeda fighters were fleeing Kandahar and melting away into the local population. US Marine and the Afghan tribal allies soon entered the former Taliban capital without resistance.

The US Navy and Marine Corps had delivered the decisive blow against the perpetrators of the 9/11 attacks. The bulk of the offensive air operations were borne by US Navy and Marine Corps jets launched from the aircraft carriers that were kept on station in the North Arabian Sea. The US Navy and Marine Corps launched some 4,900 sorties, or 75% of all strike sorties flown, compared to 701 by USAF bombers between October and December 2001. This broke down into 3,700 by F/A-18s, and 1,200 by F-14s. Naval airpower had proved decisive, and the operation had opened the door for the US Marines to establish the first major American base within Afghanistan.

Soon Afghanistan had a pro-western government and the country quickly emerged from the darkness of Taliban rule. However, the subsequent US and coalition campaign over the next 20 years failed to build up a self-sustaining Afghan government. But that is another story.

LEFT: US Air Force transport aircraft delivered the LAV troop carriers of Task Force 58 to FOB Rhino to allow the US Marines to mount raids around southern Afghanistan. (US NAVY/DOD JOINT COMBAT CAMERA)

BELOW: FOB Rhino was the first permanent US base for conventional combat forces in Afghanistan. (US NAVY/DOD JOINT COMBAT CAMERA)

Battle for the Black Sea

Ukraine's Naval War against Russia

The Black Sea has become a key theatre in the war between Russia and Ukraine, since Moscow launched its so-called 'Special Military Operation' on February 22, 2022.

For the Russians, the Black Sea was 'their lake' and critical to retaining control of Crimea. As Russia's main warm seaport, Sevastopol on Crimea was a key naval base and a vital route for civilian exports. The Russian Black Sea Fleet's warships and submarines routinely made forays from Sevastopol to launch Kalibr cruise missiles at targets deep in Ukrainian controlled territory. Domination of the Black Sea also allowed the Russians to cut off Ukrainian maritime trade, particularly grain exports.

For the Ukrainians, opening those maritime export routes was critical to keeping the country's agricultural sector in business. To break Russian control over the Black Sea, the Ukrainians embarked on a campaign to strike at the naval base in Sevastopol and drop the 17km-long road and rail link Kerch bridge, which linked Crimea with the Russian mainland. This bridge had been opened by Russian President Putin in May 2018.

The Ukrainian campaign gained momentum in 2023, with the Kerch bridge being hit twice and the headquarters of Black Sea Fleet was hit by British-supplied Storm Shadow cruise missiles in September 2023.

In the opening weeks of the Russian invasion in February and March 2022, the Black Sea Fleet

had operated with impunity against Ukraine's completely outclassed fleet. Ukraine's flagship, the frigate *Hetman Sahaidachny*, had been scuttled in Nikolayev port as Russian troops approached.

Since the opening days of the war, Black Sea Fleet warships and Kilo-class submarines launched Kalibr cruise missiles at targets throughout Ukraine, using tactics that mirrored the US Navy in Iraq and Afghanistan.

Then, in April 2022, the Ukrainians managed to sink the Black Sea Fleet flag ship, the RFS *Moskva*, with a Neptune anti-ship missile. The Russians pulled their fleet back into Sevastopol and Novorossiysk harbours, opting to rely on their shore based anti-ship missiles, combat aircraft, and Kilo-class submarines to dominate the Black Sea.

In effect this 'froze' the naval standoff in the Black Sea. The Russians could dominate the Black Sea and prevent civilian merchant ships reaching Ukrainian ports, but the Kyiv navy had no way to strike back.

The Ukrainians needed a way to get back into the fight. Building a traditional fleet of surface warships would have taken years, time the Ukrainians did not have, so an unconventional solution was needed. Drones became the latest addition to the naval warfare arsenal.

Ukrainian engineers took some basic speedboat hulls, employed commercial satellite communication technology, off the shelf sensors, and rudimentary control software to pilot unmanned vessels. Elon Musk had given the Ukrainians free access to his Starlink satellite network in the early days of the war and this cover allowed the naval drones to range far across the Black Sea.

There have been steady streams of reports of Ukrainian naval drone attacks, and they showed increasing technical maturity in the design of the robot vessels. Early on the Ukrainians realised the propaganda potential of the naval drones and made a point of releasing video clips of them in action. Video footage from the Sevastopol harbour attack in October 2022 was reported around the world and gave the impression that the Russian fleet's main port was highly vulnerable. Claims were made of many Russian warships being damaged or out of action. However, subsequent satellite and video imagery indicated that the Russia warships had not been sunk or seriously damaged.

While the naval drone attacks have not yet sunk any Black Sea Fleet ships, they have curtailed its operations. Sevastopol and Novorossiysk harbours have had to be heavily protected with booms and gun emplacements. When Russian warships leave port to fire Kalibr cruise missiles at Ukraine, they are protected by machine guns teams on the decks.

ABOVE: Snake Island has been at the centre of the duel for naval supremacy in the Black Sea. (UKRAINIAN MINISTRY OF DEFENCE)

The Kerch Bridge

Attacking the Kerch bridge was a more difficult challenge, because of its size and the strong defences around it. The first successful attack on the bridge in October 2022 involved Ukrainian undercover agents arranging for a truck bomb to be driven onto it. One span of the road bridge was dropped and a nearby train set on fire.

After the second attack in July 2023, there were no holes in the road surface that would be the tell tail signs of missile strike. However, a section of roadway was dropping away from its supports, indicating that a large explosion had occurred beneath it. Ukraine's fleet of remote-control boats, which are known as naval attack drones or unmanned surface vessels, had struck.

Later in July 2023, the Ukrainian navy invited the US news network CNN to view a demonstration of their naval attack drone during a training drill. The operators said the vessel had a range of 800km and carried a payload of 300kg of high explosives. Visible on the rear of the vessel was large satellite antenna to allow it to be controlled over long distances. A turret for electro-optical, or video, sensors was fitted near the bow of the vessel, which appeared to be about size of a small speed boat.

The July 2023 attack on Kerch bridge showed that the duel between